D1271988

Globalization
and America

Perspectives on a Multiracial America Series

R. Feagin, Texas A&M University, series editor

The racial composition of the United States is rapidly changing. Books in the series will explore various aspects of the coming multiracial society, one in which European-Americans are no longer the majority and where issues of white-on-black racism have been joined by many other challenges to white dominance.

TITLES

Melanie Bush, *Breaking the Code of Good Intentions*

Amir Mavasti and Karyn McKinney, *Unwelcome Immigrants: Middle Eastern Lives in America*

Richard Rees, *Shades of Difference: A History of Ethnicity in America*

Katheryn Russell-Brown, *Protecting Our Own: Race, Crime, and African Americans*

Elizabeth M. Aranda, *Emotional Bridges to Puerto Rico: Migration, Return Migration, and the Struggles of Incorporation*

Victoria Kaplan, *Structural Inequality: Black Architects in the United States*

Pamela Anne Quiroz, *Adoption in a Colorblind Society*

Adia Harvey Wingfield, *Doing Business with Beauty: Black Women, Hair Salons, and the Racial Enclave Economy*

FORTHCOMING TITLES

Erica Chito Childs, *Fade to Black and White*

Globalization and America

Race, Human Rights, and Inequality

Edited by
Angela J. Hattery,
David G. Embrick,
and Earl Smith

ROWMAN & LITTLEFIELD PUBLISHERS, INC.
Lanham • Boulder • New York • Toronto • Plymouth, UK

ROWMAN & LITTLEFIELD PUBLISHERS, INC.

Published in the United States of America
by Rowman & Littlefield Publishers, Inc.
A wholly owned subsidiary of The Rowman & Littlefield Publishing Group, Inc.
4501 Forbes Boulevard, Suite 200, Lanham, Maryland 20706
www.rowmanlittlefield.com

Estover Road
Plymouth PL6 7PY
United Kingdom

British Library Cataloguing in Publication Information Available

Library of Congress Cataloging-in-Publication Data:

Hattery, Angela.
  Globalization and America : race, human rights, and inequality / Angela J.
Hattery, David G. Embrick, and Earl Smith.
    p. cm. — (Perspectives on a multiracial America series)
  Includes bibliographical references and index.
  ISBN-13: 978-0-7425-6075-8 (cloth : alk. paper)
  ISBN-10: 0-7425-6075-9 (cloth : alk. paper)
  ISBN-13: 978-0-7425-6076-5 (pbk. : alk. paper)
  ISBN-10: 0-7425-6076-7 (pbk. : alk. paper)
  1. Human rights—United States. 2. Equality—United States. 3. Globalization—
United States. 4. United States—Social conditions. 5. United States—Foreign
relations. I. Embrick, David G. II. Smith, Earl, 1946- III. Title.
  JC599.U5H295 2008
  303.48'273—dc22   2007048605

Printed in the United States of America

∞™ The paper used in this publication meets the minimum requirements of
American National Standard for Information Sciences—Permanence of Paper
for Printed Library Materials, ANSI/NISO Z39.48-1992.

Contents

Acknowledgments

We acknowledge and thank the contributors for allowing us to include their research in our book, for their patience with us as we journeyed closer to completion, and for their steadfast loyalty and dedication toward issues of injustice. We are grateful for the insight and support of our editors at Rowman & Littlefield, Alan McClare and Michael McGandy.

Angela J. Hattery
David G. Embrick
Earl Smith

This book was just an idea until I met Angela and Earl, both of whom I owe many thanks that go beyond our collaboration on this project. Here's to a lasting friendship and future research possibilities. Finally, I would be remiss if I did not mention my wife Jessica, who's been understanding since graduate school and continues to be patient with me as I ride the tenure-track train, and my daughters Samantha, Brittany, and Jasmine. I love you all.

David G. Embrick

Editor's Introduction

I am pleased to have been able to work with professors David Embrick and Earl Smith, who coedited this volume. I am also grateful to the editor for the project, Michael McGandy at Rowman & Littlefield, who helped in many important ways to get this text published. An edited volume has its own set of challenges, and each of these people played a critical role in bringing it to fruition.

The major thank-you goes to the chapter contributors, who gave of their time and expertise. In many cases, they worked on tight deadlines and were required to respond to suggestions for revisions made by their own junior colleagues. This book would not be possible without their generous contributions.

I served as lead editor for the volume, reviewing and editing each chapter—front to back—but I could not have accomplished this daunting task without the tireless work of my associate editors (David Embrick and Earl Smith), each of whom took responsibility for providing an additional review of key chapters and wrote an introduction to a section.

In pulling this volume together, I constantly paid attention to the growing scholarly market on globalization and continue to believe that the approach we take here is one that significantly contributes to what Thomas Friedman calls the flattening of the world.

I know you will find the issues in this text compelling and the analyses useful as you grapple with "America's World" and "the World's America."

—Angela Hattery

1

The New Global World: America's World and the World's America

Angela Hattery, David Embrick, and Earl Smith

Globalization and America: Race, Human Rights, and Inequality provides an examination of human rights and social inequalities in the new global world. Our goal in this book is to address a wide range of topics and issues at the forefront of both scholarly and public discourse with relation to human rights and social inequalities in a global world. Our focus is U.S. based, and each chapter examines the ways in which the United States both imports and exports social inequalities as well as how the United States contributes to human rights violations both within and outside our immediate borders. In other words, this book examines human rights and social inequalities in "America's World" and in the "World's America."

In order to accomplish this goal, this book pulls together some of the leading scholars and activists writing on issues related to human rights and the global political economy and packages these into one volume that provides contemporary analyses of a changing world. Specifically, we have commissioned essays on immigration, colonialism, slavery, reparations, work, nation-state constitutions, and the prison-industrial complex. Each chapter or set of chapters—organized together in parts—explores the ways in which human rights and social inequalities that occur in the United States and abroad are connected globally and related to ideologies and practices that originate or are perpetuated in and by the United States. We note that in order to be attentive to the politization and social construction of categories of race and ethnicity, we leave it up to the individual authors to choose the language they feel is most appropriate. For example, some choose to use "African American," whereas others choose the term "black."

1

The variation across chapters is a result not of being inattentive to terms of race and ethnicity but rather of being attentive.

Our text is unique in that rather than taking a strictly cross-national or comparative perspective, which would limit its use to courses focused on cross-national or comparative approaches, it allows instructors to incorporate in their lectures issues that are many times unavailable in a typical textbook. That is, this book provides scholarly readings that are focused on contemporary issues (e.g., reparations, immigration, secret CIA prisons, and so on) that appear in the *New York Times*, *USA Today*, and other nationally recognized media outlets.

Second, these scholarly essays allow the instructor to expand the discussion of U.S.-based issues (racial discrimination, immigration, or social movements) from a strictly U.S.-based discussion to one that focuses on the ways in which many issues, including the international slave trade, the expansion of U.S. prisons abroad, and the global impact of immigration policies, are part of both "America's World" and the "World's America."

The original working subtitle of this book, "America's World and the World's America," was specifically meant to evoke this book's approach: that America's role in perpetuating inequality and failing to protect human rights is a process of both importing and exporting specific ideologies and practices. "America's World" refers to the process of exporting exploitative practices and implementing them in other nation-states, such as at Abu Ghraib in Iraq. The "World's America" refers to the importation of individuals and populations within our own borders in order to exploit them within our own institutions, such as the economy. For example, with increasing pressures on institutions of higher learning to enroll increasingly diverse student bodies, the most elite and selective colleges and universities, including Harvard, have relied on admitting black students from Africa and the Caribbean rather than native "African Americans." This and many more issues of immigration will be taken up in part 3.

Third, our approach to globalization has been reinforced by the excellent work of scholars such as Saskia Sassen, an urban sociologist at the University of Chicago. Specifically, Sassen (2008) argues that from macrosocial trends and their specific spatial patterns, the changing global urban world has been transformed by three interrelated trends: 1) growth in manufacturing, 2) huge expansions in telecommunications, and 3) acceptance among the "power elite" that the United States is not the center of the world. Globalization, Sassen (2006) contends, has increased the "area" where manufacturing, financial centers, factory production (especially car manufacturing), oil extraction, and fishing occur, thus creating the need for the reemergence and new developments of strategic research sites for careful investigation (Merton 1987).

We take up this challenge, expanding the scope of the book to address some of the most pressing sociological problems associated with expanding globalization in the new millennium.

Globalization and America: Race, Human Rights, and Inequality could be adopted and would be of use as a supplemental text in any course that focuses on inequality and/or human rights, including sociology, anthropology, race and ethnic relations, women and gender studies, and political science, among others. Specifically, what we provide here is a series of well-researched chapters that explore the ways in which social inequalities in the United States influence and are influenced by social inequalities globally: how the world becomes America and how America becomes the world.

REFERENCES

Merton, Robert K. 1987. "Three Fragments from a Sociologist's Notebooks: Establishing the Phenomenon, Specified Ignorance, and Strategic Research Materials." *Annual Review of Sociology* 13: 1–28.

Sassen, Saskia. 2008. *Territory, Authority, Rights: From Medieval to Global Assemblages.* Princeton, N.J.: Princeton University Press.

———. 2006. *Cities in a World Economy.* Thousand Oaks, Calif.: Sage.

Part 1

INTRODUCTION TO RACE/RACISM IN THE UNITED STATES

Angela J. Hattery

What is the global, racial situation as the third millennium dawns?

—Winant (2001:289)

Beginning with the "discovery" of the "new world" in 1492 by Cristobal Colon, the landmass that comprises the contemporary United States has been plagued by the issue of race. Christopher Columbus, as we in the US call him, thought he had discovered a new world, a territory he could claim for settlement by Europe. He proclaimed this despite the fact that indigenous people had been living here for at least 10,000 years prior to his arrival. The issue of race became more contentious when 150 years or so later the English sent colonists to settle Jamestown. Finding an indigenous population that was unwilling to be "conquered," the colonists set upon a mission of genocide (Wright 1997). They employed many strategies including the "sharing" of diseased blankets with the Native Americans and death marches, the most infamous being the "Trail of Tears" (Ehle 1988).

Finding an indigenous population that was not willing to be conquered meant that the colonists and early settlers needed to identify another population that they could exploit in the difficult work of "settling" the land and making it suitable for large-scale agriculture. With the European slave trade in high gear, the early settlers and colonists began bringing captured Africans to the colonies. At the beginning of the slave trade to the colonies of Virginia, Maryland, and North and South Carolina, the slave status was a contractual agreement and slaves could earn their freedom after their contracts were met. Very quickly, however, the colonists determined that it was in their best interest to re categorize the status of slave to a lifetime status. Under this new arrangement, once Africans were brought into the colonies they were slaves for life and could thus be exploited for decades. Shortly after this transition, the status of slavery was further transformed such that it became a status that was transmitted intergenerationally. In other words, any children born to an enslaved African were automatically slaves as well. This transformation of the status of "slave" was not only critical in the development of notions of race in the US but it is one of the key qualities that distinguishes slavery in the US from slavery in other parts of the world. The US system of slavery treated slaves as chattel; they were owned, they could be bought and sold, and like cattle they could be bred to increase the holdings of their owner (Franklin 2005).

But, it is not simply the system of chattel slavery alone that shapes race relations for the remainder of US history. The early settlers and colonists were devout Christians, primarily Calvinists and Puritans for whom the system of chattel slavery would have been incompatible with their religious beliefs. Thus, an ideology was necessary to justify chattel slavery. That ideology dictated that slaves were less than fully human, indeed they did not have souls (Du Bois 1973), and thus they could be held in terms that were similar to other farm-related animals. Just as mules were used for plowing, slaves were used for planting and harvesting. This ideological transformation of slaves to the nonhuman realm not only justified the system of chattel slavery for those who engaged in it, but it established a hegemonic ideology of race that was critical to the development of constructions of race that persist in the US today.

Evidence for this can be found in the fact that Lincoln's Emancipation Proclamation that freed the slaves in 1862 did not substantially alter the lived reality of the descendents of African slaves in the US. In the *Dred Scott* decision the U.S. Supreme Court upheld the official categorization of descendants of African slaves as three-fifths of a human (Hattery & Smith 2007). In *Plessy v. Ferguson*, the US Supreme Court ruled that separate but equal was constitutional. And, in the most recent decision on school desegregation, June 2007, the US Supreme Court partially overturned the famous *Brown v. Board of Education* decision of 1954; in 2007 it is no longer legal for school boards to use race when making student assignments. In other words, the Brown decision that called for school desegregation (and the desegregation of other public spaces like buses and waiting rooms) is no longer in effect; public schools may stay segregated or resegregate and this will not violate federal law.

How can we justify cases such as the resegregation of public schools (Orfield 2001; Mickelson and Heath 1999) or the prohibition on using race as a factor in college admissions (Michigan) or the exclusion of African Americans from positions of power in politics, the military, and the economic sphere? How can we justify the fact that African Americans are disproportionately likely to be poor—they are two to three times more likely than whites to live in poverty (Hattery & Smith 2007)? How can we justify the fact that African American men are eight or nine times more likely to be incarcerated than their white counterparts (Hattery & Smith 2007; Pager 2003)? Perhaps the answer lies in an examination of ideology. If whites continue to believe that African Americans are less than fully human (Pew 2003), then it is easier to justify their exclusion from educational institutions, their exclusion from positions of power, and their relegation to housing projects that lack running water or jobs that pay less than a living wage. These are the questions that Bonilla-Silva and Embrick tackle in the chapters that follow.

REFERENCES

Du Bois, W. E. B. 1973. *The Souls of Black Folk*. Edited by Herbert Aptheker. New York: Kraus Thompson, Inc.

Ehle, John. 1988. *Trail of Tears: The Rise and Fall of the Cherokee Nation*. New York: Doubleday.

Hattery, Angela J., and Earl Smith. 2007. *African American Families*. Thousand Oaks, CA: Sage.

Hattery, Angela, and Earl Smith. 2007. "Dred Scott, White Supremacy and African American Civil Rights." 445–47 in William A. Darity (ed.), *International Encyclopedia of the Social Sciences*, 2nd edition. Farmington Hill, Mich.: Thomson Gale, Inc.

Franklin, John Hope. 2005. *Mirror to America: The Autobiography of John Hope Franklin*. New York: Farrar, Straus & Giroux.

Mickelson, Roslyn, and D. Heath. 1999. "The Effects of Segregation on African American High School Seniors' Academic Achievement." *Journal of Negro Education* 68: 566–86.

Orfield, Gary. 2001. *Schools More Separate: Consequences of a Decade of Resegregation*. Cambridge, Mass.: Civil Rights Project Harvard University.

Pager, D. 2003. The Mark of a Criminal Record. "*American Journal of Sociology*" 108 937–75.

The Pew Research Center for The People & The Press. 2003. "Evenly Divided and Increasingly Polarized." people-press.org/.

Winant, Howard. 2001. *The World is a Ghetto: Race and Democracy since World War II*. New York: Basic Books.

Wright, E. O. 1997. *Class Counts: Comparative Studies in Class Analysis*. New York: Cambridge University Press.

2

"Look, a Negro": Reflections on the Human Rights Approach to Racial Inequality

Eduardo Bonilla-Silva

I begin my remarks by narrating a story. One of our neighbors, a rich Jewish woman who is a very open-minded, educated, liberal person, told us that in a recent trip to attend an opera in Washington, D.C., she was seated by the presidential box seat. Condoleezza Rice was in the box that night, a fact that fascinated many in the audience. But our neighbor was not impressed at all and told us, "I do not know why people get all excited about seeing her. She is still a nigger, isn't she?"

I anchor my comments with this story because it captures the essence of what I will suggest in this chapter. As long as the humanity of all "races" is not fully recognized, a human rights tradition (HRT henceforth) to racial matters is bound to fail. In my remarks, I will proceed as follows. First, I examine how the HRT reads classical statements on rights. Second, I discuss the limitations and racial boundaries of this and similar traditions. Finally, I pose some political challenges to the HRT and venture a few ideas on how the human rights discourse may be rearticulated to serve as a tool for the liberation of people of color the world over.

RACE AND THE HUMAN RIGHTS TRADITION

I am fascinated by how most (white) scholars writing about citizenship, human rights, and democracy ignore the centrality of race—*then* and *now*. They romanticize the emergence of democracy and Enlightenment figures such as Voltaire, Rousseau, Kant, Hume, or Condorcet. They universalize the ideas codified in the documents produced by the French and the American Revolutions when neither intended this to be the case.

They seem to forget the fact that the Athenian model of democratic citizenship was quick to exclude Others—the latter threatening "the negation of order and the rule of law" (Castles and Davidson 2000, 31). Indeed, it was Aristotle who created the mythical notion *ius sanguinis* (by blood) (Castles and Davidson 2000). With regard to the Enlightenment philosophers and to refresh the reader's memory, a few quotes will suffice.

David Hume, one of the Scottish Moralists, wrote in his 1753 *Of National Characters*, that "I am apt to suspect the negroes . . . to be *naturally inferior to the whites*. . . . Not to mention our colonies, there are Negro slaves dispersed all over Europe, of which *none ever discovered any symptoms of ingenuity*; . . . In Jamaica . . . they talk of one negro as a man of arts and learning; but it is likely he is admired for very slender accomplishments, *like a parrot who speaks a few words plainly*" (quoted in Goldberg 1993, 57).

Or consider that Kant, father of modern moral theory, also fashioned himself as an anthropologist and geographer and wrote racialized essays such as *The Different Races of Mankind*. In his *Observations on the Feelings of the Beautiful and the Sublime*, for instance, he stated that "so fundamental is the difference between [the black and white] races of man . . . it appears to be as great in regard to mental capacities as in color" so that "a clear proof that what [a negro] said was stupid" was that "this fellow was quite black from head to toe" (quoted in Mills 1997, 70).

And how can one forget that enlightened liberals in the United States, such as Benjamin Franklin, John Hancock, and James Madison (the main architect of our Constitution), as well as founding fathers, such as George Washington and Thomas Jefferson, owned people (Feagin 2000). And in France, has it been forgotten that abolitionists such as Robespierre, Lafayette, and Condorcet compromised and did not extend the so-called freedoms of the revolution to the half-million slaves in the colonies?

Hence, as my friend Charles Mills has argued, the so-called social contract of modernity was a *racial* contract. We savages, we primitive peoples, we creatures regarded as barely above monkeys, were not part of the contract (Mills 1997). The following description of the "Negro" from the *Encyclopaedia Britannica* in 1798 illustrates the era's "enlightened" thinking about race:

> Vices the most notorious seem to be the portion of this unhappy race: idleness, treachery, revenge, cruelty, impudence, stealing, lying, profanity, debauchery, nastiness and intemperance, are said to have extinguished the principles of natural law, and to have silenced the reproofs of conscience. They are strangers to every sentiment of compassion, and are an awful example of the corruption of man when left to himself. (quoted in Ishay 2004, 113)

Rousseau implied the Enlightenment's attitude of racial superiority when he stated that after years of Europeans "swarming all over the world" . . . he was "convinced that we have known no other men than Europeans" (quoted in Castles and Davidson 2000, 48).

As we well know, much evidence contradicted the putative European superiority. As Castles and Davidson (2000) point out,

> The conquest of the Americas changed the western claim to moral and ethical superiority maintained vis-á-vis the Old Worlds, since no matter how awful the Mayan and Aztec civilizations, this time the Europeans were greater in their slaughter than those with whom they compared themselves. (50)

The lands colonized by the West experienced the European warrior-citizen as someone who was a genocidal destroyer of culture and tradition (Castles and Davidson 2000). Yet the dream of the Western world has remained through today: "Why can't they be like us?"

THE (RACIAL) LIMITATIONS OF THE HUMAN RIGHTS TRADITION

There is much to say about the limitations of the human rights tradition in its approach to race. However, because of space constraints, I will enumerate only some of the major limitations of the HRT.

1. *Folks in this tradition are still stuck in the bourgeois liberal individualism that created this discourse and, accordingly, reject group-based claims or expressions unless they are relegated to the private sphere.* The HRT idealizes the autonomous individual who can be located within a universe of abstract rights, devoid of racially constraining social structures (Guinier and Torres 2002). Ironically, this color-blind stance uses the same neoconservative rhetoric that has dominated the racial justice debate since the dismantlement of Jim Crow. It focuses on a commitment to formal equality that is structured on legal and political formation. This stance so narrowly interprets the goal of human rights that it precludes concern with the consequences of real-world racial inequalities. As Guinier and Torres (2002) suggest, this denial of political race provides a cover for dominant identities that are subsumed in so-called universal categories such as "the citizen," "Americans" (see Morrison 1998; Walters 2005), or "Canadians."

This color-blind HRT stance, therefore, would solve racial inequalities by individual advancement rather than by the collective action of racial groups. Indeed, mobilization of the latter to pursue racial civil rights is viewed as racist—a threat of balkanization of modern society. The HRT logic presents us with a paradox. The reality is that agitation by people of color has made this a freer and, in a strict sense, more liberal culture. However, the universalist claim has to be that continued organizing around race will retard the liberal development of society and, thus, should be stopped because it has lost its liberationist thrust (Guinier and Torres 2002).

2. *The HRT stance assumes that modern nation-states are not deeply racialized (some admit, though, to their gender and class bias). If nation-states are also racial states, as David T. Goldberg (2001) argues, why would they provide for and guarantee full citizenship to nonwhites?*

There is a deep connection between democracy and human rights because, as Beetham (1999) states, "the guarantee of basic freedoms is a necessary condition for the people's voice to be effective in public affairs and for popular control over government to be secured" (93). Although the laws of today's democratic nation-states appear to provide universal political access, minorities in these nation-states suffer de facto exclusion from the democratic process. As Castles and Davidson (2000) point out, "They have the right to vote, but social, economic and cultural exclusion denies them the chance of gaining political representation or having any real say in the decisions that affect their lives" (11). The HRT stance attempts to mollify minorities in the United States and Canada by claiming that "blacks and women in North America do not all suffer dishonor at the same rate or intensity" as people elsewhere (Howard 1995, 159). But the reality is that, in the Western nation-state, citizenship has been and continues to be a white political category. As Dallmayr (2001) argues in his critique of Rorty's *Achieving Our Country*, the anti-identity politic, pro–melting pot stance of America was "basically a sham, disguising the hegemonic predominance of one culture—white, male, Anglo-Saxon—over women and all sorts of minorities" (101).

I agree with Beetham (1999) that there is also a deeper reason for democracy: commonality of humanity and needs. Full democratic citizenship thus implies economic and other social inclusion, not just political inclusion. As Fraga and Leal (2004) argue, "Having more rights to vote, own a home, or get an education means very little when people are provided insufficient resources to realize those rights" (298). The fact is that ascriptive racial status remains an organizing principle of Western social institutions. Social arrangements by race, such as labor market segmentation and residential segregation along racial lines produce "real-life differences that cannot be understood purely in representational terms" (Glenn 2002, 14–15). These arrangements produce and are reproduced by differential access to social capital. As Portes and Landolt (1996) suggest, social capital works through closure. The outcomes of social capital "will vary depending on what economic resources are obtained, who is excluded from them, and what is demanded in exchange" (Portes and Landolt 1996, 21). Therefore, social capital can perpetuate "exclusivity and a society in which identity, to a great extent, determines whether or not one is allowed to join" (Portes and Landolt 1996, 21).

As HRT proponents, such as Howard (1995), claim, "In a society based on human rights, human dignity consists not of acquiescence to hierarchical order but of equality and assertion of one's claims to respect" (27). The problem is that the ideology of individual choice in Western societies undermines concerns with ascriptive restrictions related to status, as status remains a private matter outside the purview of the state (Howard 1995).

3. *The HRT stance subscribes to the notion of ethical individualism—"the intrinsic value of all humans" (Howard 1995, 46), but it seems unwilling to temper this view with the fact that there are vast differences of power among individuals as individuals as well as members of social groups or nation-states.*

The idea of citizenship typically designates the two related notions of membership and equality: people who are *members* are *equal* with respect to the rights and duties associated with membership (Gaffaney 2000). Individual autonomy is the status of being enabled to participate in the governing of the state, in an ongoing democratic dialogue, or both (Gaffaney 2000). But such participation is contingent on social and economic equality. Body-Gendrot and Gittel (2003) argue that the rise of competitive national states has yielded an erosion of citizenship—that "universal policies of redistribution have masked unequal power relations and been beneficial to dominant groups . . . and less helpful to stigmatized groups, who have then demanded special treatment and affirmative action policies to combat racism and discrimination" (xi). The fact is that the poor and minorities cannot participate fully in modern nation-states. Genuine democratic citizenship and human rights can happen only when differences are no longer the basis of subordination (Pateman 1992).

4. *The HRT betrays an ahistorical understanding of the discourse of human rights and, thus, ignores the fact that the West would not have been anything without the Rest. The West reached its place, its "civilization," through "the development of underdevelopment," as authors such as Andre Gunder Frank, Samir Amin, Immanuel Wallerstein, folks in the Dependency tradition, and most writers on globalization acknowledge. Rights, citizenship, and democracy for the West exist at the expense of the Rest!*

Institutional definitions of democracy fail to say that the starting point for a democracy is popular rule and control over decision making (Beetham 1999). What the liberal discourse has sorely missed is the fact that exclusion of some groups from democratic citizenship has been, as Marshall (1994) states, "from the start integral to the entitlement of other groups" (133).

No one can deny that American "democracy" was built on the backs of its internally colonized racial and ethnic minorities, especially those of color. Besides black slavery, American Indians and their children were subject to indentured and other highly inequitable, restrictive contracts; thousands of

Chinese indentured laborers worked America's railroads and mines; and Mexican Americans were dispossessed of their lands and, in New Mexico, forced into legalized peonage (Glenn 2002). The greatest exploitation, of course, was black slavery. Black Americans were denied rights to their own labor for almost 100 years on the grounds that they were, according to the Constitution, three-fifths of a man and, to quote Chief Justice Taney in the *Dred Scott* decision of 1857, "so far inferior that they had no rights which the white man was bound to respect" (quoted in Glenn 2002, 36). Although black Americans were supposedly granted citizenship after the Civil War, they were subsequently robbed of the privileges of being full citizens by multiple laws and Supreme Court decisions. Has the decision in *Plessy v. Ferguson* that constitutionally validated Jim Crow been forgotten? "If one race is inferior to the other socially, the Constitution of the United States cannot put them upon the same plane" (Cecil 1990, 64). American blacks struggled valiantly to dismantle Jim Crow, but, as black-power activists tried, in vain, to tell America in the late 1960s and early 1970s, that gain was only a second-class citizenship.

As for Europe, their "democratic" societies can attribute their economic success to the resources they stripped from their defenseless colonies. As Cairns (1999), states, these subjects of colonial empires consequently "entered world politics not as full-fledged participants, but as people ruled by alien others on their own territories" (25). The colonial empires were hierarchical systems "based on power imbalances and on a ranking of cultures and civilizations—often equated with race—that gave a surplus of positive recognition to the ruling European peoples, counterbalanced by the non-recognition, misrecognition, or negative recognition of the people they ruled" (Cairns 1999, 25). Even the anthropologists and missionaries, the European intermediaries who "spoke for" the "subject peoples," judged these peoples as backward (Cairns 1999). Imperialism thereby defined hundreds of millions of non-Western people as politically incapable and unworthy of self-rule (Cairns 1999). As a consequence, even after their release from imperial bondage, vast numbers of these conquered people have been too poor to ever become "citizens" in the sense of full participation (Castles and Davidson 2000).

Today, imperial dominance worldwide takes the form of multinational corporations that operate outside governmental constraints. The result has been the structuring of the global system into developed and underdeveloped economies, zones of security and insecurity, hegemonic and subordinate cultures, as well as the reproduction of these inequalities within states (Beetham 1999). As Muzzafar (1993) states,

> By equating human rights with civil and political rights, the rich and powerful in the North hope to avoid coming to grips with those economic, social and

cultural challenges which could threaten their privileged position in the existing world order. What the rich and powerful do not want is a struggle for economic transformation presented as a human rights struggle, a struggle for human dignity. (39, quoted in Dallmayr 2001)

5. *The democracy, citizenship, and human rights discourses, despite their claims to universalism, often reproduce the historical paternalism of yesteryears. Many in these traditions still talk down to us, the "minorities" in the world order; they still seem burdened by the urge to civilize us. This, as Castles and Davidson (2000) argue, "can only be lived as majority oppression and provoke resistance" (215).*

The HRT stance correctly maintains that political dominance of one ethnoreligious group in a state precludes the protection of human rights. But they subscribe to the illusion that modern Western societies are now realizing homogeneity of secular citizenship, which prescribes tolerance of racial, ethnic, and religious differences (Howard 1995). Ethnic identity has become, in their opinion, a voluntary and private celebration. I argue that this may be the case for dominant identities but not for subordinated ones. Minority status is enforced in Western societies as much as differential citizenships.

In the civics of a nation-state, even reason is a national patrimony, and only the host society is believed to have its key. As Castles and Davidson (2001) point out, any attempt to debate it shows a quality that requires reeducation. This can be lived only as majority oppression and provoke resistance.

6. *HRT proponents object to political and military tactics that violate the human rights of actors, thus creating a stance that is of limited use for any revolutionary movement. Instead, they advocate "tolerance," listening to others, democratic politics, and a "Kumbaya my Lord" political practice.*

The HRT agenda is moral intervention. They envision several means: cosmopolitanism based on the ideals of Habermas, nongovernmental organizations (NGOs) devoted to human rights, international citizenship, and morally motivated, international governmental bodies.

Habermasian cosmopolitanism has perhaps the most obvious limits. How can democracies negotiate in good faith with nondemocracies even on matters that ought to concern everybody, such as environmental degradation? After all, democracies have destroyed the planet, too (Dauenhauer 1998).

The motivations of humanely motivated NGOs are more laudable. As Hardt and Negri (2000), state, "Precisely because they are not run directly by governments, [NGOs] are assumed to act on the basis of ethical or moral imperatives . . . [they] strive to identify universal needs and defend human rights" (36). These NGOs thereby "conduct 'just wars' without arms, without violence, without borders" (Hardt and Negri 2000, 36). However, as Steven Friedman (2002) warns, watch out for "civil society" interventions, as "non-state actors may thus hand control of resources to individuals and oligarchies who may limit democracy's reach and ensure that 'development' becomes a source of patronage rather than equity" (32). Moreover, the efforts of these NGOs are never sufficient. This fact, in turn, is used to justify "legitimate" interferences by external states or the international agencies they sponsor (Hardt and Negri 2000). "In this way," as Hardt and Negri (2000) state, "moral intervention has become a frontline force of imperial intervention" (36).

The idealistic notion of a global democratic citizenship is also intrinsically flawed. It ignores the fact that citizenship is still state bound and thus cannot produce internationalism (Dauenhauer 1996). As Walzer (1981) points out (paraphrased by Dauenhauer 1996, 38), philosophical knowing can be "universalist and singular," but political knowing is always "particular and plural." International citizenship, consequently, would have to be predicated on an international governing body, paving the way for another kind of imperialism.

Ironically, HRT proponents, such as Ishay (2004), document how "human rights" have ultimately been at the mercy of powerful actors, yet they maintain a faith in powerful actors as a way out. They support international governing bodies, even though history demonstrates these international actors act to maintain the exploitation of poor, less developed nations by the more powerful nations of the world system. Perhaps they need to be reminded that the League of Nations was dominated by the imperial nations and that it egregiously ignored the rights of the colonized nations. The global relationship among nations and the role of the United Nations, the World Bank, the International Monetary Fund, and the General Agreement on Tariffs and Trade in serving the interests of the dominant nations and their international corporations is not so different today. And, to quote Lummis (1996), "it is a perversion of the idea of liberation to transform it into a means for establishing the authority of a small elite of trained specialists" (20).

The fact is that liberalizing changes in the world have rarely occurred except through major social crises. In the United States, for example, revolution, Civil War Reconstruction, and World War II were, as Glenn (2002) states, "times of expanding egalitarianism typically . . . followed by periods of regression during which hard-won gains were rolled back and new exclusions put in place—the current post-civil rights period being an obvious instance" (24).

WHAT IS TO BE DONE? CHALLENGES TO THE HRT AND A FEW IDEAS ON HOW TO GET BEYOND

How can an HRT approach deal with the devastating effects of Hurricane Katrina felt along the Mississippi Gulf coast and in New Orleans? What can it do to address the fundamental racial inequities in New Orleans, Detroit, Los Angeles, Durham, and everywhere else that structure disasters such as the one wrought by Hurricane Katrina? What will HRT folks do when chocolate New Orleans is reorganized into a vanilla city?

What is the HRT political approach to the racist anti-immigration mood of American citizens? What will HRT folks do when white citizens vote in a democratic way to enforce the right for a *herrenvolk* democracy and cut programs, benefits, and resources for immigrants?

What is the HRT political strategy to deal with U.S.-led interventions in Afghanistan, Iraq, and perhaps the many more to come (and I know that many in the HRT supported these interventions against "terrorism")? How do they deal with torture, rapes, massacres of civilians, and the "collateral damage" produced by "smart" bombs?

What is the HRT approach to deal with the plight of Palestinian people? And, finally, as a Puerto Rican, I ask the reader, "What the hell is the HRT stance on the 100-plus years of American colonial domination of my island and my people?" (We are no longer a "sexy" cause, so we are all but off of the radar of folks in the HRT!)

And, more controversially, how do we feel when a 9/11 happens and many Third World people rejoice? Do we understand and empathize with their feelings? For those who still ponder the silly "Why do they hate us?" question, the answer is because "we" have done a lot of harm to "them" and "the chickens coming home to roost" is part of the equality game (Churchill 2003). If the West inflicts terror on the Rest, why does one fail to appreciate the beauty of reciprocity? Why does one not recognize the inalienable right of oppressed people to fight back? Doesn't the Bible tell us the same, "As ye sow, so shall ye reap"?

How do you feel when Iraqis rejoice after an American is killed in Iraq or elsewhere? Do you understand why they feel like that? Do you even comprehend the brutal but real logic that leaves Palestinians no recourse but to fight the Israeli occupation through suicide bombings? For every Israeli killed in this second intifada, about 3.5 Palestinians are killed.[1] Do you appreciate the sacrifice in this horrendous yet effective weapon of the weak?

Given that the world is fundamentally organized around collectivities with differential access to power and resources, there is no way we can place the resistance struggles and the tactics used by subalterns on the same plane as the offensive, imperial actions of those on the top of the world system. Taking this liberal stance ultimately helps maintain the current power arrangements in the world. Thus, liberation movements—then and now—have used the language, ideas, and spirit of the HRT but have always been ready to force the issue. Resistance, as Fanon and Malcolm X told us, can be a "cleansing force" and central in the struggle to force others to recognize our humanity (Oliver 2004).

So, what can be done to rearticulate an HRT as part of the struggle for racial equality and freedom?

1. Acknowledge the power differential among actors in the world system. Nation-states and subjects in those states are in different stations, and, thus, proclamations of rights will not be enough to overcome these differences.

2. Recognize that collectivities exist and that members of those collectivities share a similar position and set of conditions in the system. This means that if "whites" or "men" or "capitalists" have an advantageous position in society, advocating for individual-level rights for women, people of color, and workers will not do the trick. The way out is to work toward group-level solutions for the "problems" faced by the oppressed people of the world.

3. Maintain a relentless critique of empire and neoempire. Human rights advocates must always keep in mind when the empire is talking and why they must be cautious of taking the empire's talk at face value.[2]

4. Support those at the bottom of the well in social orders all over the world. Human rights advocates cannot continue their "all-people-are-the-same" nonsense. Since some people have more powers than others and are either active or passive beneficiaries of unequal social relations, human rights advocates ought to support the oppressed, period.

5. Recognize that resistance struggles are nasty. This means that in liberation struggles of any kind, excesses, brutality, and terror may happen. But we must always remember that in the tragic mathematics of death between oppressors and the oppressed, the oppressed always lose more people than the oppressors and, most often, by margins of ten to one.[3]

6. Recognize that multicultural and international citizenship and the international vigilance for the human rights of *all* will be the end product of many particular struggles. The universal and cosmopolitan dream of the HRT will come out of the particular and not the other way around.[4]

7. Finally, *real* international human rights will emerge slowly when we begin a massive redistribution of resources, recognize the historical atrocities the West did (and is still doing) to the Rest, and amend for them. Without redistribution of resources; without an end to wasteful and uncontrolled "development"; without an end to First, Second, Third, and Fourth worlds, we will not be able to see each other as members of one community (humankind) with equal rights.

I end my discussion with the words of Fanon (1968) in *The Wretched of the Earth*:

From the moment that you and your like are liquidated like so many dogs, you have no other resources but to use all and every means to regain your importance as a man [*sic*]. You must therefore weigh as heavily as you can upon the body of your torturer in order that his soul, lost in some byway, may finally find once more its universal dimension. (295)

So know that we, men and women of color, will weigh heavily on our torturers to make sure *their* soul becomes truly universal. Then "human rights" will become totally irrelevant, as we will all be equal partners in the world community of humankind. Thanks!

NOTES

This is a slightly revised version of a talk I gave at a panel sponsored by Sociologists without Borders at the 2007 meetings in Montreal of the American Sociological Association. I left the document with the character and drama of a talk because I hope to inspire readers' passions (whichever direction they go).

1. In the first intifada (1987–1992) and according to statistics from Irish and British newspapers, for every one Israeli killed by a Palestinian, eleven Palestinians were killed by Israelis. In the second intifada (2000 to the present), the statistics are more "egalitarian," as the ratio has improved for Palestinians. According to B'Tselem: The Israeli Information Center for Human Rights in The Occupied Territories, for every Israeli who has died, 3.5 Palestinians have died.

2. I gave this talk in the summer of 2006 when the state of Israel was bombing Lebanon. At the time, too many human rights advocates, including members of Sociologists without Borders, an organization to which I belong, condemned both sides for their "atrocities." This stance, I suggest, forgets the imperial role of Israel and its allies in the Middle East and does not help advance progressive politics in the area.

3. Those concerned about the "brutality" and "inhumanity" of resistance wars should always remember that empire is always more brutal and more inhumane. For example, the inequities in the moral calculations of humanity can be estimated from how much money is given in compensation when the United States admits a "mistake" in a bombing. Marc Herold, a professor of economics at the University of New Hampshire, has done the math, and, for the Italians killed or injured accidentally when a U.S. Marine jet hit aerial tramway cables in Italy not too long ago, the United States gave close to $2 million to each Italian victim; for the Chinese victims of the accidental bombing in Budapest a while ago, it gave $150,000; and for the victims of an accidental bombing of Afghanis attending a wedding party, after initially offering tents and blankets as compensation, it ended up paying $100 per victim. The relative value of life according to empire comes to this: at the top, an American (white) expects 6 million, an Italian a third of that, a Chinese a fortieth of that, and an Afghani a six-thousandth. According to Professor Herold, even if one controls for purchasing power, the relative value of life for people in the West

in terms of the Rest is staggering. See his Web page at www.cursor.org/stories/afghandead.htm.

4. The proposition that "all citizens should assume the same impartial, general point of view transcending all particular interests, perspectives and experiences" in dealing with their citizenship, as Iris Marion Young argues, is nonsense. She argues that "so long as there are disadvantaged and oppressed groups, measures should be taken to provide mechanisms for the effective recognition of their distinct voices and perspectives" through "differentiated citizenship" (quoted in Smith 1999, 142).

REFERENCES

Beetham, David. 1999. *Democracy and Human Rights*. Oxford: Blackwell.

Body-Gendrot, Sophie, and Marilyn Gittel. 2003. "Empowering Citizens: From Social Citizenship to Social Capital." In *Social Capital and Social Citizenship*, edited by Sophie Body-Gendrot and Marilyn Gittel. Lanham, Md.: Lexington Books.

Cairns, Alan C. 1999. "Empire, Globalization, and the Fall and Rise of Diversity." In *Citizenship, Diversity, and Pluralism: Canadian and Comparative Perspectives*. Montreal: McGill-Queen's University Press.

Castles, Stephen, and Alastair Davidson. 2000. *Citizenship and Migration: Globalization and the Politics of Belonging*. New York: Routledge.

Cecil, Andrew R. 1990. *Equality Tolerance and Loyalty: Virtues Serving the Common Purpose of Democracy*. Dallas: University of Texas at Dallas.

Churchill, Ward. 2003. *On the Justice of Roosting Chickens: Reflections on the Consequences of U.S. Imperial Arrogance and Criminality*. Edinburgh: AK Press.

Dallmayr, Fred. 2001. *Achieving Our World: Toward a Global and Plural Democracy*. Lanham, Md.: Rowman & Littlefield.

Dauenhauer, Bernard P. 1998. *Paul Ricoeur: The Promise and Risk of Politics*. Lanham, Md.: Rowman & Littlefield.

Fanon, Frantz. 1968. *The Wretched of the Earth*. Translated by Constance Farrington. New York: Grove.

Feagin, Joe R. 2000. *Racist America: Roots, Current Realities, and Future Reparations*. New York: Routledge.

Fraga, Luis Ricardo, and David L. Leal. 2004. "Playing the 'Latino Card': Race, Ethnicity, and National Party Politics." *Du Bois Review: Social Science Research on Race* 1, no. 2: 297–317.

Friedman, Steven. 2002. "Democracy, Inequality, and the Reconstitution of Politics." In *Democratic Governance and Social Inequality*, edited by Joseph S. Tulchin with Amelia Brown. Boulder, Colo.: Lynne Rienner.

Gaffaney, Timothy J. 2000. *Freedom for the Poor: Welfare and the Foundations of Democratic Citizenship*. Boulder, Colo.: Westview Press.

Glenn, Evelyn Nakano. 2002. *Unequal Freedom: How Race and Gender Shaped American Citizenship and Labor*. Cambridge, Mass.: Harvard University Press.

Goldberg, David T. 1993. *The Racist State*. London: Blackwell.

———. 2001. *Racist Culture*. London: Blackwell.

Guinier, Lani, and Gerald Torres. 2002. *The Miner's Canary: Enlisting Race, Resisting Power, Transforming Democracy*. Cambridge, Mass.: Harvard University Press.

Hardt, Michael, and Antonio Negri. 2000. *Empire*. Cambridge, Mass.: Harvard University Press.

Howard, Rhoda E. 1995. *Human Rights and the Search for Community*. Boulder, Colo.: Westview Press.

Ishay, Micheline R. 2004. *The History of Human Rights: From Ancient Times to the Globalization Era*. Berkeley: University of California Press.

Lummis, C. Douglas. 1996. *Radical Democracy*. Ithaca, N.Y.: Cornell University Press.

Marshall, Barbara L. 1994. *Engendering Modernity: Feminism, Social Theory and Social Change*. Boston: Northeastern University Press.

Mills, Charles W. 1997. *The Racial Contract*. Ithaca, N.Y.: Cornell University Press.

Morrison, Toni. 1998. *Beloved: A Novel*. New York: Knopf.

Muzzafar, Chandra. 1993. *Human Rights and the World Order*. Penang: Just World Trust.

Oliver, Kelly. 2004. *The Colonization of the Psychic Space: A Psychoanalytic Social Theory of Oppression*. Minneapolis: University of Minnesota Press.

Pateman, Carol. 1992. "Equality, Difference, Subordination: The Politics of Motherhood and Women's Citizenship." In *Beyond Equality and Differences: Citizenship, Feminist Politics and Female Subjectivity*, edited by Gisela Bock and Susan James. London: Routledge.

Portes, Alejandro, and Patricia Landolt. 1996. "The Downside of Social Capital." *The American Prospect* 26: 18–25.

Smith, Lynn C. 1999. "Is Citizenship a Gendered Concept?" In *Citizenship, Diversity, and Pluralism: Canadian and Comparative Perspectives*, edited by Alan C. Cairns, John C. Courtney, Peter Mackinnon, and Hans J. Michelmann. Montreal: McGill-Queen's University Press.

Walters, Ronald. 2005. *Freedom Is Not Enough: Black Voters, Black Candidates, and American Presidential Politics*. Lanham, Md.: Rowman & Littlefield.

Walzer, Michael. 1981. "Philosophy and Democracy." *Political Theory* 29, no. 3: 393–94.

3

The Diversity Ideology: Keeping Major Transnational Corporations White and Male in an Era of Globalization

David G. Embrick

> Equal rights for women is a goal that resonates with individualism and freedom of choice. Yet that goal failed because, legally, in order to be treated alike, people have to "be" alike, and the prevailing belief in Western societies is that women and men are intrinsically different.
>
> —Judith Lorber[1]

> Injustice anywhere is a threat to justice everywhere.
>
> —Martin Luther King Jr.[2]

The United States of America is a democratic, meritocratic society. In a global world, it is a shining example of freedom and equality. It is a society in which the right to work is a fundamental human right guaranteed and protected by its constitution. It is color blind, and it is gender blind. So the argument goes according to many leading conservative scholars (D'Souza 1995; Steele 1988; Thermstrom and Thermstrom 1997). Therefore, there is no need for affirmative action programs (Glazer 1987; McWhorter 2000), social welfare policies (Murray 1984), programs developed to create a more equal and fair criminal justice system (Wilbanks 1987), or diversity policies and practices (Wood 2003). The system is fair. In addition, women have made tremendous strides in the workplace. The Equal Pay Act of 1963 ensures that women and men receive equal wages in the workplace. Women are nurturers, and their need to spend more time with their family than at the workplace better explains why women are less likely to occupy high-level positions in big business (Levin 1992; Randle 1999).

23

The majority of Americans, men and women, whites and minorities, hold one or more of these beliefs.[3] After all, discrimination is against the law. The majority of Americans also have faith in the criminal justice system and believe that companies breaking the law would face stiff penalties from the federal government. And their tarnished public image would cause customers to avoid their products and services, in turn causing the company to lose money. Moreover, our current social system is a far cry from the days of Jim Crow laws when minorities faced overt racial discrimination on an everyday basis and when women did not have the right to vote. One would be hard pressed to find instances where employers explained to women that their gender was unwelcome in the workplace or responded to blacks looking for a job, "We don't hire niggers here." Hence, to most Americans, the idea that racism or gender discrimination continues to be a problem in the United States is absurd. And corporate America feeds these mainstream notions regarding race and gender in the United States by advertising themselves as "equal opportunity employers," as fair employers, and, more frequently in the past twenty years, as international, global employers that care about diversity. The central image that is portrayed to the American people over and over again is that corporations are working hard to diversify their companies. In fact, in a global system where the majority of potential customers are nonwhite, companies must be willing to diversify or face possible extinction.

Mainstream ideas regarding fairness, opportunity, and racial and gender equality in big business run into a snag when forced to face the "white male solidarity"[4] that runs the corporate world, setting barriers for minorities and women wanting to gain entry into the workplace, denying them promotions and pay raises, and denying them access to the upper levels of management. Studies by Braddock and McPartland (1982), Fernandez (1999), Kirschenman and Neckerman (1991), and Royster (2003) and others illustrate that while women and minorities have made some gains in obtaining access to previously white-dominated workplaces, many continue to be denied access and opportunity because of the structural or social elements involved in racial discrimination (see also Amott and Matthaei 2006; Reskin and Padavic 2002; Reskin and Roos 1990).

Although some access to the opportunity structure has opened up, in fact the right to work is not guaranteed or protected by the Constitution. Despite this lack of protection, I argue that most Americans believe that the right to work is in fact a "human right," that all Americans should be allowed an opportunity to make a living, take care of their families, and avoid dependency on the government. Using this understanding of human rights, I assert that the institutionalized discrimination that racial and ethnic minorities and women face in the labor market, at all levels, is indeed a violation of their human rights.

Research by notable authors, such as Sharon Collins (1997) and Anthony Stith (1998), shows that minorities who are able to enjoy the satisfaction of a "good job" are less likely to achieve upward mobility compared to their white male counterparts. When they do get promoted, they are more likely to be placed in very limited and dead-end positions (head of affirmative action, head of human resources, and so on), positions otherwise known as "glass-ceiling" positions. These positions garner little prestige, and often the managers who occupy these jobs are seen as less than competent. Anthony Stith (1998) describes the concept of the "glass ceiling" as a "visual image of people pressing up against a window, getting a tantalizing view of a wonderful world before them, but being denied entry to it" (22). For those lucky few minorities who get access to corporate jobs, researchers Ibarra (1993) and Fernandez (1981) argue that blacks and Latinos are less likely, compared to whites, to obtain mentors who will help them move to the next level. Blacks who make it to the top as chief executive officers (CEOs) of major corporations face new hardships, such as having to maneuver socially, politically, and emotionally in typically all-white settings (Davis and Watson 1982; see also Travis 1991).

THE DIVERSITY IDEOLOGY: A NEW WAY TO EXAMINE BIG BUSINESS

How are corporations able to continue excluding women and minorities in managerial, leadership, and other positions of power in the workplace? How are many companies able to get away with having an exclusive or almost exclusive white male club at the executive, board, and other positions of power in their businesses? In this chapter, I suggest that a diversity ideology has emerged since the post–civil rights era, giving many organizations an undeniable edge when it comes to maintaining the white male power structure that runs American society. Here, I am not suggesting that women and minorities do not occupy positions of power in corporate America (or other American institutions). Nor am I suggesting that women and minorities have not achieved some upward mobility in these organizations since the 1950's. What I am suggesting is that given all the past achievements and accomplishments of women and minorities in the past forty-plus years, we still have quite a way to go before we can claim that we live in an egalitarian society.

Using critical race theory and the notion of color-blind racism as theoretical anchors, I argue that a diversity ideology emerged in the late 1960s that has helped many corporations become increasingly sophisticated in their ability to portray themselves as supporters of racial and gender equality while simultaneously making no real substantial changes in their policies and practices to create real changes in the racial and gender composition of their workplaces. Specifically, corporations have systematically and strategically co-opted the notions of diversity that were established by the civil rights movement and helped to perpetuate a diversity ideology that has enabled them to advocate racial and gender equality yet maintain highly inequitable work environments and an even more inequitable chain of command. Thus, many corporations argue that they are spending huge sums of money and are working diligently to foster a corporate environment that is largely free of racial and gender discrimination, but here I present three reasons why we should suspect otherwise. First, forty-plus years after the civil rights triumphs, many companies continue to have highly segregated workplaces, segregated both racially and by gender. Second, the definition of diversity used by major corporations has become so broad that issues of racial and gender inequalities often become overlooked or completely ignored. Finally, although most senior-level managers and executives claim that their companies have diversity policies and are adamant about their companies' enthusiasm regarding diversity initiatives and practices, many are unable to adequately explain those policies and practices. The fact of the matter is that if race and gender issues do not get addressed as a central part of diversity, they do not get resolved.

Consequently, the diversity ideology has allowed many corporations to claim that they support racial and gender equality when in truth they do not. Just because there are companies that have relatively large numbers of minorities or women working for them does not guarantee that they are diverse. Nor does providing women and minorities with limited access to and opportunities in the upper managerial positions of a company confirm their commitment to diversity. Nevertheless, because corporations have developed a compelling argument centered on notions of diversity, they are able to convince the public that they are on the forefront of progressiveness. By implementing policies at the lower levels of their businesses, corporations are able to convey an ideology of equality and egalitarianism, even if only at a superficial level. By siding with affirmative action cases, promoting "best practices," and implementing diversity training programs in their workplaces, corporations are also able to generate an air of sincerity. Yet, according to Jackman (1994), "ideologies that are promoted with sincerity are more compelling" (65). Diversity, then, is used to divest rather than invest change into corporate institutions.

CLIMBING THE LADDER OF WHITE MALENESS

What does the racial and gender makeup of Fortune 500 companies look like, especially at the upper levels of the corporate hierarchy? Although a number of companies argue that they are making progress in their attempts to diversify their work environments, a number of scholars claim that corporate elites are mostly white males (Burk 2005; Domhoff 2005; Fernandez 1999; Zweigenhaft and Domhoff 2003).

Not too long ago, *DiversityInc*, a leading business-oriented magazine devoted to issues surrounding diversity, ran an article in its online newsletter announcing that sometime soon Ronald A. Williams will most likely become the sixth black CEO to run a Fortune 500 company. The mention of this news quickly made media headlines. As the news circulated in the business world that another black man was about to join the circle of high-ranked elites, newspapers and magazines such as the *San Francisco Chronicle* reported on the increasing success of blacks in the business world. In an interview with Bruce S. Gordon, fifteenth president of the National Association for the Advancement of Colored People, a *BusinessWeek* reporter asked,

> There's an unprecedented number of black CEOs in Corporate America. What has allowed them to reach a point where blacks hold such corporate power?[5]

Indeed, there is a notion floating in the business world that we are witnessing the decline of racial discrimination in corporate America. It is true that the number of black male CEOs in the Fortune 500 has tripled in the past thirteen years, from two in the early 1990s[6] to six in 2006. However, these numbers are still relatively small, just barely constituting 1 percent of the total population of Fortune 500 CEOs, especially when we consider that the number of blacks who have graduated with M.B.A. degrees has slightly increased since 2003 (Aslop 2006).[7] Second, minorities and women who occupy the position of CEO of a company are unlikely to make decisions that threaten the security and privilege of white males, especially considering that whites often make up the majority of members on a corporation's board (Zweigenhaft and Domhoff 2003). For example, consider Merrill Lynch. As a Wall Street firm, it is one of the largest and most well known Fortune 500 companies. Moreover, Merrill Lynch is regarded as one of the better models in the corporate world with respect to racial diversity, winning a number of diversity awards from *Fortune* magazine and placing forty-fourth on *DiversityInc*'s 2006 "Top 50 Companies for Diversity" (Merrill Lynch also placed number 1 in the category "Top 10 Companies for People with Disabilities," number 2 in the category "Top 10 Companies for Executive Women," and number 4 in the category "Top 10 Companies for Asian Americans"). Further, out of Merrill Lynch's eleven board members, two are African American: Stanley O'Neal, who became CEO of the company in April 2002, and Aulana L. Peters, widely known as one of the few African American women to serve on Fortune 500 boards. A superficial analysis might suggest that the racial composition of this board is not that bad. However, closer examination of the executive members of Merrill Lynch reveals a mostly white male group of people. Indeed, out of the thirty-four ranking officers, only three are women. Moreover, only one person in that group is African American. More important, this particular person happens to be head of public affairs at Merrill Lynch, a position that likely guarantees that any exposure to the media will be met by a minority face that represents Merrill Lynch.[8] Because senior-level and executive managers are the gatekeepers in their companies, the fact that the majority of these positions are held by white men creates additional barriers for women and minorities who are less likely to be mentored or given promotion or training opportunities compared to their white male counterparts (Collins 1998).

REVEALING THE TRUTH ABOUT BIG BUSINESS: EXPOSING THE DIVERSITY IDEOLOGY FOR WHAT IT IS

How do companies avoid close scrutiny? And how are they able to advertise to the public that they are sincerely interested in issues of diversity in the workplace, even in cases where they are publicly revealed as racist and sexist companies? One simple and very effective way for companies to create an illusion that they are interested in diversity is by donating money to charities and organizations whose goals specifically call for various issues of equality for women and minorities. Such charity organizations have access to the media and are well publicized. Another method used by companies is to stifle news of potential racial or gender conflicts in the company while purposely advertising news of company diversity. The diversity ideology allows companies to project an illusion of trust to the public. If businesses are willing to spend a fortune on creating diversity in the workplace and if they seem sincere enough, then why should we not believe them? An example of how the diversity ideology works to the advantage of major corporations can be found in the recent lawsuit by thirteen black employees against Tyson Foods. In this lawsuit, the employees maintained that a "white only" sign and padlock denied them access to a bathroom and break room in an Alabama plant. Even after repeated attempts to inform higher authorities of the racial discrimination that was taking place in this plant, no effort was made to stop the racial practices, and no attempts were made to investigate the incidents. In addition to the segregated bathroom and break room, plant managers frequently uttered racial epithets and used racial scare tactics, such as hanging a hangman's noose in the workplace. The lawsuit was filed in August 2005.[9] In October 2005, Tyson Foods announced that it was donating $26,000 to the Congressional Black Caucus Foundation. That same week, Tyson Foods was given a diversity award celebrating it as the "corporation of the year."

In a similar, more recent example, corporate giant Wal-Mart was forced to apologize for racially offensive movie suggestions offered on its website after being outed by bloggers who demanded Wal-Mart take responsibility for its racist actions. Apparently, customers who were interested in buying movies such as *Charlie and the Chocolate Factory* and *Planet of the Apes* were being directed to a listing of recommended movies that included *Introducing Dorothy Dandridge* and *Martin Luther King: I Have a Dream/Assassination of MLK*. Wal-Mart announced its apologies at the beginning of 2006 and announced it would make a more concerted effort to support minority organizations. In June 2006, *DiversityInc* awarded Wal-Mart number 6 on its "Top 10 Companies for African Americans" and included them in its "25 Noteworthy Companies" award.

Looking at the racial and gender makeup of managers and executive members in companies and focusing on companies' use of charities and the media to portray themselves as diverse organizations is one way to uncover the contradictions of many corporations when it comes to issues of racial and gender equality. However, these are facts that are often widely available to the public (e.g., pictures of the executive managers and board of directors of many companies can be found online). Because companies are aware of this, they need to have arguments to counter the inconsistencies between what they preach and what they practice. For example, by claiming that their work environments are not as diverse as they would like them to be while simultaneously noting their extreme interest in creating more diversity in their workplaces and efforts to make diversity a central issue for their business, a company can generate public sympathy. This tactic works well for any major institution in the United States. It downplays or minimizes the inequalities that persist in institutions. In addition, it also helps to create a favorable public image for institutions that are then seen as caring and concerned organizations.

THE CONTRADICTIONS AND VAGUENESS OF DIVERSITY

Just how sincere are corporations when it comes to diversity issues in their workplaces? Using recent interview data, I find that corporations are a lot less sincere about wanting to create an equal opportunity workplace for all employees, regardless of race or gender. For this chapter, I limit my analysis to two major findings. First, diversity has become such a broad term that issues of race and gender in the workplace have become minimized or ignored. Second, although many corporations claim that they are sincere about diversity in their workplaces, there is little to indicate that there are any actions taking place to ensure that women and minorities are given equal opportunities to succeed compared to their white male counterparts.

Data and Methods

To test my ideas regarding diversity in the corporate world, in-depth, semi-structured interviews were conducted with thirty-two middle- to senior-level managers and directors and eight executive- and corporate-level employees in top Fortune 1000 companies.[10] The interviews were conducted between May 2005 and June 2006 with approximately half the interviews being conducted face-to-face and the other half by phone. Interviews that were conducted face-to-face took place either in the respondents' office or in a secluded restaurant corner nearby the respondents' workplace, each lasting between forty-five and ninety minutes. All the interviews were race matched. Thirteen of the respondents were women, and twenty-seven were men. Three of the respondents self-identified themselves as black, two as Latina, one as Asian, and twenty-four as white. Their ages ranged from early thirties to late sixties, and all but seven of the respondents had earned at least a bachelor's degree from an accredited university. Out of the seven respondents who did not have a bachelor's degree, five reported they were close to earning a bachelor's degree but had never gotten around to finishing their course work. In all, thirty-eight Fortune 1000 companies were represented. Each respondent was asked to sign a consent form agreeing to be interviewed and tape-recorded. A transcriber was hired to transcribe the tapes verbatim, to include verbal cues and semantics. All names of respondents, as well as the companies they worked for, were then coded to protect their identities.

The Vagueness of Diversity and Minimization of Race and Gender

What exactly does it mean to be diverse? Does it mean that we should seek to include people of different racial and ethnic backgrounds in our institutions—be they colleges, corporations, or neighborhoods? Or perhaps diversity refers to class heterogeneity. What about gender, sexual orientation, age, culture, religion, or any multitude of other differences between people who live in our society?

Increasingly, diversity has come to refer to all the previously mentioned identities. Moreover, the use of the term *diversity* has seemingly expanded in the past decade so that more differences are embraced under its umbrella every day. Such broad defining of diversity has led to the decision of many companies and numerous other organizations to create support groups that celebrate people's differences in marital status, animal ownership, clothing styles, and, to invoke an old cliché, just about everything but the kitchen sink.[11]

However, with the broadening of the term *diversity* also comes a minimization or even complete neglect of issues pertaining to racial or gender diversity. By increasing the number of categories of people that fall under the umbrella of diversity, companies are able to effectively escape close examination of racial and gender inequalities that might occur in their workplaces. As long as no one brings it up, it can be ignored.

In my interviews, fewer than one-fourth of the respondents clearly mentioned race or gender when defining diversity (see table 3.1). The remaining respondents defined diversity in one of three categories: broad and encompassing, reverse discrimination, or completely off the wall.

Recognizing Race and Gender

Only eight (20 percent) respondents explicitly mentioned race or gender when asked for their definition of diversity. However, these managers were pretty clear that diversity, for them, included race and gender categories.[12] Jack, a white general manager for a large consulting business, explained diversity as follows:

A broad, just a broad spectrum of people. Typically I associate it with three areas: race, educational background, and economic background.

More typically, respondents in this category defined diversity in ways that were similar to Stephen's, an executive vice president of a large real estate corporation:

Ah, I think of it as principally as, ah, diversity with respect to ethnicity and gender.

It is worth mentioning that 30.7 percent of the respondents who answered in this category were women (compared to men at 14.8 percent), a

Table 3.1. Respondents' Definition of Diversity by Gender

Gender	Race & Ethnicity	Broadly	Negatively	Off the Wall	Total
Male	4 (14.8%)	16 (59.3%)	3 (11.1%)	4 (14.8%)	27 (67.5)
Female	4 (30.7%)	7 (53.8%)	0 (0%)	2 (15.5%)	13 (32.5%)
Total	8 (20%)	23 (57.5%)	3 (7.5%)	6 (15%)	40 (100%)

N=40

finding that is consistent with Johnson and Marini's (1998) argument that because (white) women tend to associate with minorities (at work, as neighbors, and so on) more as compared to white men, they are more likely to be sympathetic to their causes. It is also worth mentioning that a number of these respondents worked for companies that were located in politically liberal cities and states, a situation that could explain why some of these interviewees might have been more likely to give more progressive answers.

Broad Diversity

Twenty-three (or 57.5 percent; 59.3 percent of the men and 53.8 percent of the women) respondents either defined diversity as cultural or socioeconomic background or defined it so broadly (often by including a laundry list of categories) that race and gender became secondary issues or were even ignored. More often, diversity was defined in terms of individual backgrounds, socioeconomic status, or even different lifestyles. For example, Brandon, a white service director[13] of a company that specializes in information technologies, defined diversity as follows:

> Ah, when I hear the word diversity I think about, incorporating multiple life styles, philosophies, belief systems, and having them work together.

Brandon's definition of diversity does not mention race or gender, and the interpretation of what he means by "multiple life styles, philosophies, [and] belief systems" is unclear.

This is a typical pattern of respondents who fall into this category. Purposely leaving out the word *race* dilutes the importance that is placed on it and focuses attention to the other areas that are discussed. An example of a more vague form of broadness can be found in Lily's, a white branch manager of a major business specializing in electronics, definition:

> When I hear diversity, I think it's different types of people working in a working environment.

Like many of the other respondents in this category, Lily's response is short and sweet. Her definition of diversity is left wide open for interpretation. Because Lily believes that her company is diverse, it is unlikely that she would enforce policies that called for "real" diversity, even though she admitted that there were not many minorities who worked there. There were a few respondents who did mention race or gender (or both) but made sure that these notions were well mixed in with a long laundry list of other categories. For instance, Harry, a vice president of operations for a large company based in New York, interestingly said the following about diversity:

Diversity is huge. It's about status, socioeconomic standing, family background, different cultures and religions, you name it. Yes, it's about ethnicity but there's so much more to it than that. It's about allowing employees to bring their dogs to work with them, or being able to wear flip-flops to work on casual day.

The word *ethnicity* is mentioned in Harry's definition of diversity. However, its importance is diluted against the seven other categories mentioned, some of which are so outside the typical definition of diversity (e.g., being able to wear flip-flops at work) that Harry could have easily fit into my off-the-wall category.

Diversity as Reverse Discrimination

Three (or 7.5 percent; 11.1 percent of the men and none of the women) respondents defined diversity as reverse discrimination against whites. As mentioned previously, it is interesting to note that, though this definition was given by a relatively small portion of the sample, it was gendered: only men defined diversity in this manner. This is understandable given that white men stand to lose a number of privileges (i.e., white privilege and male privilege) should effective measures to create equality in the workplace ever become enforced. Respondents in this category felt that diversity meant that some people were getting a free ride and gave answers similar to Frank's, a senior-level manager and pilot for a major airline:

Uhhhh, what I think about that is lowering standards to let people in that aren't willing to, uhmmm, you know, go through the, go through the steps that it has to take or uhmmm, the people that are presently, you know, getting hired or getting promoted uhmmm have to take. Okay, I mean if someone got a job and they worked for ten years and they're up to be promoted and they just happened to be, you know a white man or a white woman and then some other person that's been there four years and says, "hey, well I deserve to get promoted," and they don't happen to be white, well, under diversity they outta get promoted so we can be a more diverse workforce, so.

Frank's answer is clear and to the point. Diversity is defined as lower standards and unfair practices that take jobs and opportunities away from white men. Frank also became very tense and angry when asked this question, as did Joseph, a director of software development for a computer company, who said the following in regard to diversity:

Um, when I was in college, diversity was kind of crammed down our throats and largely when I think of diversity I think of affirmative action, ah, yeah.

When asked to explain how he would envision diversity in the workplace, Joseph replied,

> Um, I envision diversity in the workplace as not having a predisposition to hire ah, people based on race, sex, ah, but choosing the person who is best for the job and whether as long as two applicants are qualified for the job or which ever one performs or the interviewer feels will be best for the job and fits the position best and not taking into account any type of race or sex.

Since affirmative action is a heated topic in today's public debate and often not well received by the general public, defining diversity as affirmative action (or as reverse discrimination) allows managers to portray (and even justify) diversity as a bad idea or, worse, as one that further exacerbates discrimination rather than resolves it.

Off-the-Wall Diversity

Finally, seven (or 15 percent; 14.8 percent of the men and 15.5 percent of the women) respondents defined diversity in terms so different compared to the other respondents that I labeled them as "off-the-wall diversity." While this is not as common a reply compared to the broad interpretation of diversity, it still indicates that a large portion (in this case, close to one-sixth) of the definitions of diversity given by higher-level corporate managers completely neglect racial or gender equality and may reflect the fact that these individuals and/or their companies have little or no interest in pursuing a company agenda that calls for racial and gender equality. One of the oddest replies was given by Ryan, a district manager of a large international corporation who defined diversity more in terms of one's ability to do different job tasks:

> Not putting all your eggs in one basket, you know just, just having things spread out. It's kinda like laying on your back trying to float on water instead of trying to stand straight up. Uhmmm, the employees having more than one job that they're required to do.

Ryan's explanation of diversity ignores not only the issue of race and gender completely but also other institutionalized forms of inequalities that occur in the workplace (e.g., ageism, discrimination against gays and lesbians, and so on). In other instances, it was quite clear that the manager being questioned really did not understand what diversity meant. For instance, Brianna, a general manager of a company specializing in hospitality management, had this to say when asked to give her definition of diversity:

You know, I honestly don't think much about it, ah, I don't know. Nothing comes to mind. If I had to pick out a specific term or whatever it's just that, I don't have a problem with it, it just hasn't occurred to me very much.

Either Brianna honestly could not define diversity in even the simplest manner or she felt uncomfortable with the topic and did not want to provide her thoughts on it. Similar to the other examples, race and gender were not mentioned.

A Special Look at Minorities' Definitions of Diversity

Although the sample size of my minority respondents is small, it is useful to compare their definitions of diversity to the responses given by white interviewees. One would suspect that managers of color might be more sympathetic to the plight faced by women and minorities, given that they have more of an inside understanding of the hardships faced by women and minorities on an everyday basis. However, the data illustrate that black managers, for the most part, held similar views to their white counterparts (see table 3.2).

Only one (16.7 percent) of the six minority respondents explicitly included race and gender as a crucial part of diversity. One respondent (16.7 percent) gave an answer that was off the wall. And although none of the minority managers described diversity as reverse discrimination, four (66.6 percent) gave broad answers that minimized or ignored the importance of racial or gender equality.

Chad, a branch manager in Houston, when asked his definition of diversity, gave an off-the-wall definition not too different from that of Ryan:

Diversity just means you're just diverse just because you're smart enough to figure out that, you know, you need eight totally different types of people to really and truly give you a good think tank. So it's not all redundant. You know, if you really want to really build something, then everyone's gonna come up with different ideas and different perspectives.

Table 3.2. Respondents' Definition of Diversity by Race

Race	Race & Ethnicity	Broadly	Negatively	Off the Wall	Total
White	7 (20.6%)	19 (55.9%)	3 (8.8%)	5 (14.7%)	34 (85%)
Minority	1 (16.7%)	4 (66.6%)	0 (0%)	1 (16.7%)	6 (15%)
Total	8 (20%)	23 (57.5%)	3 (7.5%)	6 (15%)	40 (100%)

N=40

Monique, a black senior manager of employee relations at a major airline company, defined diversity as individuality. In doing so, she made sure to broaden the definition widely, thereby minimizing the importance of race and gender in her reply:

> I think about, uhhh just accepting individuality and that's my definition of it whether it's race, sex, sexual orientation, uhmmm national origin, or whether it's, you know, one person's from the country, one person's from the city, one person's from a different region, or whether it's age, generational differences, it, to me it's just accepting individual's different work styles. Uhmmm I have people who are more introverted. I have people who are extroverted and ahhh to me it's just respecting those differences and understanding that they all have some value and not looking negatively upon one just because that's not something that you, yourself may exhibit or subscribe to.

The fact that minority managers have similar definitions of diversity as their white counterparts is not a startling finding. Previous studies have indicated that minorities who are promoted to higher levels within the corporate structure tend to have similar political, economic, and social mentalities as white managers (Zweigenhaft and Domhoff 2003). This does not mean that minority managers who have different political and social views than their white counterparts will not be successful in the business world. However, it does imply that, given a choice, whites will tend to support minority managers who are of like mind rather than those who threaten their dominant and privileged status in the company.

Diversity Policies and Practices—or Something Else?

My second finding is much more direct and to the point compared to the first finding. It speaks volumes about the insincerities many corporations have with regard to issues of diversity and provides a clear indicator that while some companies may claim that they are interested in diversity, the likelihood that any "real" effort has been made to ensure (or enforce) diversity in the workplace is minimal.

Corporate websites are notorious for publicizing their "take" on diversity. Few companies are willing to admit that they are not interested in diversity. In fact, most companies include a diversity and inclusion mission statement on their websites. Fewer still are managers who are willing to admit that their companies are not diverse or not interested in diversity. This is one reason why it is so hard to find accurate data on whether companies are really interested in diversity or are merely selling a favorable public image. Everybody says that her or his company is diverse. In my interviews with forty middle- to upper- and executive-level managers, 75 percent of the respondents answered yes to the question that asked whether their com-

Table 3.3.   Respondents' Knowledge Regarding their Company's Policy on Diversity, by Gender

Gender	Did Not Know	Answer: No	Answer: Yes–Could Explain	Answer: Yes–Could Not Explain	Total
Male	2 (7.5%)	5 (18.5%)	4 (14.8%)	16 (59.2%)	27 (67.5%)
Female	2 (15.3%)	1 (7.9%)	2 (15.3%)	8 (61.5%)	13 (32.5%)
Total	4 (10%)	6 (15%)	6 (15%)	24 (60%)	40 (100%)

N=40

pany currently had a diversity policy or set of practices in place[14] (76.8 percent of the women and 74 percent of the men; see table 3.3). Even the few respondents who responded angrily or negatively to the question asking them to define diversity said that their company had a diversity policy. Fifteen percent of the respondents replied that they did not know whether their company had a diversity policy in place (15.3 percent of the women and 7.5 percent of the men). And 10 percent of the respondents said that their company did not have a diversity policy (7.9 percent of the women and 18.5 percent of the men).

Although the importance of diversity in the workplace is often stressed by company managers and executives, excluding those respondents who claimed that their company did not have a diversity policy or set of practices, 70 percent did not know or could not explain their company's policy or practices to me. To break it down further, of the 75 percent of men and women who answered yes to the question of whether their company had a diversity policy, 60 percent were unable to describe or elaborate on their company's diversity policies or practices (61.5 percent of the women and 59.2 percent of the men).

One might understand how workers, uninterested in reading company policies or perhaps not yet exposed to diversity workshops, might not be able to elaborate on such policies. However, it is quite alarming when higher-level managers are unable to do so, especially if they are working for companies that claim to be concerned about diversity.

Black and other minority respondents were also often unable to explain or elaborate on their company's diversity policies or practices (approximately 66.7 percent could not; see Table 3.4), although all of them insisted that their company had one. As discussed previously, the fact that blacks have similar views as whites on diversity is not unusual. Because ideologies become normative, they are likely to affect, albeit in an indirect way, those they try to subject. As Bonilla-Silva (2006) has argued, "An ideology is not dominant because it affects all actors in a social system in the same way and to the same degree. An ideology is dominant if most members of a social

Table 3.4. **Respondents' Knowledge Regarding their Company's Policy on Diversity, by Race**

Gender	Did Not Know	Answer: No	Answer: Yes–Could Explain	Answer: Yes–Could Not Explain	Total
White	4 (11.7%)	6 (17.6%)	4 (11.7%)	20 (59%)	34 (85%)
Minority	0 (0%)	0 (0%)	2 (33.3%)	4 (66.7%)	6 (15%)
Total	4 (10%)	6 (15%)	6 (15%)	24 (60%)	40 (100%)

N=40

system have to accommodate their views vis-à-vis that ideology" (152). Thus, in order for the diversity ideology to work, a segment of the minority community must also buy in to its language.

IN CONCLUSION: WHAT DOES THIS MEAN IN TERMS OF MAINTAINING WHITE SUPREMACY IN A GLOBAL AGE OF BUSINESS?

In this chapter, I presented several reasons why corporations' preaching of diversity is inconsistent with their practices. First, I illustrated that while many companies may have a few women and minorities seated on the board of directors, when taking into account the executive managers, those who run the day-to-day operations of the company, and even the middle- to senior-level managers of a company, the number of women and minorities are almost nonexistent. Considering these are the gatekeepers for the next generation of upper-level managers, unless there are dramatic changes in the structures (i.e., more practice and less talk) of many companies to address the need to promote and mentor more women and minorities, white males will continue to dominate these corporations.

Second, I discussed the impact of the media on helping many corporations project an image of themselves as equal employment employers who are interested in having a diverse workforce even when they are not. Finally, I presented two key findings from my data that suggested that many large companies were not as interested in promoting racial and gender equality as they publicly claim. In the first of these findings, I illustrated that managers were excluding, intentionally or otherwise, race and gender from their definitions of diversity. Because race and gender are not discussed, these issues get ignored, leading to policies that do not address the racial and gender discrimination that still occur in the workplace.

In the second finding, I found that many managers, including executive and human resource managers, could not effectively elaborate on their company's diversity policies or practices even while insisting that their company had such plans. This is a clear indication that many companies are not concerned with ensuring equal opportunity in the workplace so much as their portrayal as equal opportunity employers.

The question we should be asking is not whether corporations are sincere about diversifying their workplaces to create more opportunities for women and minorities. We already know the answer to that question. Forty-plus years of civil rights triumphs have not produced any significant changes in terms of who controls big business. A better question to ask is, What are the implications of these major corporations maintaining their white male power structure? As more of the Fortune 1000 companies become major transnational players, there is a greater likelihood that the inequalities that women and minorities faced (and continue to face) in the United States will become a problem of global proportions. Already we know that major corporations like Nike and Coca-Cola outsource most, if not all, of their labor overseas. In many instances, the policies and practices, such as the fact that the products are made in sweatshops or by using child laborers, violate various fundamental aspects of human rights. In even the best scenarios, workers overseas are paid a very small fraction of what their labor is worth. Further, for decades, major corporations have been exporting toxins to other, mostly Third World countries. As more corporations outsource their labor overseas and are able to thwart U.S. pollution guidelines, countless more people will face the deleterious effects of not having fresh air to breathe or clean water to drink. And what face are we able to put to these corporate culprits who would deny American workers a living wage and engage in countless violations of human rights, across the globe, in order to increase their bottom line? Finally, the immigration debate in the United States is exploding. I fully anticipate that, coupled with the export of human rights violations via outsourcing, immigration policies and practices will also have detrimental effects on both those trying desperately to reach the United States and find employment and those, especially minority men and women, who are already here. Will U.S. corporations attempt to protect the human rights of those immigrating to work in their plants and factories? Will the human rights of racial and ethnic minorities currently working in factories on U.S. soil be compromised? We do not yet know. What we do know is that times have changed. Yet the faces remain the same.

NOTES

1. This quotation is taken from Judith Lorber, "Dismantling Noah's Ark," in *Paradoxes of Gender* (New Haven, Conn.: Yale University Press, 1994), 282–302.

2. This quotation is taken from Martin Luther King Jr.'s *Letter from a Birmingham Jail, April 16, 1963*.

3. For data on racial attitudes in the United States, see Howard Schuman, *Racial Attitudes in America* (Cambridge, Mass.: Harvard University Press, 1997), or Paul M. Sniderman and Edward G. Carmines, *Reaching beyond Race* (Cambridge, Mass.: Harvard University Press, 1997). For data on gender attitudes in the United States, see Judith Blau, *The Declining Significance of Gender?* (New York: Russell Sage Foundation, 2006).

4. "White male solidarity" refers to the tight-knit bond that white males have developed that enables them to be more effective at creating and maintaining white male privilege in the workplace. Thus, white male managers back up white male workers at the lower levels whenever possible, and at the upper-level company positions, white males have developed practices that exclude minorities and women from being included in their group. Thus, minorities and women are kept out of the loop in regard to office politics, discretions, and other inside information that is beneficial for success in the business world. For examples of how white male solidarity keeps women and minorities out of the power structure of big business, see Landon Thomas, Jr., "A Path to a Seat on the Board? Try the Fairway," *New York Times*, March 11, 2006, and Martha Burk, *Cult of Power: Sex Discrimination in Corporate America and What Can Be Done about It* (New York: Scribner, 2005).

5. See Jason B. Johnson, "Black CEOs Gaining in Corporate America, Numbers Growing: 18 Join Magazine's List of Top Execs," *San Francisco Chronicle*, February 10, 2005.

6. The two African American CEOs were Richard Parsons (Dime Savings Bank of New York) and Clifton R. Wharton Jr. (TIAA-CREF). Further information can be found in *Black Enterprise* magazine (January 21, 2005).

7. According to Aslop (2006), the number of blacks, Latinos, and Native Americans who have graduated with M.B.A. degrees plummeted by 20 percent from the early 1990s to the early 2000s. However, since 2003, there has been an increase of roughly 6 percent.

8. Such positions are often glass-ceiling jobs that do not lead to positions of power in the company (Collins 1997).

9. For more information, check out the website of the U.S. Equal Employment Opportunity Commission at www.eeoc.gov/press/8-11-05.htm.

10. By mid- to high level, I am referring to positions within the corporate structure that are responsible for enforcing company policies as well as delegating and overseeing the day-to-day operations in the workplace. Examples of these positions include store, branch, regional, area, and senior managers or directors. By executive level, I am referring to the highest-ranked positions within the corporate structure. Examples of these positions include vice president, president, comptroller, any of the chief executive positions (e.g., chief financial officer), or any of the corporate board positions.

11. According to a 2003 article in *Workforce Management*, the increasing number of groups that are covered by diversity initiatives have helped to trivialize racial discrimination in many companies. Some examples of more recently created groups in various organizations such as Microsoft are groups, among others, for single parents; for people with attention deficit disorder; for dog owners; for any number of ethnic, cultural, or national identities; and birth order.

12. I should note that just because a respondent identified race and gender as key components in their definitions of diversity did not necessarily mean that their company had a diversity policy or set of practices in place, nor did this mean that companies that had diversity policies or practices enforced them.

13. The responsibilities of a service director are equivalent to those of a director of sales or regional/zone manager. Managers who occupy these positions are usually responsible for overseeing a department in a company or a region or zone where the company has a number of branches set up.

14. A preliminary analysis of a survey addition to this project also indicated that only two of the returned survey questionnaires had answered no to the question asking whether their company currently had an official diversity policy or set of practices in place. Five hundred surveys were sent out to each of the Fortune 500 companies. Thus far, over seventy have been returned for a response rate of 14 percent.

REFERENCES

Amott, Teresa, and Julie Matthaei. 2006. *Race, Gender, and Work: A Multi-Cultural Economic History of Women in the United States.* Boston: South End Press.

Aslop, Ronald J. (with Harris Interactive). 2006. "Minorities in M.B.A. Programs." In *The Wall Street Journal Guide to the Top Business Schools 2006: The Only Guide to What Corporate Recruiters Really Think.* New York: Simon & Schuster.

Bonilla-Silva, Eduardo. 2006. *Racism without Racists: Color-Blind Racism and the Persistence of Racial Inequality in the USA.* Boulder, Colo.: Rowman & Littlefield.

Braddock, Jomills, and James McPartland. 1982. "Applicant Race and Job Placement Decisions: A National Survey Experiment." *International Journal of Sociology and Social Policy* 6: 3–24.

Burk, Martha. 2005. *Cult of Power: Sex Discrimination in Corporate America and What Can Be Done about It.* New York: Scribner.

Collins, Sharon. 1997. *Black Corporate Executives: The Making and Breaking of a Black Middle Class.* Philadelphia: Temple University Press.

———. 1998. "Black Mobility in White Corporations: Up the Corporate Ladder but Out on a Limb." *Social Problems* 44, no. 1: 55–67.

Davis, George, and Glegg Watson. 1982. *Black Life in Corporate America: Swimming in the Mainstream.* New York: Anchor Books.

Domhoff, William G. 2005. "Interlocking Directorates in the Corporate Community." sociology.ucsc.edu/whorulesamerica/power/corporate_community.html (accessed March 11, 2007).

D'Souza, Dinesh. 1995. *The End of Racism: Principles for a Multiracial Society.* New York: Free Press.

Fernandez, John P. 1981. *Racism and Sexism in Corporate Life.* Lexington, Mass.: Lexington Books, D. C. Heath.

———. 1999. *Race, Gender and Rhetoric: The True State of Race and Gender Relations in Corporate America.* New York: McGraw-Hill.

Glazer, Nathan. 1987. *Affirmative Action: Ethnic Inequality and Public Policy.* Cambridge, Mass.: Harvard University Press.

Ibarra, Herminia. 1993. "Personal Networks of Women and Minorities in Management: A Conceptual Framework." *Academy of Management Review* 18: 56–87.

Jackman, Mary R. 1994. *The Velvet Glove: Paternalism and Conflict in Gender, Class, and Race Relations.* Berkeley: University of California Press.

Johnson, Monica Kirkpatrick, and Margaret Mooney Marini. 1998. "Bridging the Racial Divide in the United States: The Effect of Gender." *Social Psychology Quarterly* 61, no. 3: 247–58.

Kirschenman, Joleen, and Kathryn Neckerman. 1991. "'We'd Love to Hire Them but . . .': The Meaning of Race for Employers." In *The Urban Underclass*, edited by Christopher Jencks and Paul Peterson. Washington, D.C.: Brookings Institution.

Levin, M. 1992. "Women, Work, Biology, and Justice." In *Equal Opportunities: A Feminist Fallacy*, edited by C. Quest. London: IEA Health and Welfare Unit.

McWhorter, John H. 2000. *Losing the Race: Self-Sabotage in Black America.* New York: Free Press.

Murray, Charles. 1984. *Losing Ground: American Social Policy 1950–1980.* New York: Basic Books.

Randle, Valerie. 1999. "The 'Glass Ceiling': An Illusion." *Interdisciplinary Science Reviews* 24, no. 2: 105–9.

Reskin, Barbara F., and Irene Padavic. 2002. *Women and Men at Work.* Thousand Oaks, Calif.: Sage.

Reskin, Barbara F., and Patricia A. Roos. 1990. *Job Queues, Gender Queues: Explaining Women's Inroads into Male Occupations.* Philadelphia: Temple University Press.

Royster, Deirdre A. 2003. *Race and the Invisible Hand: How White Networks Exclude Black Men from Blue-Collar Jobs.* Berkeley: University of California Press.

Steele, Shelby. 1998. *The Content of Our Character: A New Vision of Race in America.* New York: HarperPerennial.

Stith, Anthony. 1998. *Breaking the Glass Ceiling: Sexism and Racism in Corporate America: The Myths, the Realities and the Solutions.* Los Angeles: Warwick Publishing.

Thernstrom, Stephan, and Abigail Thernstrom. 1997. *America in Black and White: One Nation, Indivisible.* New York: Touchstone.

Travis, Dempsey J. 1991. *Racism American Style: A Corporate Gift.* Chicago: Urban Research Press.

Wilbanks, William. 1987. *The Myth of a Racist Criminal Justice System.* Monterey, Calif.: Brooks/Cole.

Wood, Peter. 2003. *Diversity: The Invention of a Concept.* San Francisco: Encounter Books.

Zweigenhaft, Richard L., and G. William Domhoff. 2003. *Blacks in the White Elite: Will the Progress Continue?* Boulder, Colo.: Rowman & Littlefield.

Part 2

INTRODUCTION TO REPARATIONS ISSUES

David G. Embrick

The reparations debate is an old one. It is a debate that transcends American geography but also questions the sincerity of color blindness in a country that supposedly exports (or is interested in exporting) equality and democracy. Hence, on the one hand, the United States epitomizes notions of freedom, opportunity, democracy, and fairness. On the other hand, and in the eyes of many countries, the United States represents a tyrannical oppressor that is unable to solve its own internal racial and class struggles and that has no business allowing its government leaders to dictate moral arguments to the rest of the world. At the forefront of unresolved issues that stem back to chattel slavery lies the due compensation owed African Americans for the forced removal of their ancestors from their homes, for their forced labor and the profits derived from that labor, and for the unquestionable physical and psychological suffering at the hands of mostly white men. The history of the rapid rise and success of the United States as a world power is one of racial amnesia. As noted scholar Manning Marable (2000) has succinctly argued, the United States has made a successful living off the sweat and toil of African Americans and other racial minorities. According to Marable (2000, 2), "Each advance in white freedom was purchased by black enslavement" and oppression.

The issue of reparations is also especially crucial because the legacy of slavery continues to have present-day effects on the lives of many African Americans, economically, socially, and psychologically. Considering the fact that the majority of wealth in the United States lies in the form of property that can be transferred intergenerationally or used as a form of equity to pursue higher education, to pay bills, or to improve one's socioeconomic status, it is no wonder that many African Americans today continue to lag behind whites in the land of equal opportunity (Conley 1999; Oliver and Shapiro 1997). According to leading scholars William Darity Jr. and Dania Frank, if we were to take a conservative estimate of the amount owed to the descendents of African Americans who were enslaved, the amount today would exceed $1.3 trillion.[1]

However, the issue is not whether the United States will be able to pay reparations for their atrocious violations of human rights but, rather, why attempts to even engage in a national debate over the issue of reparations continue to get dismissed or minimized. Rather than questioning the economic feasibility of underwriting such a grand yet long-overdue project, we should be directing our attention to the central issues surrounding reparations: race and racism. The bottom line is that if the United States is unwilling to even consider paying reparations to African Americans for past (and, incidentally, current) injustices inflicted on them by their government, there is little hope of ever getting past the color line (see Robinson 2000).

The following chapters provide context to the new ways that we should examine (and actively pursue) the issue of reparations. They offer fresh commentary on the political, economic, and even moral justifications for thinking about and acting on the issue of reparations. The chapter by Thompson-Miller and Feagin presents counterarguments to prevailing antireparations assertions and claims. Further, they examine the often-overlooked ramifications of legal segregation on the lives of today's African Americans. Thomas and Brunsma examine American hypocrisy and the moral implications and need to redress the grievances of the African diaspora, especially given the fact that across the globe, other nonblack reparations movements have garnered reasonable success. Finally, Ansell's chapter brings the issue of reparations home by examining the obstacles that the reparations movements currently face as well as prospects and increased global activism that may help revitalize a racial and social justice issue that has long been ignored.

The issue of reparations is central to understanding human rights in the global era because it represents a long-standing debate that continues to stymie progress toward total equality and egalitarianism. If the issue of redressing past wrongs committed by governments toward their citizens cannot be adequately addressed or continues to be ignored, how are we able, as a global community, to move forward and deal with the new challenges of global human rights? How are we able to view current crises of human neglect if we ignore past injustices?

NOTE

1. William Darity Jr. and Dania Frank. 2003. "The Economics of Reparations," *American Economic Review* 93, no. 2 (2003): 326–29. A more in-depth analysis of the amount of reparations owed descendents of African Americans can be found in William Darity Jr.'s paper that was presented at the South Africa–United States Civil Society Forum that was held on December 9–13, 2003, titled, "Forty Acres and a Mule in the 21st Century" (www.igpa.uillinois.edu/lib/data/pdf/FortyAcresMule.pdf).

REFERENCES

Conley, Dalton. 1999. *Being Black, Living in the Red: Race, Wealth, and Social Policy in America.* Berkeley: University of California Press.

Marable, Manning. 2000. *How Capitalism Undeveloped Black America: Problems in Race, Political Economy, and Society.* Cambridge, Mass.: South End Press.

Oliver, Melvin L., and Thomas M. Shapiro. 1997. *Black Wealth/White Wealth: A New Perspective on Racial Inequality.* New York: Routledge.

Robinson, Randall. 2000. *The Debt: What America Owes to Blacks.* New York: Penguin.

4

Jim Crow and the Case for Reparations: Lessons from the African Diaspora

Ruth Thompson-Miller and Joe R. Feagin

In 1619, the first enslaved Africans arrived in the state of Virginia. Subsequently, for several centuries, European slave traders kidnapped millions of African men, women, and children from their homeland; enslaved them; and forced them to work to generate prosperity for the European colonists. The majority of these enslaved Africans, throughout the African diaspora, were not allowed to maintain their language, religion, and cultural beliefs. In 1807, the British were the first to outlaw the slave trade. The United States abolished the institution of slavery in 1865, nearly sixty years later (Franklin and Moss 2000).

However, the social, economic, and psychological injuries that the people of the African diaspora suffered are still riveting today. The human rights violations that an estimated 10 million Africans who survived the Atlantic slave trade endured is beyond comprehension. The enslaved Africans and their nine to fifteen generations of descendants worked to make the United States wealthy. Presently, the descendants of those enslaved Africans have never received an apology or reparations for the years of stolen labor. The fight for slavery reparations has so far resulted in very modest results for African Americans.

Here we explore the legal and political arguments for reparations, uniquely examining the idea of substantial reparations for the era of *legal segregation*. The system of legal segregation in the United States was deep and pervasive. It influenced similar segregation elsewhere, including the rigid apartheid system in South Africa. While in this chapter we can focus only on the U.S. system of legal segregation, this U.S. system and its white apologists had a significant effect on segregation in other countries, such as South Africa. The U.S. segregationist and South African segregationist had a lovefest, they got together, and the white racist frame was imported lock, stock, and barrel to South Africa.

The advocates of reparations have mostly ignored reparations for Jim Crow segregation, even though millions of living African Americans who suffered extreme oppression under legal apartheid before 1968 can provide some details on the great damage that white-owned companies and white individuals did to them and their families.

THE HISTORY OF LEGAL SEGREGATION: JIM CROW

The legalized system of racial segregation was developed by whites soon after slavery. Jim Crow's function was to continue the system of servitude, the racial caste hierarchy, and economic control of African Americans. Jim Crow began in the 1880s and ended only in the late 1960s. Legal, state-sanctioned Jim Crow practices, as well as informal practices, meant subordination and an imposed badge of degradation on African Americans in southern and northern areas (Feagin 2006; Packard 2002; Smythe 1948). The 1896 *Plessy v. Ferguson* decision affirmed the fiction that public accommodations for blacks and whites could be "separate but equal." This included segregated schools, health care facilities, and many other aspects of public life. The Constitution and later federal court decisions legitimized these racist institutions, many of which are still functioning today (Thompson-Miller and Feagin 2006). Racial violence, actual and threatened, was central to enforcing the blatant injustices of Jim Crow. Huge numbers of African Americans were compelled to flee homes, families, and communities because of everyday occurrences of racialized violence (Tolnay and Beck 1992).

THE CENTRALITY OF RACIAL VIOLENCE

Bufacchi (2005) explores the strengths of two definitions of violence, "violence as an act of force" and "violence as a violation of a person's rights" (197). Bourdieu and Wacquant (1992) viewed the power dynamics that occurred between powerful and powerless as a form of violence, including "symbolic violence," the act of imposing the cultural views of the dominant group through the educational system on the less powerful, who often internalized that oppression (167–68). Racial violence during legal segregation involved acts of force, violation of individual rights, and internalized symbolic violence. This racial violence was utilized to control the political, economic, and social lives of African Americans and sympathetic whites (Brundage 1997; Tolnay and Beck 1995). Scholars have documented the reality and legacies of lynching, the ultimate form of racial violence in the United States (Dray 2003; Ginzburg 1988).

OUR DATA

Our data are from nearly 100 interviews with African Americans who lived through part of the Jim Crow era. Using key informants, such as community leaders and ministers, in four communities, we secured names of older African Americans who were willing to participate. Our narratives indicate experiences of elderly African Americans in everyday life during legal segregation. We received accounts of encounters with whites that took place in public and private spaces. These older black respondents cleared up numerous misconceptions and contradictions in historical representations of everyday practices of whites and experiences of African Americans during Jim Crow.

We interviewed fifty-two respondents in the Southeast (thirty-seven women and fifteen men). The majority (65 percent) were over seventy, with the rest between fifty-two and sixty-nine. In the Southwest, we interviewed forty respondents (twenty-five women and fifteen men). The majority (75 percent) of the latter were over seventy, with the rest between fifty-eight and sixty-nine. In both regions, about two-thirds held relatively low-paying jobs (such as domestic worker or hospital aide) during their primary work lives under legal segregation, and most of the rest held modest-paying jobs (such as schoolteacher in a segregated school). From the interviews, we learned that all were strongly committed to education, and a majority managed to secure at least a high school diploma. (The requirements for a diploma then often differed from present-day high school diploma requirements.)

REPARATIONS AND AFRICAN AMERICANS

African Americans have struggled to get reparations for centuries. More than a century ago, ex-slave Callie House fought for reparations. She and the Reverend Isaiah H. Dickerson "established the National Ex-Slave and Mutual Relief Bounty's Pension Association in 1894 and actively promoted reparations to ex-slaves until the movement fizzled when House and other members of the Association were indicted for mail fraud in 1916" (Verdun 1993, 3). In addition, Verdun (1993) notes that during five eras of black activism, the issues of reparations for slavery have arisen: during the Civil War and Reconstruction era, from the National Association for the Advancement of

Colored People in the early 1900s, from the Marcus Garvey movement, from the civil rights movement of the 1960s, and now during the post–civil rights movement era. African Americans have been fighting for reparations for extreme oppression for many decades.

For example, after the Civil War, many thousands of impoverished former slaves organized, supported each other, and vehemently fought for reparations in the form of land and educational opportunities. The white-run governments, white elites, and some elite African Americans ignored their pleas; however, they continued to struggle tirelessly for reparations (Berry 2005). In none of these eras have white elites or governments agreed to provide any significant reparations.

THE CHALLENGES OF FIGHTING FOR REPARATIONS FOR SLAVERY

The leading arguments proposed against reparations for African Americans almost always focus on slavery, ignoring eras of oppression since. We see five such erroneous, usually whitewashed, arguments about reparations: 1) too much time has passed without reparations redress; 2) all the victims of slavery are dead, and living African Americans do not deserve reparations; 3) whites today and their descendants are not responsible for the injuries inflicted on African Americans in the past; 4) locating the victims and calculating reparations is impossible; and 5) African Americans need to be more independent of government and enterprising (Verdun, 1993).

Even otherwise savvy white scholars do not perceive the need to compensate for extensive oppression clearly, as in this recent comment by political scientist Ira Katznelson (2005): "The brutal harms inflicted by slavery and Jim Crow are far too substantial ever to be properly remedied. . . . There is no adequate rejoinder to losses on this scale. In such situations, the request for large cash transfers places bravado ahead of substance, flirts with demagoguery, and risks political irrelevance" (157–58). He goes on to mock calls for reparations for slavery as being too abstract and even ignores the catastrophic and compensable impact of the Jim Crow era that he brought up.

We now examine how viable the usual arguments against reparations are when we shift the terrain of discussion to the nearly 100-year era of Jim Crow segregation.

The argument that too much time has passed without reparations redress (Verdun 1993) would not be so effective against those seeking reparations for legal segregation. Official segregation ended only in the late 1960s with the significant implementation of three major 1960s civil rights laws, the final one being the 1968 Civil Rights Act. In addition, for a time these laws did not end some Jim Crow segregation, which lasted openly into the mid-1970s in numerous areas (sometimes later). Thus, the *extreme* apartheid of the Jim Crow era ended no more than four decades ago. Vivid memories of this bloody era of white-imposed segregation are still very alive in the minds of African Americans. The pain still destroys lives.

A related argument is that all the victims of slavery are dead and thus living African Americans do not deserve reparations (Verdun 1993). This allows whites to focus on slavery, and they ignore the more recent era of *semislavery* called Jim Crow. Millions of *living* African Americans lived through some part of legal segregation, many for a long period. They are still living and willing, in most instances, to relate their oppressive experiences. They recall who did the harm, which companies treated them discriminatorily, and which government officials participated in that discrimination or stood by while they were abused. The actions and laws of state and federal governments in the United States sanctioned the essentially totalitarian oppression African Americans faced.

In our view, thus, researchers should be documenting the accounts of extensive discrimination by living African Americans, with a clear vision of the need for major government reparations. These Americans are growing older, and it will not be long before whites can once again say accurately that all African Americans who were alive during legal segregation are dead and that there is no way to make amends. Time plays into the hands of oppressors.

RAPE AND OTHER VIOLENCE DURING JIM CROW

Another antireparations argument goes this way: whites today and their descendants are *not* responsible for the injuries inflicted on African Americans so far in the past (Verdun 1993). Again, there are African Americans alive who can identify the white person or persons who injured them. For example, they can name the white man who raped their daughter, son, mother, wife, or sister. One of our respondents in the Southwest, a woman in her late seventies, recalls such a white rapist:

> In later years, my mother and her sisters would never tell us anything but I have . . . a cousin, I called her Aunt Bell. . . . She told me, that this white prostitute across the street, Ms. Ann, my Auntie worked for her and she was over there working one day and this [white] man, that owned a store a block up the street, came to see Ms. Ann. . . . He was married. Ms. Ann wasn't there, he raped my Aunt [pauses] and my Aunt got pregnant and when she got pregnant she told [her family] what happened, she told them that he had raped her that day. And they went to talk to him, and you know what [whites] did? They made her leave town. They said you have to send her out of town, and my Aunt said that

is what they did to Blacks. The white men would rape the Black girls, and if the Black girls got pregnant the families would have to send them out of town to have the babies.

The raping of black women was an everyday occurrence in much of the South and some border states, a part of U.S. history almost universally covered up today. African Americans like this woman can identify the white men, including public officials, who participated in such targeted violence. Much violence that occurred during legal segregation was sanctioned, witnessed, or assisted by law enforcement officials or other government officials. This reality makes it harder now to get to the historical truths. Indeed, a thorough investigation of the hundreds of thousands of such rapes in the Jim Crow era would likely take a major outside investigation, much like that done for the Nuremberg trials of German Nazi criminals.

This older woman continues in her interview with another story of rape in her community by white men:

> I remember this little boy across the street named Charlie, he was one of my friends, we was the same age. And he was white, but his mother was lighter then I am, his mother looked white but she was Black and she married a Black man and they had a daughter who was about my complexion. Then Charlie came here with blonde hair and snow white just really, really, white. The daddy said, "I'm outta here." He left and he said, "That's not my baby." Charlie went to school with us through about the first or second grade and his mother got such flack, you know in the neighborhood they said, "He was the ice man's baby." . . . You didn't have refrigerators then, it was iceboxes, and they said, "That Charlie's daddy was the ice man." His mother finally after about a year or two she just packed him up and moved to [names place]. [She] reared him as a white boy and then when he got grown he moved back to [names place] and left him. . . . He never accepted the fact that he ever had any Black in him, but his mother reared him that way, and when his mother died that's the only time he ever came back to [names place]. His sister was living there and the mother was there. He came for the funeral, his sister said, "He got there just in time for the funeral, went to the funeral, and when it was over he told her goodbye and that was it."

Black women, their husbands, and the children of these rapes often suffered subsequent feelings of shame, abandonment, or isolation. Shame is evident when the respondent adds, "It was not his fault, but the kids teased him." Over centuries, many biracial Americans and their mixed-racial descendants have descended from the commonplace, institutionalized, and sanctioned rapes of black women during slavery and Jim Crow segregation. Census data provide some clues to the scale of this rape by white men during slavery. The 1850 census was the first time that the (white) census takers counted people with multiracial ancestries; they counted 406,000 people as visibly "mulatto" out of a total African American population of 3,639,000 (Williamson 1995). These mixed-racial people made up more than a tenth of African Americans, nearly 2 percent of the national population. Such large numbers for an era when interracial marriages were *all but impossible* in most areas suggest the extent of rape and sexual coercion targeting African American women. Such rape and coercion by white men continued on a large scale during the Jim Crow era, although the data for this era are not as accessible (Feagin 2006).

In the Southwest, a respondent in her late sixties responds to a question about white rapists in her community when she was growing up:

> There *were rapes*! The white man would rape girls. . . . If a white man see a halfway decent woman, if he wanted her, he went up and just grabbed her and start doing whatever he wanted to do to her. You know, she would fight, and say no, but he would beat her up, slap her, knock her down, and just, just take her. That was the norm back then for the white man to do.

Violence again is cited as central to the experience. White society pushes the extreme oppression of black Americans back hundreds of years, but these women remember the rapes and how women fought, often unsuccessfully, against white men. The psychological and physical injuries sustained by those who experienced rape and heard about it are unmistakable in these accounts.

Similarly, a respondent in the Southeast in his late sixties recalls a rape in his community:

> This lady's name was Elizabeth Smith and she was going to the sanctified church around the corner from Mt. Carmel Church and she got kidnapped by a white guy and he took her out in the woods and [he] sodomized her and raped her. . . . He never served a day in jail. . . . She wasn't even married or anything at the time.

The argument that some antireparations analysts make to the effect that whites today and their descendants are not responsible for injuries inflicted on African Americans in the past (Verdun 1993) does not apply, for the man who did it (or his immediate descendants) can be identified and targeted for reparations to this woman and her family.

In this excerpt, a custodian in the Southeast in his late seventies uses the term *dipping* to signal how common such rape and coercion were during legal segregation. Hesitantly, he expresses how he realizes black women had no choice:

> My mamma was a maid. She used to work with a lot of white folks. . . . My mamma had gray eyes and red hair. . . .So, when he [my brother] come out, with blonde hair, they ain't no goodwill where he come from. . . . He come

from a [white] man who'd . . . been dipping into my family a long time ago. . . . White folk, they love the [black] women especially. . . . Bring them in and their wives couldn't say nothing. . . . And so you know about these kids, coming up with the light skin, you know. They know where they come from.

Painfully, this respondent shared his understanding of how his brothers were born with blonde hair. His statement that "they ain't no goodwill where he come from" relays the feelings that black men had about the raping of their wives. The African American family was strong, and most husbands supported their wives; they usually remained in the household after rapes. However, some men could not live with the reality that they could not protect their loved ones and decided to leave; the harm done is immeasurable. In many instances, the respondents did not realize what had occurred to their mothers, aunts, grandmothers, or sisters until they were older and reflected on the different phenotypes present in their families.

The raping of African American women in the Jim Crow era provides justification for significant reparations. These rape accounts are not isolated, for they are similar to many other accounts during segregation. The women raped often know who did them harm, and they have a right under U.S. laws to seek redress for their pain and losses, including loss of familial support and pain to children of the rapes abandoned by white fathers. The women who had to leave town, shrouded in shame, bearing children away from their families, friends, and social networks, have a right to government help and action in seeking redress for such extreme and recurring pain and suffering. The white rapist was usually able to carry on with his life without being prosecuted for a criminal offense. If the victim had been white, the crime would have warranted several years in prison. Had a black man raped a white woman, in most instances he would have faced death. These recurring and institutionalized experiences with violence clearly require reparations. The statute of limitations should be irrelevant because the justice system at the time sanctioned these acts of brutality.

MURDER AND TORTURE: OTHER WHITE VIOLENCE OF JIM CROW

Whites conveniently forget the genocidal history of the first half of the twentieth century in regard to black men and women. The latter were often lynched, mutilated, and burned to death during legal segregation. Numerous respondents noted that black men would disappear, as in the totalitarian regimes of the old South Africa, Chile, and Argentina, and that no one would know what happened to them. Families never heard a word, never discovered the body, and never received assistance from police to locate missing loved ones. Some family members were even forced to watch as loved ones were *tortured to death*. Social science research has shown that African Americans were (and still are) psychologically affected by lynchings, even those who did not witness one. White mob lynchings of black men and women (even occasionally children) were common during the Jim Crow era. In the Southwest, a respondent in her eighties shares a painful recollection:

> There was a man, a black man. He was a janitor, he cleaned up the place, and he went and told this white man that was so mean to me. . . . That he didn't have to treat me the way he was treating me. He [the white man] took and pushed me over one of the tables . . . he [black man] got tired of him doing that, before I know it he leaned back and hit that white man and beat him up. It scared me so bad because I didn't know what he [the white man] was going to do to him. When the police come, he [the white man] had almost beat him to death. You know. So anyways, my parents raised enough money to get him out of jail. [pauses, then starts to cry] Somebody back then, you, could go up and down the highway, and see the Black boy hanging from the tree, and he was dead. They killed him on the tree. . . . I didn't think that I could live to see somebody beat somebody like that man did and not [have anyone] do anything about it. [cries harder] . . . the white men, they took hot water, they boiled that water, and they put him in the water, and cooked him. How could somebody treat somebody, a human being, and just threw them in the pot, they had a big ol' pot they used to make soap out of it. And they just throw them in there [the pot]. Whenever you use to do stuff, you were dead. You couldn't do anything, you had to just stand there and watch them do him like that, and every time his head would come up like that, they pushed him right down in the pot. God brought us through all of that, he sure did. . . . It didn't help his family to see him tortured down there . . . it was a black pot, a cast iron . . . they rejoiced. Can you believe that they [whites] rejoiced about what they did to him in the black pot, they rejoiced.

The vivid details of a black man being boiled while the family watched demonstrates the often routine atrocities of legal segregation. This respondent's reference to God displays how she feels her spirituality helped sustain them through it, yet frequent crying shows that she did suffer much psychological distress. The respondent continues:

> When you walk back into your backyard and see your grandfather hanging from an oak tree [cries harder]. He still should have stayed in jail. Those were some hard times. . . . Back in those days, you could be standing back there, in your backyard, and see your grandfather and grandmother, and anybody in your family, hanging on a tree. And when you saw one hanging on a tree, they would come to the church real soon; and they would set the church on fire. . . . To white people that was fun. And all you could do was stand there and look.

Again we see whites inflicting physical and psychological injuries. Such African American targets of violence have a right to significant reparations for damage, including pain and suffering, that they and their families endured. This respondent died within a month of this interview—which indicates both the necessity for immediate reparations and the continuing oppression of whites intentionally delaying such compensation for damages. We also see the importance and urgency of documenting experiences of African Americans who survived legal segregation.

A respondent from the Southeast in her eighties recalls lynchings:

> The Ku Klux Klan. . . . If you had sons, you were just frightened. . . . People were hung right here. . . . It was a place called Lynch Hammock. They would take people out and lynch them. They would take those kids out and you would find a Black body hanging any day. Any time. People were frightened. There was nothing they could do.

This witness references an area in the Southeast where at least half a dozen African Americans were lynched by white mobs over several decades of the twentieth century. The place was used so much and the brutal lynchings were so institutionalized that the area was named Lynch Hammock.

The torture of a family member forever affects the family and all those around who witnessed it or heard about it. Another respondent in the Southeast in her seventies describes how:

> [The Ku Klux Klan] . . . did use to hang people. . . . The last two I know was [names two young men] . . . caught them with a white girl. I think they were fooling around with the girl all the time and she just got caught. . . . They hung them. . . . I don't know too much about it because they didn't put it in the paper, and I just heard mom and them talking about it in the house. They [whites] just went, broke into the house, and just grabbed them while they was sleeping. They say that, the girl say that they raped her. [Was there a trial?] No. I might have been thirteen or fourteen. . . . Those boys were teenagers, they might have been about nineteen, twenty. . . . They were young!

Here whites distribute mob "justice" without a trial, and the damage is done off the record. The only accounts are in the memories of those alive at the time. As we see here and in the next account, perceived offenses that triggered the white murders of young and old were wide ranging. A respondent in his late seventies in the Southeast recounts thus:

> There was a fellow named John. Now we can't prove it, but we know that white folks had something to do with taking him out in the woods and burn[ing] him up in the house. . . . This was right around here . . . somewhere, but it was out in the woods. . . . They burned him up in the house. [Why?] [whispers]

White girls. White girls. You didn't cross no lines. That was automatic death. And there was nothing nobody could do about it.

African American men who were just *suspected* of sleeping with white women were often murdered by white men. This contrasts with the black women who were actually raped by white men and had no legal recourse. Whites often acted under cover of night or in wooded areas. Throughout the accounts, the respondents indicate that they know who murdered, raped, and tortured loved ones and that they had nowhere to turn for assistance, justice, or reparations.

VIOLENT RACIAL EXPULSION

The argument that locating the victims and calculating reparations are impossible tasks (Verdun 1993) does not work for much of the damage done under legal segregation. David Swinton, Gerald Chachere, and Bernadette Chachere estimate a cost of many billions of dollars for racial discrimination in the labor markets of the Jim Crow era (Darity and Frank 2003). Such economists can probably estimate roughly how much was lost to African Americans in a particular area as a result of stolen land, forced labor, violence, and the birth of children who never received financial support. A recent study by Jaspin (2007) analyzes the racial expulsion of African Americans from several hundred counties in Texas, Arkansas, Tennessee, Georgia, Kentucky, North Carolina, and Indiana. The residents were forced by whites to flee their communities under threat of extreme white violence. This study documents white expulsions, and similar studies could be used as part of the process of determining how much compensation is due to many African Americans who suffered similar fates. One of our respondents in his late fifties recalls stories of African Americans losing land and lives in the Southwest:

> My grandmother said, "At one time a lot of blacks owned the land that is now owned by whites and that they were forced to sell their land." Those who did not sell lost their lives. Or the land was taken from them by means of taxation and indebtedness that they had incurred and they weren't aware that they were incurring. . . . Some of them were killed to take the land; they [whites] killed some of them to take the land. . . . Some drownings that were later said accidental, but they didn't kill them accidental.

As in the Southeast, this respondent recalls the land of African Americans stolen by whites through an array of techniques. Whites killed African Americans to steal their land. Their families can still identify those whites who killed relatives or burned houses down. They can identify, in many instances, those whites who put on Klan robes and rode through their communities terrorizing them. At the least, they can identify their immediate descendants. Why has there been so little redress for these obvious and documentable crimes?

Similarly in the Southeast, a retired nurse, in her seventies, recalls how her aunt was living in a home that whites deemed to be nice and how that leads to collective, physically violent actions:

> My aunt came here to visit us and they set the house on fire and they burned him [cousin] up in the house, when he tried to get out the window, they pushed him back in the house. They just nasty and mean. . . . Black people, weren't suppose to live in no, really nice area like that. She was living on this lake, and they wanted it and, and they probably knew that, she was here in [names town], and, so they went there and he was, 'cause they left him home by himself. My cousin, he was a young man. . . . And they just burned . . . the house down and burnt him up in the house. She left that place. She didn't want nothing else to happen. . . . They know who did it, but wasn't nothing they can do about it. All the white people, they stuck together. . . . Back in the forties. Just like Rosewood. They burned him alive.

With tears in her eyes and sadness in her voice, she describes how her family suffered for striving for the American dream. Her cousin was burned alive, and she and other family members can identify the white perpetrators. This is not an isolated incident, for several respondents shared similar stories of how, if whites wanted a property, they would assault the black owners or kill them. Indeed, Rosewood, an African American town in Florida, was destroyed in the 1930s by a white mob seeking to remove the African Americans; they killed numerous residents. Throughout the South, an undocumented number of African Americans suffered great physical and material injury in such white expulsion. Significantly, the descendants of African Americans who lived in Rosewood received nearly $2.1 million in reparations from the state of Florida, almost the only such compensation ever paid by a U.S. government (Brophy 2006). Clearly, similar brutality, murder, and land theft occurred against African Americans across many states during the Jim Crow era. Many African Americans lost lives, property, and family members to racial violence by whites, and most of this violence is undocumented and uncompensated to the present day.

THE GREAT PSYCHOLOGICAL HARM

One white antireparations argument suggests that African Americans need to be more "independent" (Verdun 1993). The argument that African Americans must be more independent of government and more enterprising is again neglectful of U.S. history, for African Americans have had to be independent and enterprising to survive racial oppression that makes them subordinated and dependent. In spite of the oppression and consequently severe damage and pain, they have frequently organized to protest state and private oppression. Calls by whites do little to guarantee solutions to inequality, for independence would not address the overwhelming magnitude of current disparities that have continued for fifteen generations now. It is too easy for whites to minimize the long-lasting effects of discrimination by referencing a few visible African Americans, such as Oprah Winfrey and Bill Cosby. Yet the same whites ignore or do not know the truncated and harmed lives of the many millions of African Americans who have struggled with discrimination, unemployment, and poverty. Whites routinely turn a deaf ear and a blind eye not only to the historical reality of systemic racism but also to the severe psychological impact on African Americans (Westley 1998). Full independence was not allowed by the system of racism.

During the Jim Crow era, most African Americans found themselves dealing daily with extreme social, political, and economic constraints as well as serious psychological impacts of fear, anxiety, anguish, and shame. As Jackman (2002) notes well, "Public humiliation, stigmatization, exclusion, imprisonment, banishment, or expulsion are all highly consequential and sometimes devastating for human welfare" (393). We see this in an account by one southwestern respondent in her late sixties, who discusses witnessing a lynching:

> The [black] guy that was down there wasn't with us, but spoke to, [he] just said "Good evening" to a white girl, and she all freaked out and things went from there. She went screaming and yelling . . . like somebody killed her. Some other white guys came along and asked what was going on . . . and they took him right then and there, took him away, and hung him. Got the rope off the truck and just hung him right there in front of us and told us, "This is what happens to ninnies who get out of line and speak to people they're not suppose to speak to." This happened a lot, throughout the South. . . . It was something that was just the norm back in those days. I had brothers during that time that we always, always, always begged them: Whatever you do, do not speak to white women.

White hallucinations about black men being potential rapists of white women doubtless led to this man losing his life. The psychological injury to numerous blacks here is clear as this respondent recalls vividly the details of Nazi-like brutality and notes emotionally that her brothers were "always, always begged . . . not to speak to white women." In such situations, state, local, and federal judicial agencies almost always failed to prosecute whites for racial violence, helping to promote more such violence.

Severe psychological injuries suffered by black citizens are evident throughout the narratives. Another respondent shares an account of how some were lynched:

> They [blacks] had a fear that if they did something that aggravated the white folks, that that night about midnight, they would come to [find the person]. They would knock on the door. . . . "Is [names person] in there? Well send him on out here." They would take him to a tree. . . . Then you found the person dead the next day.

Constant control of one's everyday actions, as well as those of one's children and other relatives, was necessary for survival. Black citizens knew that almost anything they did that incited white anger could result in death. Stress associated with negotiating white spaces—and the documentable harm done to those who experienced, heard about, or witnessed white-racist atrocities—remain uncompensated to the present day.

Contemporary discrimination has been shown to have a negative effect on the physical and psychological health and other types of African American well-being (Feagin and McKinney 2003). Thus, the extreme racial violence of legal segregation has created much immediate and systemic stress. This systemic impact in the black community of decades of economic, social, and educational deprivation, fundamental to legal segregation, should be obvious to all Americans, though they often are not. Large-scale government reparations are one way for white society to flood impoverished black areas with an abundance of much-deserved and much-needed resources to overcome some of that systemic impact (Williams and Collins 2004). Consequently, linking the current mental health and physical health of African Americans to the extremely destructive past is one avenue to make a strong case for governmental reparations.

THE GLOBAL FIGHT FOR REPARATIONS

The U.S. and Canadian governments have paid modest reparations to Japanese Americans for concentration camp oppression during World War II. These governments have given some land back to indigenous peoples as a type of reparations. The Austrian and German governments have compensated some Jewish and other Holocaust survivors in the form of monetary reparations (Howard-Hassmann 2004; Winbush 2003). Native Americans and Japanese Americans received reparations in the 1970s and 1980s. New Zealand took land from the Maori people and are considering the issue of reparations (Brophy 2006). Truth and reconciliation trials in South Africa offered South Africans the opportunity to have their voices heard;

however, they did not receive reparations. The United Nations endorsed the convening of other truth and reconciliation commissions in Sierra Leone, Uganda, East Timor, Ghana, and Nigeria. The United Nations recommended that these countries consider the issue of reparations for the bloody wars that have occurred there (Brophy 2006). In 2006, Prime Minister Blair apologized to the people of Britain for slavery but offered no plans for reparations.

Certain groups have thus been very successful in capturing the moral sense of many people outside their groups. Even some perpetrators have somehow been brought to identify with the long-term pain, suffering, and economic losses of their or their ancestors' victims (Brooks 2004). We suggest that African Americans need to gain support from some such groups that have received reparations in the past.

CONCLUSION

Recent lawsuits filed against specific corporations—Aetna Insurance Company, JP Morgan, and Brown & Williamson Tobacco Corporation—and John Conyers's yearlong battle in Congress to pass House Resolution 40 show evidence of the various strategies being utilized to fight for African American reparations, but almost always only in reference to slavery (Brophy 2006). Considering slavery, some in the African American community want an apology with substantial reparations, while others seek only reparations. Assessing slavery, Randall Robinson argues that no particular white person could or should be held personally responsible for the ills of his ancestors. Yet Robinson adds that "crimes by governments against people" are "crimes that should not be touched by statutes of limitations, because when governments commit such crimes, they have a certain immortality" (quoted in Winbush 2003, 73). The victims of the Nazi Holocaust, thus, were successful in fighting against legal statutes of limitations because the crimes were genocidal crimes against humanity.

While nonviolent racial oppression under Jim Crow was widely and legally sanctioned, violent crimes committed against African Americans were usually not officially sanctioned by law. Indeed, the laws mandated separate but equal accommodations, and these were almost never equal. Even in the Deep South, it was unlawful for black individuals to be raped, murdered, lynched, and terrorized. The state governments had the *responsibility* to protect all citizens under their jurisdiction. Local, state, and federal officials were paid by the taxes of African Americans to protect them. However, these officials and ordinary white citizens frequently disregarded the laws of separate but equal and committed large-scale violence against African Americans.

The case of *Altmann v. Republic of Austria* (317 F.3d 954 [9th Cir. 2002]) set a precedent that can be seen as applying to African Americans seeking reparations for the unjust enrichment of whites at their expense through centuries of past wrongdoing. The U.S. Supreme Court held that certain legislation can be applied retroactively so that a (successful) lawsuit could be filed by Maria Altmann against the government of Austria to recover a painting stolen by German Nazis. In this and similar cases involving the Nazis, the statute of limitations does not apply because of the severity of crimes against humanity, including murder and torture. Such reasoning can now be applied to the case of African American suffering and loss during the legal segregation era with its widespread murder and torture, during which time black citizens could not even become plaintiffs seeking such reparative justice (Winbush 2003).

In this chapter, we have given an overview of the history of Jim Crow segregation, the centrality of racial violence in that era, and some arguments against reparations for African Americans. We have shown the importance of making a case for reparations for the era of legal segregation.

Remedies for Jim Crow could be quite specific and designed to compensate for specific wrongs to specific living individuals by specific living whites or white-controlled companies. Millions of living African Americans suffered through apartheid, and millions of living whites participated in acts of violence and other racial oppression. The arguments used to deny African American reparations are here addressed and dispelled because the era of legal segregation is relatively recent. The white perpetrators and the black victims and their immediate descendants are often not difficult to identify. Many living African Americans can tell what actually happened to them, where it was done, and who did it, and they can give many details necessary for legal redress. The issue is why the U.S. government and local governments do not see this as necessary or urgent. Time is of the essence, for these African Americans are growing older. We as social scientists should document and disseminate their stories, for they do indeed make a powerful case for what are long-overdue reparations for African Americans. The African American experience with legal segregation is of global importance as the people of South Africa and of the African diaspora continue their struggle for human rights and restitution.

REFERENCES

Berry, Mary Francis. 2005. *My Face Is Black Is True: Callie House and the Struggle for Ex-Slave Reparations*. New York: Vintage Books.

Bourdieu, Pierre, and Loïc Wacquant. 1992. *An Invitation to Reflexive Sociology*. Chicago: University of Chicago Press.

Brooks, Roy L. 2004. *Atonement and Forgiveness: A New Model for Black Reparations.* Berkeley: University of California Press.

Brophy, Alfred L. 2006. *Reparations: Pro and Con.* New York: Oxford University Press.

Brundage, Fitzhugh W. 1997. *Under Sentence of Death: Lynching in the South.* Chapel Hill: University of North Carolina Press.

Bufacchi, Vittorio. 2005. "Two Concepts of Violence." *Political Studies Review* 3: 193–204.

Darity, William Jr., and Dania Frank. 2003. "The Economics of Reparations." *American Economic Review* 93, no. 2 (May): 326–29.

Dray, Phillip. 2003. *At The Hands Of Persons Unknown: The Lynching of Black America.* New York: Modern Day Library.

Feagin, Joe R. 2006. *Systemic Racism: A Theory of Oppression.* New York: Routledge.

Feagin, Joe R., and Karyn McKinney. 2003. *The Many Costs of Racism.* Lanham, Md.: Rowman & Littlefield.

Franklin, John Hope, and Alfred A. Moss Jr. 2000. *From Slavery to Freedom: A History of African Americans.* New York: McGraw-Hill.

Ginzburg, Ralph. 1988. *100 Years of Lynchings.* Baltimore: Black Classic Press.

Howard-Hassmann, Rhoda E. 2004. "Getting to Reparations: Japanese Americans and African Americans." *Social Forces* 83, no. 2 (December): 823–40.

Jackman, Mary. 2002. "Violence in Social Life." *Annual Review of Sociology* 28: 387–415.

Jaspin, Elliot. 2007. *Buried in the Bitter Waters: The Hidden History of Racial Cleansing in America.* New York: Basic Books.

Katznelson, Ira. 2005. *When Affirmative Action Was White.* New York: Norton.

Packard, Jerrold. 2002. *American Nightmare: The History of Jim Crow.* New York: St. Martin's Press.

Smythe, Hugh H. 1948. "The Concept of Jim Crow." *Social Forces* 27: 45–48.

Thompson-Miller, Ruth, and Joe R. Feagin. 2006. "Building a Theory of Racial Violence: Violence and Legal Segregation" (under review).

Tolnay, Stewart E., and E. M. Beck. 1992. "Racial Violence and Black Migration in the American South, 1910–1930." *American Sociological Review* 57 (February): 103–16.

———. 1995. *A Festival of Violence: An Analysis of Southern Lynchings, 1882–1890.* Urbana: University of Illinois Press.

Verdun, Vincene. 1993. "If the Shoe Fits, Wear It: An Analysis of Reparations to African Americans." *Tulane Law Review* 67 (February): 597–668.

Westley, Robert. 1998. "Many Billions Gone: Is It Time to Reconsider the Case for Black Reparations?" *Boston College Law Review* 40 (December): 429–76.

Williams, David R., and Chiquita Collins. 2004. "Reparations: A Viable Strategy to Address the Enigma of African American Health." *American Behavioral Scientist* 47, no. 7 (March): 977–1000.

Williamson, Joel. 1995. *New People: Miscegenation and Mulattoes in the United States.* Baton Rouge: Louisiana State University Press.

Winbush, Raymond A. 2003. *Should America Pay? Slavery and the Raging Debate on Reparations.* New York: HarperCollins.

5

Bringing Down the House: Reparations, Universal Morality, Human Rights, and Social Justice

James M. Thomas and David L. Brunsma

The black reparations movement in Amerikkka[1] has been and continues to be unsuccessful. Ever since General William T. Sherman's infamous Special Order 15 ("forty acres and a mule") was overturned by President Andrew Johnson in 1865, blacks in the United States have received nothing in the form of material compensation or symbolic reprieve while enduring all the structural, cultural, political, material, and psychological costs of such disregard. Deep-rooted notions of human rights (harkening back to African culture) remained dormant in this postemancipation period while liberalism and individual rights plowed ahead as the cornerstone of the expansion of the capitalist world economy. Contemporarily, the courts have ruled against separate claims for reparations in Chicago (Carillo 2005) and Tulsa (Burroughs 2005), and the federal government (and much of its white constituency) simply fail to see the point of even discussing the issue (Coates 2004)—all this in a post-UN era when the United States is a rogue state fully disregarding human rights. The black reparations movement in the United States has been unsuccessful, and a new approach is needed.

The reparations movement has focused primarily on judicial and legislative action; however, as we argue here, this is counterproductive to the movement. By and large, American judges and juries, senators and representatives, as well as presidents and cabinet members are rooted in the illusory (but, for them, no less real) enlightenment social contract and notions of individual rights. Playing on the card of abstract liberalism and a pseudolibertarian philosophy as a means of avoiding collective responsibility, the United States has continuously proven to be behind the rest of

65

the world when it comes to creating programs of restitution in response to violations of human rights. Through the deepest exploitation, whites retain the power in dominant American institutions *because* blacks lack power in them. On closer inspection, the otherworldly "social contract" cements an utterly real *racial contract* (Mills 1997) with whiteness as its moral and legal foundation. In order for blacks in the United States to have any success in attaining reparations, the movement must recognize and articulate this fact, step outside this contract, and ultimately center its efforts within the realm of universal morality and human rights. Only then can a legitimate dialogue be opened up as a precursor to actual social justice for blacks in the United States.

This chapter seeks to begin charting such terrain. To map this out, several things must occur. First, we briefly examine comparative movements for reparations and consider the vacuous response to blacks' claims. Second, we provide the reader an understanding of how the black reparations movement can be (has been) framed *within* the context of the racial contract. Third, we develop a brief discussion of how legal structures and arguments concerning reparations are constantly besieged by the United States through the racial contract in the desire to protect whiteness as an investment; thus, failure is ensured. Fourth, in order to plant the argument for reparations on more solid ground, it will be framed within the broader context of morality as a universal ideal.

Ultimately, the United States, as an entity directly responsible for the wrongs against its nonwwhite citizens, has a prima facie obligation to address those wrongs (McCarthy 2004), allowed through its simulated morality. Through an analysis of morality as it relates to the wrongs committed by the United States against its black citizens, the racial contract is deconstructed as illegitimate. It is through this moral argument that reparations are then framed in the context of social justice. Social justice, as a living extension of morality, is the basis of all reparations movements. Simply stated, not only do those who receive direct compensation for wrongs committed benefit from the principle of social justice, but the entire society inherits these benefits as a collective body. Recognizing the fact that discussions of universal morality and human rights fall on primarily deaf ears in the American context, we consider the necessary changes that are imperative in the U.S. context for success.

THE BLACK REPARATIONS MOVEMENT

The black reparations movement, as a form of social justice, has long struggled for a consistent definition of its purpose. The National Coalition of Blacks for Reparations in America has defined reparations as the "money, land, scholarships and other goods owed Black people in the United States for slavery and 100 years of discrimination after slavery" (Carillo 2005). Here, reparations seek to address a debt to *all* blacks for specific wrongs committed during slavery and the Jim Crow era. However, some conservative pundits (e.g., Thomas Sowell and David Horowitz) have sought to narrow this argument to specific times and geographical locations in order to limit the argument legally and logistically (no living victims/perpetrators) (Sowell 2001). In the realm of electoral politics, reparations have become talking points. For example, earlier in his career, Republican Allen Keyes referred to reparations as an "insult to our ancestors," but during a 2004 senatorial run, he posed a federal tax exemption for slave descendants as reparations (Carillo 2004). In both instances, it was unclear what Keyes meant when he spoke of reparations. Such definitional inconsistency gives reparations little solid ground to stand on. In order for reparations as a movement of social justice to withstand the assaults from its opponents, it must be firmly planted. What is it? What is it not? From a lens of social justice and human rights, we define reparations as *any social project that carries with it an explicit intent to correct a specific wrong through collective action*. A social project is any project that carries with it the best interests of the society at large.

Scholars within the debate have also limited the discourse on reparations by reducing claims of restitution to claims for material compensation—questions of "how much" and/or "in what form" reparations will come—an individualistic and contractually rooted notion. While material compensation is certainly a part of the reparations movement as a whole, it is unjustly portrayed as *the* goal. This focus fails to address the *why* of reparations: why is there a *need* for material compensation? If our definition of reparations is applied, reparations are not limited only to material compensation; other forms are possible, such as symbolic reparations (Coates 2004). While a formal apology is the most common symbolic reparation, it can also be established through commemorative exhibits and national holidays.

The concept of symbolic reparations is important for two reasons. First, it places a much greater emphasis on the *why* of the movement in that it allows for dialogic reflection by both the oppressor and the oppressed. A formal apology, while seemingly superficial, implies a sense of guilt by the party extending the apology as well as a sense of entitlement by the receiving party. This leads to the second point: symbolic reparations *specifically address guilt*. As such, a relationship between the two parties is potentially (re)created where previously it was nonexistent or covered up via immoral ideology and political rhetoric (Posner and Vermeule 2003). Once this relationship is established, further action can be taken to achieve the material compensation due to the offended party, as it creates a legitimate approach to a remedy: "You are wrong, you admitted that you are wrong, now how will you make this right?"

"WE THE WHITE PEOPLE . . ."

In 1997, Charles Mills published *The Racial Contract*. This work took to task the epistemological foundation of white supremacy, exposing the modern social contract as one wrought with racial hegemony and white supremacy. The racial contract, among other things, describes how society is structured, how government functions, how morality is constructed, and how public morality guides institutional practice. This contract rests on three basic tenets: white supremacy is global, white supremacy is a political system, and, as a system of domination, white supremacy can be illustrated as a contract between whites. Because those living and benefiting from such a system will fail to comprehend such a fact (their misconstrued cognitive maps serving as socially functional ones), exposing this racial contract as foundational in the denial of reparations to blacks will no doubt draw criticism. We turn to these next.

First, libertarian frameworks, rooted in Enlightenment individuals, often claim that there can be no contract that was not signed. Such an argument, however, is a non sequitur. Just because the contract is unlike any other does not mean that it is not a contract (much like a human contract, which does not need signing but benefits all). When we sit down at a restaurant to eat, though no paper is signed, we have agreed with the restaurant that we will use their goods and services in exchange for our money. A code of conduct is understood by both parties, making this a contractual agreement between both the restaurant and the patron.

Second—and relevant to understanding reparations as social justice—are arguments that state that a contract does not bind later generations to its principles when those later generations had not agreed to sign it (Mills 1997). However, Mills shows how Locke's notion of tacit consent plays a key role in countering this claim. Later generations who have decided to partake of the goods and services provided by the previous system have implicitly agreed to the tenets of the contract. Those who have agreed to live in a society have implicitly agreed to abide by the rules of that society. Particularly, in the case of the racial contract, whites have chosen to accept the privileges acquired through the use of the contract; thus, they have consented to the contract by consenting to the benefits given through the contract.

What of those who may be oblivious to the contract? How is one able to consent to a contract that they do not realize exists? Such an argument is naively apologetic and serves to underscore just how deep the racial contract runs. The fact that the racial contract has constructed a means whereby racial oppression can be narrowed to a specific time and place, without taking into account the effects of a racist ideology put into practice, shows the true scope of its terms. Whites who do not realize that they have benefited from a legacy of racial oppression are not excused from what they have inherited from the past 500 years, including the inheritance of the legacy itself. While they may remain ignorant of present and historical racial reality and even actively construct counternarratives, their privileges are real and exist in concrete forms. For example, Mills and others have described the white body as being the somatic norm (Mills 1997; Puwar 2001, 2002). This somatic body allows for whites to "shape-shift" in the appropriation of material resources without having to take on the hegemonic consequences to such appropriation. White women on Fifth Avenue can wear the cultural fashions native to women of Southeast Asia and turn such cultural fashions into high-brow cultural objects. Yet when those same fashions are worn on the women to whom these garments are indigenous, their bodies are subject to the racialized gaze of these same white women, turning these bodies into the somatic Other (Puwar 2002).

What of those whites who wish to fight for racial justice? Mills (1997) states that "all whites are beneficiaries of the Contract, though some whites are not signatories to it" (11). Even those whites who spend their entire lives fighting for racial justice and who acknowledge their privileges on a daily basis are still responsible for the privileges they maintain because they have made a choice to accept those privileges. There is an alternative: to deny every identified privilege and metaphorically "walk away" from their whiteness. Such a struggle may seem unbearable for such individuals. Their struggle, however, is relative when placed alongside the duress suffered by nonwhites, whose particular struggles as a group are in large part due to whites' creation and maintenance of the racial contract. The racial contract flows through the heart of American society. From this foundation, institutions emerged (e.g., government, law, health care, education, and so on) that have served to overtly protect and then covertly conceal 500 years of mass exploitation. One cannot separate the life process from the mode of production of material life. It is the mode of production that is determinant in the life process. The mode of production that has shaped the historical life process of our society was racist in its foundation and has determined America's white supremacist ideology and structure.

HISTORY, HYPOCRISY, AND HEGEMONY

So powerful and so fundamental is the racial contract that any movement for reparations *must* be developed (ideologically and structurally) outside it. However, the failures of the black reparations movements have indeed occurred largely within this epistemological framework of human injustice. However, in this context, there have been other groups, having been wronged in the past and having sought redress, who have won some success.

We wish to briefly understand such movements and the continuing failure of the black reparations movement. It is important when framing an approach to reparations to pay special attention to whom and by whom reparations are paid.

Globally, reparations movements have had some success over the past sixty years. Since 1947, Germany has paid over $100 billion to the state of Israel and Holocaust survivors, descendants, and organizations (Posner 2003). Here, a state, through legislation (*Wiedergutmachung*), reckoned moral responsibility for the destruction caused by a previous administration against a target population. Germany felt a moral obligation to the global Jewish Diaspora for the genocide committed against Jews who were within the reach of the Third Reich. Such responsibility was not forced by international law or coerced by Allied pressure. The principle for this legislation states that when a legitimized government, through its own legitimized structures and institutions, victimizes its own inhabitants, that state has a moral obligation to compensate that group for the wrongs committed by that state (Westley 2003).

While the Jewish movement for reparations from Germany may stand as the most successful in terms of material compensation and global recognition of Germany's moral responsibility for redress, it is by no means the only success story. In 1992, a Chilean commission enacted a monthly pension of 140,000 pesos, plus benefits, to the survivors and descendants of the brutalities enacted under the Pinochet regime against over 200,000 Chilean citizens (Posner 2003; Van Dyke 2003). New Zealand has established a process to address the wrongs committed by the British government during its colonial rule against the indigenous Maori during the late 1800s, including returning indigenous Maori property and transferring property accumulated at the expense of the Maori (Van Dyke 2003). Australia has established a National Sorry Day to address the Australian governmental program of taking aboriginal children from their families and having them raised by white families (Posner 2003). Canada, responsible for similar acts of government-sponsored kidnapping of its indigenous population, awarded $350 million in various aid to its First Nation children (Posner 2003; Van Dyke 2003). As of the writing of this chapter, the postapartheid South African government is currently undergoing a nationwide land reform meant to address the ill effects of colonization and racist doctrine under its previous administrations.

While moral arguments for these reparations are typically not explicitly made, they are implied through the agreement of these political entities to correct past wrongs. They felt responsibility for the crimes committed against those to whom reparations were paid. This moral obligation is key when addressing the morality of reparations pertaining to the responsibility of the United States as a political entity in addressing blacks' claims.

Over the past thirty-five years, the United States has enacted various strategies to address the wrongs committed by previous administrations against diverse Native American tribes since this country's inception. In 1946, the United States granted over $800 million through various programs to Native American tribes as reparations for land taken by force or deception (Posner 2003). In 1971, the United States awarded $1 billion, along with 44 million acres of land, to Native American tribes in Alaska (Coates 2004; Posner 2003; Winbush 2003). From 1980 to 1986, the United States awarded over $231 million to various tribes, including the Lakota, the Seminoles, and the Chippewas (Winbush 2003).

Japanese Americans have received recompense as well. On February 19, 1942, President Roosevelt issued Executive Order 9066, effectively interning over 120,000 people, including 77,000 American citizens of Japanese descent, from 1942 to 1946 (Howard-Hassman 2004). In 1988, in an attempt to redress the incident, the United States awarded approximately 80,000 survivors a total of $1.6 billion, which amounted to about $20,000 per individual (Howard-Hassman 2004; Posner 2003).

While a very small minority of Native American tribes as well as Japanese Americans have received some recompense, two points are in order. First, the reparations paid out in these various cases do not come close to what was lost by each of these groups during their subjugation. Native Americans lost their land, their culture, and much of their identity because of systematic genocide committed by the United States in the name of territorial expansion. Many of the Japanese Americans interned during World War II lost their businesses, their homes, and their families as a result of racist, exclusionist doctrine. Such "redress" amounts to little more than trivial acknowledgment. Nevertheless, it was acknowledgment, and other forms of symbolic reparations have taken place since then, such as an official apology that was included in the Civil Liberties Act (Howard-Hassman 2004).

Second, the acknowledgment of specific wrongs committed by previous administrations of the U.S. government and then specific actions taken by administrations many years after the fact underscore a hypocritical position by the U.S. government when it comes to addressing its wrongs committed against its black population. Since 1890, blacks as well as a few influential whites have argued for reparations for wrongs committed against the black population of the United States, with little to no success (Coates 2004). Their arguments have been very similar to those of other reparations movements: that a wrong was committed, that a certain group suffered, and that a certain entity was the perpetrator of this wrong. The United States has worked very hard to protect itself against these claims, and opponents of black reparations often cite trivial reasons (e.g., who is a victim?) rooted in the racial contract, amounting to a running away from the collective responsibility that the United States has toward its black community.

This "bob-and-weave" strategy takes the emphasis off the *why* of reparations. Choosing to discuss victim status and identification in a limited manner does not excuse the act from being immoral. It is hypocritical to shirk the American responsibility for acts committed by a government legitimized by its very citizens when these same citizens lavish praise and commemorate previous administrations for the benefits they have attained over the past 250 years. Celebrating the benefits attained from previous administrations (e.g., the Fourth of July) while at the same time declaring that we cannot hold those same administrations responsible for the atrocities they committed in establishing this very nation is abhorrently illogical and anti-human. Such contradiction is the lifeblood of the racial contract. We cannot approach black reparations through the institutionalized racial contract—this we learn from *Cato v. United States* (1995), from recent cases in Chicago and Tulsa (Burroughs 2005; Carillo 2005), and from John Conyers's fifteen-year failure to have House Resolution 40 (H.R. 40), his reparations study bill, make it out of committee. In order to effectively make a case for reparations, we must frame this case outside the racial contract, deconstruct this contract as immoral and illegitimate, and then frame our argument around a human contract in which *all* men and women are inherently equal in moral qualities. Only then are reparations for the wrongs committed against blacks in this society and around the world possible.

LAW AS METHOD

At least two different approaches to reparations have been taken within the legal system. One such approach is to attempt to legislate reparations. This method did not start with John Conyers and H.R. 40 but actually dates back to General Sherman's "forty acres and a mule" Special Order 15 (Coates 2004)—quickly rescinded by President Andrew Johnson (Coates 2004; Farmer-Paellman 2003). Between 1897 and 1917, the Ex-Slave Mutual Relief, Bounty, and Pension Association, founded by Callie House (Coates 2004), lobbied the government to enact legislation for pensions to ex-slaves. The governmental response to this lobbying was to prosecute House and others within this organization on fraud charges, arguing that they were collecting money for a lobbying effort that instilled false hope that ex-slaves would receive a pension (Farmer-Paellman 2003). The concern was not whether this argument was legitimate in its approach but whether the government, legitimized by its white citizens, would recognize the moral and legal claims of its now "free" population of second-class citizens. It would not. Eighty years later, U.S. Representative Tony Hall's resolution (asking for Congress to formally apologize for slavery) and Conyers's H.R. 40 (asking for Congress to simply study reparations) have never made it out of committee.

Even though the door to legislative discussion concerning reparations for blacks continues to remain shut, the door to judicial hearings has remained opened. However, this door often leads to a series of obstacles and legal jargon that prevent the movement from ever gaining any momentum or even marginal success. In *Cato v. United States* (1995), the Ninth Circuit Court of Appeals, one of the most liberal federal courts in the nation, ruled that the plaintiffs had no grounds to sue the U.S. government for reparations for slavery due to a "surpassed statute of limitations" and the principle of sovereign immunity (Farmer-Paellman 2003). Sovereign immunity essentially declares that the government cannot be sued unless *it* gives permission to be sued.

The African-American Slave Defendants Litigation, led by activist and lawyer Deadria Farmer-Paellman, brought a case against eighteen different U.S. companies whom the plaintiffs claimed benefited from the enslaved labor of their direct ancestors (Carillo 2005). However, in 2005, this case was dismissed by the U.S. district judge because he ruled that the plaintiffs had not suffered any "personal injury" due to the enslavement of their ancestors (Carillo 2005). Things have happened more recently for Farmer-Paellman's case. In December 2006, the federal appeals court upheld fraud claims against major U.S. banks, insurers, and transportation and other corporations that concealed their slave-trading histories from consumers. Such a recent case appears to have ushered in a shift in the legal environment for reparations—only time will tell. There is reason to be skeptical of such "gains," however. The tenets behind the racial contract, combined with an epistemology of individualization inherited from the same "enlightened" doctrine that produced the racial contract, make the argument for reparations within the contract as one about individual compensation and redress rather than collective restoration and justice.

Even in this brief analysis of the history of legal reparations, a pattern emerges: that, though appearing open, the courts and the legislative process remain closed to proponents of black reparations. The deeper meaning behind this, however, is found in the construction of the racial contract. This contract, while formally extending basic *individual* rights to its black citizens, acts on blacks as a *collective* (while not grounded in collectivist, human rights), virtually denying them access to legal redress for the immoral acts that the U.S. government perpetrated against them since their enslavement. When unable to discuss reparations within the legislative body, it is taken to the judicial branch. This branch, however, has in effect told them that their case has no place in its halls either. Earlier it was mentioned that all laws are structured around a basic morality of the society that these laws protect. However, when the moral code becomes racialized, it legitimizes immoral actions against a population by the state (Mills 1997). Immoral actions by the state are legitimate even when their principles are irrational.

Thus, the racial contract allows for state monopolization over what is moral and what is not. If the state agrees that to enslave one group is morally right, then enslavement becomes legitimate. If the state agrees that this group will be set free but subject to discrimination de jure, then this discrimination becomes legitimate. When the state finally decides to slowly extend basic formal rights to this same group (i.e., individuals) yet deny them the appropriate fundamental changes needed to establish their right to self-determination, this group's inferior social position in society becomes legitimate as well. This, then, is the range of the racial contract. Past reparations movements have focused on the project of slavery as the center of their argument for reparations, but that argument fails to see the interconnectedness of racist practices into one big racial project that is underwritten by the racial contract. Reparations proponents must step outside this contract and into the realm of human rights and universal morality in order to fully understand what this project has truly meant.

MORALITY AS METHOD

How is it that 500 years of oppression and domination has come to be justified in the annals of history? How can the founding fathers of our modern-day moral scope claim a moral egalitarianism by which all men are created equal yet argue, as Kant did, that skin color in itself is a measure of moral superiority (Mills 1997)? Universality, as an ideological framework, has its foundation in human production. Society is a human product. However, when the world became globally connected, with the discovery of the African continent, and its many resources of material wealth for Europe, universal morality was reconstructed as a means to exclude. Then the subsequent exploitation was rationalized as moral. Thus, the concept of universal morality was not abandoned so much as it was rearticulated. The morality that existed for whites was limited to whites because blacks were framed as objects by the racial contract (Mills 1997). Morality then became a simulation, a creation of a reality without a concrete origin. As Baudrillard (1983) puts it, "At the beginning of colonization, there was a moment of stupor and amazement before the very possibility of escaping the universal law of the Gospel. There were two possible responses: either to admit that this law was not universal, or to exterminate the Indians so as to remove the evidence" (20). Yet, a third possibility was presented at this time: construct those seen as different as subpersons through *Herrenvolk ideology* (Mills 1997).

Through this ideological frame, the principles of morality did not have to apply to this subhuman category. Rather than acknowledging that the morality here was nothing but a simulation of actual moral principles, whites not only exterminated those groups that stood as evidence against this simulation but also, through Herrenvolk ideology, were able to justify the immoral treatment of indigenous populations they encountered. This extermination, then, was not only physical extermination but also extermination of a people's humanity. The order of the imperial world had to remain intact by any means necessary. How else can a law remain universal? Make no mistake, however; the simulation of morality constructed through the racial contract was not simply conjured out of thin air—it was by design. Universality came to include some, not others.

The morality within the racial contract started off as a reflection of basic reality, of that which was agreed on in the social contract of all humanity. In other words, the language was the same; however, the application was color coded. Once populations were found to exist outside white European society and were differentiated, morality under the social contract became a perversion of its former self. The exploitation of nonwhite populations became justified when morality was able to mask this reality of exploitation; whiteness came to be redefined as natural domination over a nonwhite world. It was at this point that the racial contract allowed for this new color-coded morality to become its own "simulacrum": it bears no relation to basic reality whatsoever (Baudrillard 1983). The European powers attempted to disguise this domination as the spreading of democracy or, more to the point, a simulation of democracy, based on a simulated morality. American democracy does not exist, nor has it ever existed. Unless nonwhites and, within the focus of this chapter, blacks in America are included within this representation of democracy—and because they are not—democracy as it stands is a mockery of what it seeks to represent. W. E. B. Du Bois (1940) knew this all too well: "The democracy which the white world seeks to defend does not exist. It has been splendidly conceived and discussed, but not realized" (169).

When discussing reparations as a moral claim, it cannot be framed in relation to a single immoral act or a single immoral era. Rather, it has to be framed as a continuing immoral act, of which there has been no moral response to remedy it. Two wrongs are distinct only "if they have nothing to do with one another" (Hughes 2004, 251). While Hughes causally links slavery and present-day discrimination by racism, Omi and Winant (1994) offer a much clearer perspective of this linkage through their concept of the racist project. A racial project is racist "if it creates or reproduces structures of domination based on essentialist categories of race" (71). Using this concept, it becomes much easier to see how the racial contract is a *metacontract*. It has constructed an immense racist project that links essentialist representations of race to social structures of domination.

This racist project began with a reconstruction/reframing of morality as universal only to those who are "human." Blacks, as "nonhuman," were commodities to be exploited. Slavery was not the racist project but rather the first manifestation of action called on by the greater project itself. When it was no longer in the best interests of white America to continue to enslave its black population, whites extended formal freedom to blacks and in effect reconstructed morality again, with blacks as human but not quite as human as whites. All men are free, but under this reconstructed morality, all men cannot be equal. The racist project continued, manifesting itself through Jim Crow legislation and the black codes throughout the United States. Again, Jim Crow was not the racist project itself and cannot be conceived of as a separate racist project if this moral argument for reparations is to hold any weight. It was but a continuation of a much larger racist project, set up by the racial contract and manifesting itself in different forms throughout U.S. history. When the laws of Jim Crow were no longer able to withstand the pressure of civil disobedience and changing public morality, these laws were struck down, and formal civil rights legislation came swooping in. This legislation was, as mentioned, only a formality, though. There was no fundamental change in the effects from the previous system of explicit de jure discrimination.

Thus, even the civil rights legislation of 1964 can be argued as a continuation of the racist project in that it only reproduced racial domination in the form of color-blind racism and abstract liberalism (Bonilla-Silva 2001). Morality was reconstructed to include blacks as equals, but there was no effort to assist them in becoming objective and structural equals. Programs such as affirmative action, for instance, in this project are ambiguous and do not call for specific action to address specific wrongs. They merely present an illusion of change based off of a reconstruction of the racial contract. If the black reparations movement is to attain any success, it must acknowledge this time line of racial discrimination as one metaproject, underlain by the racial contract and founded on the principle of a simulation of universal morality.

One consistency in socially situated morality concerns the actions of one person against another person or one group against another group. These actions can be judged as moral or immoral, and this judgment withstands the test of time. If the actions of one harm another or prevent another from attaining a certain level of success, then those actions are immoral. Opponents to this line of thought have sought to attribute racist practices and ideology to the context of the times in which they took place, such as John McWhorter (2003), who criticizes Randall Robinson (2001) for attacking Hegel and other thinkers of that era for their racist ideologies. McWhorter argues that by doing this, Robinson and others miss the bigger picture: these men's societal contributions. However, we argue that it is illogical to conclude that these men were only behaving in ways that were justified during their times rather than attributing their behaviors to a racist ideology that has withstood the test of time.

As Robinson (2001) dares to ask, who isn't a man of his time? If Thomas Jefferson or George Washington are overlooked for their immoral acts as men of their time yet celebrated for their contributions as men of their time, we again run into a hypocrisy of commemoration. Such an argument does not, ever, reduce the immorality of their actions as any less savage. Aside from extremists, it is hard to imagine anyone commemorating the unprecedented efficiency with which Hitler exterminated his victims during the Holocaust, nor is it likely that we will hold a conference celebrating the medical information that was gained through the deliberate deceit of black men by the U.S. government during the Tuskegee syphilis experiments. These acts, immoral then, remain immoral now, as there has been no redress for the ongoing racist project.

Approaching the issue of reparations from the standpoint of a universal morality and human rights allows us to construct a specific perpetrator of harm as well as specific recipients of harm. The United States is the legal entity that has existed throughout this immoral act, and each generation of citizens, native or not, inherits the burden of membership and national debts along with the benefits of membership (McCarthy 2004). Stepping outside the racial contract allows us to see, from a bird's-eye view, just how whites have consented to this immorality throughout American history. Residence as a form of tacit consent was but one form of whites' legitimization of U.S. practice of racial hegemony. While most whites "did not own slaves," the collective failure of whites to reject the U.S. government's immorality resulted in the citizens of this country consenting to this immorality (Boxill 2003). Blacks as a group have suffered harm solely because of their membership in a racially classified group, based on a constructed morality of inferiority grounded in an illusion of reality that manifested itself as a racial contract between whites (Mills 1997). Responsibility for this racial construction falls squarely on the shoulders of the state. It is not surprising, then, that an immoral code of conduct, sanctioned by an immoral state, created an immoral society. What is surprising, however, is that in a day and age in which we claim to live by a higher moral code than our forefathers, we find ourselves either denying the existence of there ever being an immoral society from which we sprang or minimizing the transgressions of the past and their residual effects on the present.

HUMAN RIGHTS AND EPISTEMOLOGIES OF SOCIAL JUSTICE

The black reparations movement is not about punishing whites or punishing the U.S. government. The movement is about acknowledgment and awareness. Most important, it is about social justice, that extension of morality that calls for action. Current policies that claim to address racial inequalities created by an ongoing racist project only suppress the conditions of racial inequalities (Coates 2004). They do not attempt to remedy them. Compensating one who has been harmed involves bringing them to a level of well-being that a person would have attained had they not been harmed (Boxill 2003). Had all things been truly equal, blacks in this society would have achieved the same level of "success" as whites had they been allowed to participate fully in this society, had the racial contract not constructed them as subhuman, and had the racist project that has unfolded over the past 500 years never begun. This does require awareness and acknowledgment first.

In order for social justice to be achieved for blacks, the society in which we live needs to redress its past and current wrongs and establish a condition of justice for a society that is "scarred by enduring and pervasive effects of these wrongs" (McCarthy, 2004, 751). As of this writing, the Virginia General Assembly voted unanimously on February 24, 2007, to express "profound regret" for the state's role in slavery—this is but a small start at the state level. Redress does not stop with governmental acknowledgment of immorality, however. These atrocities, while sanctioned and committed by a legitimate government, were also committed by persons, and any account of responsibility and atonement for wrongs done to others that omits persons from this moral responsibility falls short of social justice (Hughes 2004). What good do reparations do if coming in the form of a reluctant handout or in an adversarial position to whites who cannot understand how they are responsible or even understand how reparations will benefit them? As a form of social justice, reparations benefit the entire society by elevating a group within from a position of subordination to one of equal footing. A chain is only as strong as its weakest link, and in an era in which we are constantly bombarded with messages of meritocracy in the face of inequalities, it is to the image of the chain that we must refer back. Duress for some is duress for everyone (Sacks 2005). That is the principle on which human rights and human unity stand, and it is a principle that our society alludes to but rarely demonstrates. This movement has a chance to become the ground on which our society can firmly stand as *the* moral agent of the free world, but only if we are willing to accept the responsibility in the first place.

The black reparations movement is asking not for handouts or quick fixes but for human rights. Whatever form reparations come in, it will require a great deal of effort and resources. What it will not stand for, however, is the continuous application of "Band-Aids upon hemorrhaging wounds" (Coates 2004, 854). Those who argue for reparations within the realm of the courts and legislative bodies are, in the end, only to be given more Band-Aids. This is the nature of the racial contract. It seeks to protect whiteness as an investment and thus has created a bomb that continues to explode in the faces of those who argue for social justice in relation to the continuous racist project that is the foundation of our society (Boxill 2003). Boxill (2003) begs the question, "Why has nobody diffused this bomb?" (66). The answer is because it has not been convenient for those who have planted it to do so. As long as this bomb continues to go off, the smoke and ash that rise up from it offer shade for those perpetrators who would attribute its explosion to its target's lack of awareness in walking across a minefield rather than take responsibility for planting the bomb themselves.

Racial oppression has no place in a regime of international human rights doctrine. The global human rights community has mechanisms in place to offer redress from states engaging in racial oppression. Aside from the Universal Declaration of Human Rights, the United Nations adopted the International Convention on the Elimination of All Forms of Racial Discrimination on December 21, 1965. The United States holds a "ratified" status with this convention (that was to be enforced by January 4, 1969) and has done nothing. There exists an optional protocol to this convention that sets up tribunals for the pursuance of reparations and the satisfaction for any damages suffered from state-sponsored racism. Not only has the United States eschewed these mechanisms, it has also turned aside from the varied World Conferences Against Racism (1978, 1983, and most recently 2001) and, indeed, the international human rights committee itself.

The point here is that, should the international community keep the United States accountable, reparations may become a reality. Yet, again, we must acknowledge that human rights discourse receives little airplay in the United States—what must happen? The human rights revolution requires an epistemology of justice. Claims of truth within a system of knowledge rooted in the racial contract will not be effective. We need to root our claims to truths (epistemologies) within the struggles of the oppressed in such systems. The oppressors cannot be in charge of doling out justice, as our argument here has made excruciatingly clear. Truth and reconciliation commissions could be encouraged bringing both the oppressed and the oppressors to the table (Freire 1988).

NOTES

We would like to thank Charles Mills and Rodney Coates for their exceptional comments on previous drafts of this manuscript.

1. We use the term "Amerikkka" instead of "America" following the lead of scholar Eduardo Bonilla-Silva of Duke University. We also agree with him that we will remove the Ks from this word when the United States removes racial oppression from this country.

REFERENCES

Baudrillard, Jean. 1983. *Simulations*. Translated by Paul Foss, Paul Patton, and Philip Beitchman. Cambridge, Mass.: Semiotext[e].

Bonilla-Silva, Eduardo. 2001. *White Supremacy and Racism in the Post Civil Rights Era*. Boulder, Colo.: Lynne Rienner, 2001.

Boxill, Bernard. 2003. "A Lockean Argument for Black Reparations." *Journal of Ethics* 7, no. 1: 63–91.

Burroughs, Todd. 2005. "1921 Tulsa Riot Survivors Denied Reparations." *Crisis (The New)* 112, no. 4. findarticles.com/p/articles/mi_qa4081/is_200507/ai _n15665595 (accessed January 15,2007).

Carillo, Karen. 2004. "Anybody for Reparations? Republicans and Democrats Share a Disinterest." *New York Amsterdam News* 95: 38.

———. 2005. "Lawsuit Seeking Reparations Fails in Chicago." *New York Amsterdam News* 96: 29.

Coates, Rodney. 2004. "If a Tree Falls in the Wilderness: Reparations, Academic Silences and Social Justice." *Social Forces* 83, no. 2: 841–64.

Du Bois, W. E. B. 1940. *Dusk of Dawn: An Essay towards an Autobiography of a Race Concept*. New York: Harcourt Brace.

Farmer-Paellman, Deadria C. 2003. "Excerpt from Black Exodus: The Ex-Slave Pension Movement Reader." In *Should America Pay for Reparations? Slavery and the Raging Debate on Reparations*, edited by Raymond A. Winbush. New York: HarperCollins.

Freire, Paulo. 1988. *Pedagogy of the Oppressed*. Translated by Myra Bergman Ramos. New York: Continuum.

Howard-Hassman, Rhoda. 2004. "Getting to Reparations: Japanese-Americans and African Americans." *Social Forces* 83, no. 2: 823–40.

Hughes, Paul. 2004. "Rectification and Reparation: What Does Citizen Responsibility Require?" *Journal of Social Philosophy* 35, no. 2: 244–55.

McCarthy, Thomas. 2004. "Coming to Terms with Our Past: On the Morality and Politics of Reparations for Slavery." *Political Theory* 32, no. 6: 750–72.

McWhorter, John. 2003. "Against Reparations" In *Should America Pay for Reparations? Slavery and the Raging Debate on Reparations*, edited by Raymond A. Winbush. New York: HarperCollins.

Mills, Charles. 1997. *The Racial Contract*. Ithaca, N.Y.: Cornell University Press.

Omi, Michael, and Howard Winant. 1994. *Racial Formation in the United States: From the 1960s to the 1990s*. 2nd ed. New York: Routledge.

Posner, Eric, and Adrian Vermeule. 2003. "Reparations for Slavery and Other Historical Injustices." *Columbia Law Review* 103, no. 3: 689–747.

Puwar, Nirmal. 2001. "The Racialized Somatic Norm and the Senior Civil Service." *Sociology* 35, no. 3: 651–70.

———. 2002. "Multicultural Fashions . . . Stirrings of Another Sense of Aesthetics and Memory." *Feminist Review* 71: 63–87.

Robinson, Randall. 2001. *The Debt: What America Owes to Blacks*. New York: Penguin.

Sacks, Jonathan. 2005. "We Are in Danger of Forgetting That Waiting Comes before Wanting." *The Times*, November 12.

Sowell, Thomas. 2001. "Victimizing Blacks." www.townhall.com/columnists/thomassowell/ts20010802.shtml, August 2.

Van Dyke, Jon M. 2003. "Reparations and the Descendants of Slaves under International Law." In *Should America Pay for Reparations? Slavery and the Raging Debate on Reparations*, edited by Raymond A. Winbush. New York: HarperCollins.

Westley, Robert. 2003. "Many Billions Gone: Is It Time to Reconsider the Case for Black Reparations?" In *Should America Pay for Reparations? Slavery and the Raging Debate on Reparations*, edited by Raymond A. Winbush. New York: HarperCollins.

Winbush, Raymond A. 2003. "And the Earth Moved: Stealing Black Land in the United States." In *Should America Pay for Reparations? Slavery and the Raging Debate on Reparations*, edited by Raymond A. Winbush. New York: HarperCollins.

6

Paying for the Past: Prospects and Obstacles Facing Reparations Politics in the U.S. and South Africa

Amy E. Ansell

The last thing one would expect to hear these days is discussion of racial reparations. As citizens of the United States approach the end of eight years of the presidency of George W. Bush, itself part of a continuum of conservative rule that began with Ronald Reagan's election in 1980, progress that had been made in the civil rights era has been gradually eroded. A new spirit of social meanness is apparent, albeit voiced in the laudable language of individual rights, equal treatment for all, and race liberalism.[1] The manner in which the new conservatism has engaged global human rights discourse has delivered results that are deleterious to progress toward racial equality and justice. For example, affirmative action has been curtailed out of respect for the right of whites to equal treatment and may be on its way out with the retirement of Justice Sandra Day O'Connor, antidiscrimination law has been retailored narrowly to cases of proven intent (as opposed to consequences), and statements of political will supporting the goal of diversity are increasingly substituted for discourses of redress. So why all the talk of reparations?

Talk there is, especially among academics interested in the study of race and ethnicity and among media and cultural critics as well as bodies such as Human Rights Watch and the Center for Constitutional Rights.[2] Several reasons can be proffered for this burgeoning interest:

- Beginning in the 1990s, the demand for recompense for past wrongs on the part of a variety of ethnoracial groups has exploded on the international scene, fueled by a collective identity of victimization.

- The establishment of truth commissions questing after transitional justice as societies in Eastern Europe, Latin America, and South Africa exited from authoritarian rule has spurred the debate surrounding reparations.
- The waning prospects for affirmative action as an effective policy of redress have resulted in growth in the movement for reparations as a partial substitute, especially as affirmative action discourse increasingly turns on diversity as a rationale.
- The shift from the transformative movement politics associated with the civil rights/antiracist era to today's era of identity politics has fueled the concern for recompense for past victimization as opposed to more universal and collective hopes for the future.
- The success of legal suits brought on behalf of victims of World War II–related atrocities has provided a template of sorts for the growing movement for reparations, especially among juridical activists interested in pursuing the logic of these legal precedents.

The latter two contextual factors in particular—cultural and legal—beg for greater amplification. In terms of cultural context, if one can speak of an emergent global political culture, it is one marked by the end of the transformative politics characteristic of the post–World War II context and the march toward a more authoritarian form of liberal democracy. The demobilization of progressive coalitions for change has gone hand in hand with the rise of identity politics and the triumph of diversity-oriented forms of multiculturalism that celebrate ethnoracial particularity and a politics of difference—often organized around collective identities based on the articulation of past grievances—over a future-oriented agenda for equality and justice based on notions of universal human sameness and "common dreams."[3] In an environment wherein a supposedly robust economy has delivered a few economic winners and a growing number of losers, it is far more comfortable to construe oneself as victim than as one who might bear some historic responsibility or be accused of relative privilege. The emergence of the movement for reparations is therefore coincident with a global symbolic currency that places high value on the status of victimhood.

In terms of the legal context, the success of suits brought on behalf of victims of World War II–related atrocities helps explain the recent burgeoning of reparations politics. Suits on behalf of Holocaust victims and Japanese American and Japanese Canadians interned during World War II have provided a template of sorts for so-called reparations lawyers to bring subsequent claims on behalf of a wide variety of groups, among the most notable of which are comfort women sexually exploited by the Japanese during World War II, African Americans enslaved and then discriminated against during Jim Crow, the Herero in Namibia decimated by the Germans in 1904–1907, and nonwhite South African victims of the apartheid state. Added to the power of precedent, is the sense on the part of human rights lawyers of the potential usefulness of the formerly obscure eighteenth-century Alien Tort Claims Act as a vehicle to litigate human rights and reparations claims regardless of whether any of the parties (individuals, states, corporations, or religious institutions) are U.S. based, a topic that will be pursued further in the last part of this chapter. The rise of legal activism concerning reparations also relates to the demobilization of transformative politics noted previously, making law seem a more fruitful avenue to pursue racial justice.

The remainder of this chapter examines the mix of obstacles and prospects facing the growing movement for reparations. The analysis remains mindful of the previously mentioned contextual factors as well as the terrific variety of claims and differences in origin and focus that are in need of unraveling. Reparations can entail monetary payments to individual victims or descendants, public funds put toward sources of inequality inherited from the past, or the offering of apologies or other expressions of regret to the communities aggrieved. The national comparative aspect of the analysis aims to draw attention to the impact of variables such as 1) the variety of goals ranging from material (individual monetary settlements as well as redress of systemic inequalities) to symbolic (discursive apologies or expressions of regret and commemoration); 2) differences due to whether the victims of past wrongs are still living, with implications for whether the focus is on perpetrators or beneficiaries on the one hand or on victims or the disadvantaged on the other; 3) the role of institutional context, whether it be the courts in the case of class-action monetary settlements or the court of public opinion and politics in the case of antisystemic reparations and apology; and 4) the two contrasting versions of rights, multiculturalism and citizenship at the heart of reparations politics, the one lending itself to common universal goals of equality and justice, as in antisystemic reparations, and the other more attuned to identity politics and the cultural recognition of ethnoracial differences, as in the discourse of apology and commemoration. In order to ground the study empirically, I present data from two sources—one from the United States and the other from South Africa—in order to capture white narratives on reparations and the obstacles such narratives present in terms of growth in the movement for reparations. The chapter concludes with an evaluation of prospects for a legal approach to reparations, with a special case study focus on the apartheid-era lawsuits most recently argued before the U.S. Second Circuit Court of Appeals in January 2006.

REFUSING RESPONSIBILITY: WHITE
NARRATIVES ON REPARATIONS

In the abstract, making good on past wrongs is a laudable act. Yet in concrete instances marked by contestation over what exactly is owed and by whom, the degree of repair already achieved, and the appropriate principles to guide ensuring that the wrong is not repeated in the future, then proposals for reparations enter a fray that necessitates calculation of the unintended consequences of making amends. Chief among these potential consequences is that paying for the past might unwittingly fuel racial divisiveness and even white nationalist sentiment.[4] This is especially pertinent in the United States, as surveys of white public opinion have found that a majority of whites believe that discrimination against racial minorities no longer exists and that the playing field between whites and blacks is now level.[5] Such opinion helps make sense of a 1997 poll that found that 88 percent of white respondents in the United States opposed the notion of paying reparations and that two-thirds resisted even an apology.[6]

Undoubtedly, part of the challenge of reparations politics in the United States has to do with the historical distance between present generations and those wronged by the institution of slavery. White opposition to proposals for reparations is of course a discourse of denial, a statement of personal and social innocence. But the fact of historical distance makes the issue particularly thorny, for, in their protestation of nonresponsibility, white Americans refuse guilt for that which they can never literally be accused of, namely, the ownership of slaves or the initial subjugation of Africans. Reparations politics in South Africa are freed to some extent from this challenge since many of the victims and perpetrators of gross human rights violations during apartheid are still living. On first glance, it would be reasonable to assume that the prospects for reparations politics are more promising in postapartheid South Africa, not only because of the more recent timing of the dismantling of institutional racism and segregation but also as a result of a political culture more accepting of the constitutional violation of race neutrality.[7] Yet data surveying South African white opinion toward racial reconciliation presents a puzzle of discursive congruence with the attitudes expressed by Euro-Americans. One aim of the presentation of empirical data here is to demonstrate how white discourse opposing reparations in the two countries is surprisingly congruent, revealing either an effect of the deliberate mutual sharing and transatlantic cross-fertilization of the public framing of racial issues, the importation of American racial discourse into the South African scene, or the formation of a pan-white diasporic consciousness emergent in response to a shared global context wherein white racial privilege and dominance is faced with a challenge.

The shared context here is one that can be characterized as an era of apology. Indeed, the decade of the 1990s witnessed a virtual explosion of political apologies from around the globe: in the United Kingdom for the English role in the Irish potato famine, in Australia for the forcible removal of fair-skinned aborigine children and adoption in white homes and orphanages, in Germany for genocide against the Herero of Namibia, in Japan for having kept Korean women as army sex slaves during World War II, in France for its collaboration with Germany during World War II, and so on. It is reasonable to surmise that part of the story behind this explosion of apologies is the highly publicized model of South Africa's Truth and Reconciliation Commission (TRC) that more than anything came to embody the so-called South African miracle. Archbishop Desmond Tutu, TRC chairman, understood apology as the cornerstone of reconciliation. During his appeal to former state president P. W. Botha, Tutu said,

> I want to appeal to him to take this chance provided by this court to say that he himself may not have intended the suffering to happen to people . . . [but] the governments that he headed caused many of our people deep, deep anguish and pain and suffering. Our people want to be part of this country and be part of reconciliation. If Mr. Botha is about to say "I am sorry the policies of my government caused you so much pain"—just that—that would be a tremendous thing.

Apology as a means of recompense for the nation's racist legacy also became salient in the United States. In 1997, President Clinton apologized on behalf of the nation to black men who were the unwitting experiment subjects in the government's Tuskegee Syphilis Study and also for not awarding Medals of Honor to African American soldiers in World War II. That same year, and no doubt partly on the basis of the 1988 precedent represented by the U.S. Congress both apologizing and paying economic reparations to Japanese Americans who were interned in the United States during World War II, Representative Tony Hall (D-Ohio) proposed a one-sentence resolution (House Concurrent Resolution 96):—"A concurrent resolution apologizing for those who suffered as slaves under the Constitution and Laws of the United States until 1865." The motivation for Hall's proposed apology seems to have been almost entirely religious in inspiration and moral in character. Nevertheless, the proposed apology hit the headlines in what became a national debate about the nation's racist legacy.

The discourse of apology in both national contexts raises difficult questions with respect to reparations politics, such as the following: To what degree is an unwilling or unwitting beneficiary accountable for the sins of perpetrators of the past? What is owed to those who are not themselves victims but who suffer from disadvantages associated with the unintended consequences of historical injustice? Apologies, even those absent a linked economic dimension, can wield enormous emotional and symbolic power for all parties concerned. Presented next is a brief summary of findings concerning white popular opinion with regard to racial reparations, reconciliation, and apology. The first data set is from the United States, drawn from a set of public submissions ($N = 518$) sent in to the Congressional Office of Representative Tony Hall in 1997 in the wake of his call for Congress to issue an apology for slavery. The second data set is from South Africa, drawn from a set of public submissions ($N = 154$) sent to the South African Human Rights Commission as both follow-up to the work of the TRC and in preparation for the National Conference on Racism held in 2000, itself a precursor to the International Conference on Racism held in Durban in 2001.

Submissions in both societies manifest a remarkably similar sequence of ideological and political themes, organized around opposition to the demand for reparations based *within* the overlapping frameworks of human rights, color blindness, multiculturalism, and race liberalism. The shared themes are 1) selective acknowledgment of the racist past, 2) denial of the continuing impact of the legacies of the past, 3) assertions of unbiased innocence, 4) complaints of white communal victimization, and 5) reliance on idealistic definitions of racism that emphasize the need to combat prejudice and protect the individual from nondiscrimination over more structural definitions that highlight systematic relations of power and disadvantage. Operating together, they contribute to an oppositional discourse on reparations without, importantly, departing from global human rights ideals.

The question of how to deal with the racist past is especially thorny for whites in both societies. Here the difference in timing is crucial, as one would expect the more recent exit from apartheid (as compared with the end of slavery or even the dismantling of Jim Crow in the United States) to contribute to a greater degree of acknowledgment of the crimes and violations of the very recent past. Denial is not an option given that both perpetrators and victims are still living. Yet the manner in which the past is acknowledged is very selective, as demonstrated in this chapter. Acknowledgment of the racist past is less contested in the United States since the institution of slavery existed so many generations ago. Consequently, in this context, the question of how to deal with the racist past revolves more around whether the legacies of the past still impact on the present.

The debate over reparations in South Africa is closely tied to the framework of national reconciliation. Many submission authors regard reparations and reconciliation as opposing and mutually exclusive components in the making of a democratic society. A common refrain in the files is the expressed belief that in order to reconcile, South Africans must forget about the divided past and focus instead on building a common future. For example, submission author M. S. M. cautions that politicians who comment on the injustices of the past cause "more bad feelings like all the commissions and recriminations. . . . Why keep bringing up the past, forget what happened, who was wrong and who was right, just get on with the job and work together instead of causing a state of reverse apartheid." Some submission authors assert that while statutory racism ended in 1994 with the transition to democracy, the legacy of apartheid racial classifications is dangerously present in the rule of the contemporary African National Congress (ANC). Among self-identified whites, a central concern is that Afrikaner nationalism is being replaced by African nationalism, with all the attendant negative consequences in terms of a racially divided and hostile society. Gerhard P. writes,

> You would agree with me that two wrongs do not make a right, but distort matters even further. I certainly do acknowledge the serious wrongs of apartheid, and have in fact opposed it all my life. I continue to be against it, also now that the role players have been swapped around and the policy of race differentiation is being labeled "affirmative action." Under the policy of apartheid, particularly the Afrikaners sought to obtain certain privileges and protection for themselves. Today the black majority seeks to do likewise.

Far from representing a simple denial of the racist past, these authors acknowledge the injustices of the past and state their objection. But the acknowledgment is selective in the sense that commitment to redress the socioeconomic legacies of apartheid is avoided, indeed trumped, by rhetorical commitment to nonracialism and human rights. So it is a particular kind of denial—denial of the cumulative benefits of being white. In her study of white identity in a changing South Africa, Melissa Steyn writes,

> A desire to close the discussion of the past is one strand within a general pattern of denial. The appeal to let sleeping dogs lie hides the crucial issue of which dogs are still holding onto the bones. It is an evasion of the extent to which the past permeates the present, of how the legacy of social injustice continues into the future. It is a refusal to acknowledge that sustaining "normal" white life perpetuates the disadvantages of others. Complacency, even indifference, is passed off as liberality.[8]

It is this evasion of how the legacy of past racial injustice permeates present-day race relations that is the most salient in the U.S. discussion. Fueled by the historical distance between the era of slavery and today, whites in the United States protest reparations for two reasons: one is the assertion of unbiased innocence on the part of present-day whites for culpability for crimes of the past, and the other is denial that contemporary patterns of racial disadvantage are due to historical oppression. Submissions in the Hall files reveal the extent to which many white people are currently focused in their dealings with the question of their responsibility for and/or complicity with the historical consequences of racism. One letter writer states,

> I have never owned any slaves, neither have my grandfathers and great grandparents. I do not know any living slaves. Hence, is my elected official supposed

to make an apology for me, for something I am not responsible for, but for the fact that I am white? That, Congressman, sounds racist to me. I do not accept blanket responsibilities for events of history beyond my control.

Similarly, a letter writer from California states,

I wasn't alive then; had nothing to do with it; you weren't; and neither was anyone in any position of government today! So why should those of today apologize for something which they had nothing to do with? Back off!

The fact that slavery was abolished in the nineteenth century allows white Americans to offer various disclaimers of responsibility. One common disclaimer is organized around renditions of immigrant histories rehearsed in order to absolve authors from accountability for the institution of slavery. Such assertions symbolically construct white innocence in decrying that the present generation should be forced to pay for the sins of the parent generation. In the South African context, similar sentiments are sometimes voiced, most often in relation to children. But more typical are disclaimers based on assertions of personal histories of antiapartheid activism. Yet in both contexts the need for whites to establish innocence appears as a kind of fetish.

Despite differences between the United States and South Africa due to differences in historical timing as well as other factors, a new pattern of meaning construction on the part of whites in both societies is evident. Rhetorical accommodation to color blindness is combined with denial of the continuing relevance of the legacies of the past. Such a combination allows whites to claim the moral high ground of being "beyond race" while refusing sacrifice of the accumulated benefits of racial privilege inherited from the past.

Whites in both societies express feelings of victimization in the face of equality-promoting programs. Loss of privileged status is understood not only as discriminatory against them but also, in diasporic identification with global whiteness, as deleterious in signaling falling standards, increasing corruption, and the decline of meritocracy. Tales of reverse discrimination abound. In the United States, such tales are, for the most part, limited to complaints of not getting a job or university admission because one is white. In South Africa, no doubt because of vastly different demographic realities, the political hegemony of the ANC, and more intense employment equity programs, added to such complaints are allegations of media bias against whites, discrimination on the job, and other tales expressing a sense of marginalization. In the South African files, Wendy M. feels that she and her colleagues have been the victims of open racism on the part of the South African Broadcasting Corporation (SABC), which was allegedly not interested in covering overseas victories in 1999 of a school pipe band:

I personally was told that as there were not blacks in the band they were very sorry but they could not cover it. I have since then seen choirs and sports teams covered by the SABC and they have all been almost exclusively black school children. . . . We all feel that these children, no matter their race or colour work very hard to be the best . . . and they are being denied opportunities for exposure and even sponsorship on the basis of their colour. . . . Give us what you promise—non racist treatment for ALL SOUTH AFRICANS IRRESPECTIVE OF RACE OR COLOUR OR CULTURE. These children did not have anything to do with the OLD REGIME OF APARTHEID and most of us (their parents) were even too young to vote for the racist regime of the past. They should not be made to suffer for the mistakes made by others.

Similarly, Mrs. M. F. B. identifies herself as a female white South African who was overjoyed in 1994 but has since become cynical:

I feel myself part of a discarded minority who is getting blamed for all conceivable wrongs in the country. . . . At present only one side of racism in South Africa is seen and recognised as such, ie white-on-black racism. The existence of its mirror image and twin brother, black-on-white racism, which is just as rampant, evil and destructive, is not even acknowledged, let alone condemned. Thus, tragically, the very perception of racism in South Africa is racist.

In a similar vein, Hugh W. writes,

It would be unthinkable in the new South Africa for someone to form an Association of White Plumbers. But it seems quite acceptable for there to be a Black Lawyer's Association . . . and no-one calls that "racist."

In the U.S. files too, belief borrowed from the color-blind framework that the mission of eradicating racism has been accomplished and the opportunity structure is open and fair slides easily into adoption of the attitude that whites are in fact the new victims of the current racial order. Indeed, evidence suggests that there is a growing sentiment on the part of relevant social groups that the white male is being treated unfairly at the hands of women and people of color—that is, that they are in fact the new victims of discrimination. The sense that the current playing field has been skewed to black advantage is expressed in the following letter to Tony Hall:

Do you really think that we as white Americans really need to apologize to the Black Americans or the so-called African Americans? I never had slaves nor did any of my relatives. And I'll just be damned if I'm going to apologize for being white!!! . . . I do not apologize for the black TV shows that don't have to have a white person in it but white TV shows that have to show at least one black person in it or it will be called racist!!! The black people have their own College fund for blacks only!! Whites can't have this because it would be racist!!! Blacks have the NAACP [National Association for the Advancement of Colored

People] to protect them from racist white people. But if white people did this
it would be racist!!! I don't apologize for something I or my ancestors had ab-
solutely nothing to do with."

Such accounts of white victimhood both reflect and help shape an increasingly hegemonic right-wing consensus that celebrates abstract notions
of equal opportunity and individualism over demands for recognition of
difference and group rights at the heart of demands for reparations. The potential exists for such victim discourse to be reorganized into a form of
white subnationalism (more likely in South Africa) or white identity politics modeled on multiculturalism (more likely in the United States).

The failure to secure a new consensus in this interregnum between the
now-defunct white supremacist social order and an ostensibly postracist
one relates in part to a definitional struggle over what constitutes racism in
the first place. Superficially, the notion of race neutrality is consistent both
with what I label *idealist* definitions of racism that are concerned with prejudice and attitudes of racial hatred and what I label a *structural* definition
that brings to bear systemic relations of power, class, and inequality. During
the apartheid and Jim Crow eras, the distinction was less relevant as the
two—prejudice and racial inequality—worked together, more or less in tan-
dem. However, one of the defining characteristics of the postapartheid and
post–civil rights eras is how systemic patterns of racial inequality and disadvantage have persisted, even worsened, despite the dramatic increase in
egalitarian sentiment. The ideological battle over the meaning and opera-
tional consequences of race neutrality is given purchase in this definitional
fissure.

One of the most surprising aspects of discursive congruence between the
two countries is the degree to which white South Africans, a mere decade after the end of apartheid and with every major socioeconomic indicator still
cleaved profoundly by race, have adopted an American-sounding, idealistic
language to opine about racism. Whereas reparations politics operates on
the basis of an assumed structural definition of racism wherein the legacies
of the racist past continue to shape present-day patterns of racial disadvantage, racism is talked about in the submissions in terms that are moral, religious, and highly individualistic. It is this severance of racism from concern with the reproduction of systemic advantages inherited from the past
that allows whites to claim victim status despite the fact that they continue
to wield enormously disproportionate social and economic power. Many
submission authors rely on abstract, universalistic themes to define racism
as any and all unfair treatment based on skin color, regardless of whether
the color is white, black, or other. George E. writes, "Any definition of
racism that is based on specific racial categories is itself racist and should
not be countenanced." In this view, racism is not a structural problem in

need of redress but a psychological condition that can best be eliminated through programs of resocialization, multicultural education, and opportunities for intercultural exchange. Robert M. proposes implementing a national "Dialogue Project" in order to provide "the opportunity and the process for people to engage empathetically on the issue of racism." Connie D. suggests that "getting to know each other" socially is important and that people of different racial groups need to intermarry. Others, such as Faith G., employ religious metaphors in pleas for love and interracial friendship. Dr. G. concludes, "Racism . . . is a mind set problem. . . . I think we need to accept one another first as human beings." Here the vocabulary of nonracialism serves to impoverish the political imagination so that acting against racism means changing mind-sets and not structures of power.

Added to the general universalistic and humanistic rhetoric cited previously is a civics discourse in the United States that emphasizes race neutrality and a culture of personal (not group) responsibility as necessary for national cohesion. For example, a columnist for a Cleveland newspaper rejects Hall's proposed apology with the argument that the very definition of what it is to be an American would be jeopardized if racial groups were to be held accountable for past wrongs:

> We are not the generation responsible for slavery; nor are we the generation that was enslaved . . . it is simply unjust for one person to pay for the crimes of another, whether he be related or not. If the United States were to adopt a system of justice based on group rather than individual responsibility, there would be no end to the rancor among the Balkanized groups. Grievances would be nursed from one generation to another. No longer would we be worthy of the slogan "E Pluribus Unum."

Despite the many differences that exist between the United States and South Africa, there does exist a common set of white narratives on reparations. Narratives that employ selective aspects of a universal human rights model are invoked to counter alternative constructions, such as one based on inequality or the need to repair legacies of the past. Rhetorical accommodation to color blindness and defense of the principle of equal protections for all individuals (not groups) is combined with appeals for the need to be forward looking in order for racial reconciliation to succeed, together with denial of the persistent purchase of the legacies of the racist past. Such a combination allows whites to refuse recompense for the accumulated disadvantages of racial subordination inherited from the past.

Such refusal draws on a triumphant liberal ideology today that accepts and naturalizes gross economic disparity, thereby bracketing and deleting the structural dimension of racial discourse, rendering race—like ethnicity, national origin, religion, or sexual preference—simply a social identity, a cultural/historical marker in a diverse globalizing society. Recognizing the obvious vast differences in economic circumstance, it revels in moral narratives of impoverished individuals—black and white, native born and immigrant—who, through talent, tenacity, and luck, have overcome immense obstacles to join the ranks of the powerful, rich, and famous. The emergence of a wealthy and connected black elite in South Africa—the so-called patriotic bourgeoisie—and the visibility and prominence of extraordinarily successful African Americans in popular culture serve as apparent empirical validation of liberal ideology. In this way, white narratives opposing reparations are buoyed by a global discursive context in which claims for group redress and racialized advantage appear as carping, regressive, discordant, and profoundly antidemocratic, antithetical to the very principles and ideals assumed triumphant in the victories over apartheid and Jim Crow.

The fact that this perspective enjoys global ubiquity is not to say that it goes uncontested. Evident in both files are countercurrents to the sentiments surveyed previously. There do exist submissions that support especially symbolic forms of reparations, such as apology, for their potential to heal wounds, bring closure, and confront the amnesia and evasion represented by the "postracism" consensus. In so doing, these currents of opinion represent a powerful antidote to the previously presented narratives in that they manifest acceptance, not of personal responsibility but of a collective and often moral sense of accountability for both nations' past racist legacy. This recognition of accountability carries tremendous power, as evidenced by the enormous hostility and criticism that proposed apologies often evoke. The power of apology derives partly from the profound emotional effects it can wield on its recipient constituency but also from the extent to which an apology remaps symbolic boundaries. The discourse of apology thereby raises difficult questions, such as the following: To what degree is an unwilling or unwitting beneficiary accountable for the sins of perpetrators of the past? What is owed to those who are not themselves victims but who suffer from disadvantages associated with the unintended consequences of historical injustice?

Despite its effectiveness in countering the methodological individualism and race blindness of those opposing reparations, the discourse of apology remains a limited response to the demand for redress. It remains limited because, in deploying abstract liberal humanist or moral principles against systematically asymmetrical relations of racial power and advantage, the discourse of apology unwittingly slides back into collusion with those who evade the power dimensions of race and racism. In the context of the United States, although Hall's proposed apology does acknowledge the historical relationship of white privilege and black disadvantage, it attempts to resolve this unequal power relationship at a moral level (via apology), not a political or material one. In doing so, critics from across the political spectrum agree, the discourse of apology fails to effectively combat racial inequality and injustice. Jesse Jackson complains, "It is like you drive over somebody with a car, leave the body mangled, then you decide to come back later to apologize with no commitment to help them get on their feet. There is something empty in that. It is just more race entertainment." Other critics agree and argue that substantive policy measures are required if racial reconciliation is to be achieved, not symbolism that distracts from real healing. Roger Wilkins said, "I think it's a bad idea. There are real things that need to be done. The problem with the apology is that it makes people think they've done something when they haven't really done anything significant about the problems that face real American human beings that are alive and in need of help today."[9] Even the likes of House Speaker Newt Gingrich dismissed the proposal as mere symbolism, "an avoidance of problem solving" and "a dead end."[10]

In the South African context, too, there is an argument to be made that the South African TRC has similarly attempted to "exorcise the ghosts of apartheid" via symbolic gestures and diffuse apologies that fail to resolve, even name, the systemic crimes and abuses of apartheid that continue to shape the postapartheid socioeconomic and political terrain.[11] Although it is no doubt important and beneficial to deal with the past in a transparent manner, to air the events and crimes that were hidden from public view for so many years, and for those who are deemed accountable to apologize, there is the danger that in attempting to satisfactorily put to rest the memories, identities, and the anger of past antagonisms, current-based forms of systemic subjugation will be obscured. It is true that the South African TRC recommended monetary reparations to complement the efforts on the more symbolic front, although only a fraction of what the commission recommended was ultimately awarded to victims (see the discussion later in this chapter). Nevertheless, to the degree that the TRC has attempted to construct a discourse of national unity through the minimization, mystifications, or denial of the traces of historical victimization and oppression on the present postapartheid settlement, it has revealed not only the limits of saying I'm sorry without justice but, more important, the danger of substituting substantive means of redress that upset structural relations of power and powerlessness with postmodern symbolic theater that mistakes emotional catharsis for real change in the world.

The survey of white narratives on reparations presented here demonstrates that there is tremendous contest and opposition to reparations, even of a symbolic or commemorative type. The acknowledgment of responsibility or accountability for human rights violations implicit in the act of apology is not at all straightforward for the beneficiaries of crimes of the past, and what is acknowledged is often very selective. The selectivity is oriented around protecting white innocence in terms of the sins of generations past, thereby relieving any sense of rightful debt. Demands for recompense or equality-promoting schemes are understood by whites as victimizing them and, as such, contrary to the very liberal notions triumphant in the struggle to dismantle apartheid and segregation. In this way, the universal human rights construction, while principled in the abstract, can act practically to obstruct policies aimed at racial reparation, equality, and justice. White responses to symbolic forms of reparation make it very difficult to imagine much viability for more ambitious monetary or antisystemic types of reparations, a hunch born out by growing opposition to affirmative action in the United States and the fact that a proposal for a one-off wealth tax in South Africa never got off the ground. Indeed, across all types of reparations and whether or not the victims/perpetrators are still living, it seems that the movement for reparations faces an uphill battle. White narratives on reparations demonstrate that the human rights model is more than amenable to universal constructions that seek to protect the abstract individual, thereby relieving beneficiaries of the racist past from a sense of debt and disempowering the more particularist demands for recompense on the part of ethnoracial groups.

LITIGATING ACCOUNTABILITY: AN ALTERNATIVE PROSPECT FOR REPARATIONS

Reparations will not be delivered by proclamation of majority public opinion, certainly not in the context of the demographic realities of the United States. However, not all policies result from swells of popular support. Some, such as affirmative action, which in a certain sense represents a systemic form of reparations, emerged as a result of complex bureaucratic and executive action in the context of consistent public opposition.[12] It is therefore worthwhile imagining alternative avenues for reparations politics. The remainder of this chapter examines the prospects for novel legal strategies in pursuit of monetary damages as a form of racial reparations based on a case study of what has become known as the "apartheid-era lawsuits."

The apartheid-era lawsuits emerged as the TRC's work came to a close and its limits and failures became more evident. Critics have argued that the process delivered more to perpetrators, in the form of amnesty, than to victims of apartheid-era crimes.[13] Perpetrators were offered amnesty for confession, the idea being that the act of fessing up to their crimes would be rewarding and cathartic for victims, thereby facilitating the nation's movement toward racial reconciliation. This assumption has proved problematic and has been deservedly scrutinized. Critics have pointed out that only a tiny fraction of victims were allowed to speak during the TRC hearings. Others point out that the act of granting victims the floor to rehearse the traumas of the past served in some ways, especially given the lack of redress, to revictimize them and their families. Others write of how the overriding mission of reconciliation served to voice victims' testimonies in patterned ways. Still others complain of the limits of the process given that the TRC focused solely on those victimized by gross human rights violations, thereby bracketing off the millions more *disadvantaged* by pass laws, forced removals, labor restrictions, and so on. By the same token, *beneficiaries* of apartheid were off the hook with attention only to those who perpetrated gross human rights violations. In terms of monetary reparations, too, the success of the TRC proved only partial: the commission recommended to the president and Parliament that a financial grant of reparations in the amount of 375 million rand be paid to 22,000 victims identified through the TRC process, although President Mbeki ultimately settled on a one-time payment of 74 million rand to 19,000 victims. A portrait therefore emerges of a process that was more successful at granting amnesty to those perpetrators who came forward than delivering healing or justice to participating victims.

It is in this context that a lawyer named Ed Fagan brought suit on behalf of apartheid-era victims in June 2002. Fagan was one of the lawyers who helped pioneer the pathbreaking lawsuits against corporations, banks, insurance companies, and others that were alleged to have profited from property and labor stolen during the Holocaust. A controversial figure, Fagan also initiated what became known as the slave labor lawsuits, bringing suit to recover damages caused by slavery to all African Americans enslaved in the United States between 1619 and 1865. The suit in South Africa was conceived in similarly broad terms, defining *plaintiffs* as that class of persons alive in South Africa between 1948 and 1993 who were affected by the apartheid regime and *defendants* as banks, corporations, and other bodies that profited from the apartheid regime as well as (most controversially) the current South African government under Mbeki for the continued economic exploitation of black South Africans. Not surprisingly, the tactic provoked stiff opposition on the part of the Mbeki government as well as within legal, political, and business circles because of the difficulties associated with litigating indirect injury defined in such a broad and vague manner. The legal team for the apartheid-era lawsuits eventually split into two rival camps: the one led by Fagan, the other by a lawyer named Michael D. Hausfeld.

The suits have earned enormous attention in legal and human rights circles, in part because they were filed under a formerly obscure 18th Act—the Alien Tort Claims Act (ATCA). The ATCA dates back to 1789, with an original design to protect against piracy. Applied contemporarily, the statute essentially allows foreign victims of serious human rights abuse to sue, in U.S. courts, the perpetrators and those who aid and abet them. After having sat dormant for the better part of two centuries, the ATCA was rediscovered as a potential tool in 1979 by the Center for Constitutional Rights in a case that successfully brought suit in the U.S. courts against the torturer of Joel Filartiga in Paraguay. With this important precedent established and with the general increase in international concern with human rights issues, cases alleging violations of human rights law filed under the ATCA have ballooned to more than 100. Many of these suits are oriented to the prosecution of individuals for torture and other abuses and have included defendants such as Zimbabwe's President Robert Mugabe; Bosnian Serb leader Radovan Karadzic; Chilean army officer Amando Fernandez Larios; the former president of the Philippines, Ferdinand Marcos; the former dictator of Haiti, Prosper Avril; and many others.

A recent development that has brought heightened attention to the ATCA is its use against multinational corporations for violation of international law outside the United States. Suits have been filed against corporate defenders in sectors such as banking (e.g., Citigroup and Barclays Bank), oil and gas (e.g., Shell, ExxonMobil, and Unocal), transportation (GM, Ford, and Chrysler), and technology (IBM and Unisys) in countries such as Colombia, Ecuador, Egypt, Guatemala, India, Indonesia, Myanmar (Burma), Nigeria, Peru, Saudi Arabia, and Sudan. The cases have been pursued with varying degrees of success, with complex precedents, never more so than in *Sosa v. Alvarez-Machain* (2004). As the Supreme Court's most recent ATCA ruling, critics and proponents alike have examined its implications for future suits, with both sides proclaiming vindication. For proponents, *Sosa* demonstrated that the court is prepared to send a message to multinational corporations and the Bush administration that international human rights law cannot be ignored. For critics, *Sosa* signals that the court intends to exercise great caution to limit the scope of liability and availability of relief.

It is in this post-*Sosa* context that the pending appeal of the apartheid-era lawsuits assumes great significance, oral arguments for which were heard in the Second Circuit Court of Appeals in New York City on January 24, 2006. It is likely that the ruling will settle some of the ambiguities left open by the court. In fact, in the *Sosa* ruling, the justices went out of their way to reference the apartheid reparations case in what has become widely referenced as "footnote 21." The footnote asserts the principle that the claimant needs to have exhausted remedies available in domestic legal systems before pursuing damages internationally and that serious weight needs to be given to the views of other political branches, especially the executive, regarding the potential impact on foreign policy. While the central aim of the suits remained unchanged—to hold numerous corporate defendants accountable for their complicity in apartheid-era crimes—the appeal sought the opportunity to revise the complaints based on the limitations suggested by the *Sosa* decision. These revisions involved demonstrating a tighter connection between plaintiff and defendant and harm, identifying discrete acts against which the claim for damages could be pursued, and setting a clearer standard of what exactly constitutes aiding and abetting.

Simply demonstrating that a corporate defendant conducted business with the apartheid regime is not going to fly in the face of the new standards (nor would they have likely before). Corporate defendants assert that they were involved in legitimate activity as part of a strategy of constructive engagement. In order to meet the more rigorous aiding and abetting standard, the appeal aims to demonstrate that corporate defendants were willing collaborators with the apartheid state, engaged in joint action that led to systemic human rights abuses. Evidence for such a symbiotic relationship does exist and in many cases has already been documented by the TRC, including demonstration that corporate defendants benefited from apartheid crimes such as forced removals, forced labor, and labor repression. So the sorts of actions the lawyers for the plaintiffs aim to hold liable for civil damages include, for example, the granting of financial assistance by defendant banking institutions or the provision of technical support for security and law enforcement provided by defendant companies such as IBM. The legal challenge is to prove that the sort of knowing practical assistance lent by corporate defendants renders them responsible for apartheid crimes as the actual perpetrators.

The appeal is also based on rebuttals to foreign policy concerns expressed in footnote 21. In *Sosa*, the court justices cautioned that an ATCA ruling could carry deleterious consequences for U.S. foreign policy and urged that due attention be granted to the views of the executive branch of government. The views of the Bush administration (especially the State Department and Justice Department) could not be clearer: the ATCA should be gutted. Not only does the ATCA potentially deter the international business community from conducting business with failing or rogue regimes, but it also ties the hands of the State Department in its ability to use foreign policy for positive change, including improvement in the arena of human rights. Notwithstanding the irony that the Bush administration holds those aiding and abetting terrorists to be as guilty as the terrorists themselves in the context of the War on Terror, it has sought to protect corporate defendants from any accountability in the context of ATCA-related claims. With regard to the apartheid-era lawsuits, the administration has been assisted by statements by South African President Mbeki opposing the suits. The State Department submitted an amicus brief asserting that the United States should not interfere with South Africa's chosen route of confession and reconciliation as opposed to racial reparations or some other form of victors' justice.

Lawyers for plaintiffs counter that the South African position is not so self-evident. Besides the fact that many of the prior statements opposing the suits were in reference to the broadly drawn pre-*Sosa* allegations, fresh bases of support for the plaintiffs on the part of South African stakeholders are evident. Perhaps the most notable is an amicus brief submitted by the TRC. Commissioners minced no words: the chosen route of the TRC should not be used to relieve aiding and abetting liability for corporate defendants. Commissioners complain that corporate defendants not only never petitioned for amnesty (thus not relieving them now for civil liability) but also refused to participate in TRC hearings, even those specifically investigating the role of business in supporting apartheid-era abuses. The idea that multinational corporations could invoke the TRC process as a shield from civil damages is clearly upsetting to commissioners who conclude with a statement that the apartheid-era lawsuits not only are consistent with but also flow from the TRC's findings regarding the role of business during apartheid.

CONCLUSION

In sampling the mix of prospects and obstacles facing reparations politics in the United States and South Africa, this chapter has pinpointed intriguing parallels between the legal logic of corporate defendants on the one hand and white public opinion on the other. In both arenas, the thorny questions surrounding what exactly constitutes responsibility, accountability, or aiding and abetting the racist crimes of the past are deeply felt and contested. Evident is worry that answering these questions too broadly may open a Pandora's box with destructive potential. Principles with which to determine liability and proportionality are sought in order to answer the refrain, "When do we stop paying for the past?" In this search for principles, we have seen that the human rights frame is drawn on by whites in both nations in order to refuse payment. A discourse of universal human rights can therefore operate against the movement for reparations and disempower alternative discourses oriented around redress or inequality. Even more, the human rights frame can sustain a regressive logic that it is in fact whites who are the ones now wronged in the present racial dispensation. Perhaps the best hope for reparations politics today is that individual victims of human rights abuses will win civil damages through the U.S. courts, although as we have seen in the case of the pending apartheid-era lawsuits, even here a host of actors (political, business, and state) seek to limit access to such redress.

NOTES

1. For elaboration of this context, see Amy E. Ansell, *New Right, New Racism: Race and Reaction in the United States and Britain* (New York: New York University Press, 1997).

2. Examples of this burgeoning interest in reparations include John Torpey, *Making Whole What Has Been Smashed: On Reparations Politics* (Cambridge, Mass.: Harvard University Press, 2006); Elazar Barkan, *The Guilt of Nations: Restitution and Negotiating Historical Injustices* (New York: Norton, 2000); Human Rights Watch, "An Approach to Reparations," www.hrw.org, July 19, 2001 (accessed April 18, 2007); Janna Thompson, *Taking Responsibility for the Past: Reparation and Historical Justice* (Malden, Mass.: Polity Press, 2002); Roy Brooks, ed., *When Sorry Isn't Enough* (New York: New York University Press, 1999); Martha Minow, *Between Vengeance and Forgiveness* (Boston: Beacon Press, 1998); John Torpey, ed., *Politics and the Past: On Repairing Historical Injustices* (Lanham, Md.: Rowman & Littlefield, 2003); and Nicholas Tavuchis, *Mea Culpa: A Sociology of Apology and Reconciliation* (Stanford, Calif.: Stanford University Press, 1991).

3. This point is elaborated by John Torpey, *Making Whole What Has Been Smashed: On Reparations Politics* (Cambridge, Mass.: Harvard University Press, 2006). Torpey here builds especially on the work of Todd Gitlin, *The Twilight of Common Dreams: Why America Is Wracked by Culture Wars* (New York: Henry Holt & Co., 1996).

4. For more on white nationalist sentiment, see Carol Swain, *The New White Nationalism in America* (Cambridge: Cambridge University Press, 2002).

5. For this statistic and more on surveys of public opinion on race relations in the United States, see Charles Gallagher, "Color-Blind Privilege: The Social and Political Functions of Erasing the Color Line in Post-Race America," in *Rethinking the Color Line: Readings in Race and Ethnicity* (2nd ed.), edited by Charles Gallagher (Boston: McGraw-Hill), 575–87.

6. See Joe R. Feagin and Eileen O'Brien, "The Growing Movement for Reparations," in Brooks, *When Sorry Isn't Enough*, 343.

7. For more discussion of the comparative similarities and contrasts between the United States and South Africa, see Amy E. Ansell, "Casting a Blind Eye: The Ironic Consequences of Color-Blindness in South Africa and the United States," *Critical Sociology* 32, no. 2–3 (2006): 333–56.

8. Melissa Steyn, *Whiteness Just Isn't What It Used to Be: White Identity in a Changing South Africa* (Albany: State University of New York Press, 2001), 112.

9. Roger Wilkins, "Slavery: Should the Nation Apologize?" *USA Today*, June 18, 1997.

10. Newt Gingrich, "Speaker Scoffs at Proposal for Apology on Slavery," Associated Press, June 14, 1997.

11. James M. Statman, "Exorcising the Ghosts of Apartheid: Memory, Identity and Trauma in the 'New' South Africa" (paper presented at the International Society of Political Psychology, Washington, D.C., 1995); Adam Habib, "South Africa—the Rainbow Nation and Prospects for Consolidating Democracy," *African Journal of Political Science* 2 (1997): 13–37.

12. See John Skrentny, *The Ironies of Affirmative Action: Politics, Culture and Justice in America* (Chicago: University of Chicago Press, 1996).

13. The criticisms surveyed here were elaborated at an academic conference, "The TRC: Commissioning the Past," held at the University of Witwatersrand in June 1999. Further discussion of these and other criticisms can be found in James M. Statman, "Performing the Truth: The Social-Psychological Context of TRC Narratives," *South African Journal of Psychology* 30, no. 1 (2000): 23–32.

Part 3

INTRODUCTION TO IMMIGRATION ISSUES

Angela J. Hattery

One of the key issues facing the contemporary United States is the issue of immigration. As critical as the issue is, it is hardly new. The first immigrants arriving to what is now the United States were the men and women who crossed the frozen terrain taking advantage of the Bering Strait ice bridge that connected the frozen tundra of what is now Russia to what is now Alaska. Nearly 400 years ago, the first immigrants from Britain arrived in Jamestown, Virginia, in order to colonize the "New World." And in less than a decade, these colonizers began bringing captured Africans to work as chattel slaves in order to grow the infant agricultural economy of the colonies. In short, the flow of people in and out of what are now the borders of the United States has existed for at least 10,000 years and has been steady and constant for at least 400 years.

As scholars, historians, political scientists, sociologists and journalists have noted, immigration has been a hotly contested issue across most of the history of the United States, and this debate has been raging out of control since the beginning of the twentieth century (Kerber 1997). Beginning in the late 1880s, as immigration increased from China, the United States began to develop and enforce immigration policies. The Chinese Exclusion Act of 1882 was not only one of the first immigration policies developed and enforced but was the first that targeted a specific racial or ethnic group. Thus, it is apparent that immigration policy quickly became racialized; it was a mechanism by which the U.S. government could exercise some control over the changing racial/ethnic composition of the population. Simultaneously, attempts to control the racial/ethnic composition of those who were already living in the United States took the form of eugenics. According to scholars on the issue (Davis 1983; Schoen 2001), as many as 60,000 racial/ethnic minorities and poor whites were sterilized either forcibly or without their consent (see Hattery and Smith 2007). And across the remainder of the twentieth century, a number of immigration policies that established quotas on immigration from the "third world" were enacted and enforced. This is especially true for countries like Haiti.

When we examine the symbiotic relationship between immigration policies and eugenics practices, we can see more clearly the ways in which these policies and practices both were racialized and violated individual and group-level human rights.

At the time of the writing of this book, the immigration debate is once again at the center of U.S. politics. Although the debate is presented as if it centers on the legality of immigration, guest worker programs, and "paths to citizenship," as President George W. Bush is fond of proclaiming, a careful analysis reveals that the debate continues to be racialized and designed to control the racial/ethnic composition of the U.S. population.

Most notable in the recent debates is the focus on increasing the number of immigrants from India and China who possess technology skills and advanced degrees (e.g., Ph.D.s) that can enter the United States and apply for citizenship while severely restricting the number of immigrants from the global south (namely, Mexico) who come here to clean our houses, mow our lawns, and build our infrastructure (Friedman 2006; Mills 2007). These Asian immigrants with technology skills and advanced degrees will likely gain access to the racial/ethnic hierarchy as "honorary whites" (Bonilla-Silva 2001, 2003), whereas those whose immigration we seek to limit will remain as "black" or "brown" in this system.

In terms of human rights, one of the key issues of these new immigration bills that will likely be signed into law (Mills 2007) is that they will allow new immigrants with the appropriate skills to enter the country legally while turning back thousands of individuals who are already living and working here and contributing positively to the economy. For example, researchers at the University of North Carolina at Chapel Hill note that Hispanic immigrants in North Carolina alone pay $455 million in state and local taxes, they have access to $8.3 billion in buying power, and their total consumer impact is estimated at $9.2 billion (Kasarda and Johnson 2006). This raises the issue of the value of individual human life as well as the value of contributions to the economy. When immigration policies are developed such that individual lives and individual contributions are valued differently, then these policies pose a threat to maintaining human rights at both the individual and the societal level.

This part of the book is the largest, and all the chapters address different issues related to immigration. The chapter by Golash-Boza and Parker addresses many of the questions raised in this introduction: the ways in which guest worker programs violate the human rights of individual men and women who contribute significantly to the U.S. economy. Goldsmith and Romero examine specifically the ways in which "Mexicanness" can be used, legally, as a status for police profiling. Rubio and Lopez examine the ways in which immigrant status, language acquisition, and education impacts the ability of Hispanic immigrants to gain access to the American dream via home ownership. The chapter by Morales and Bejarano examines the ways in which factories set up on the Mexican side of the U.S.–Mexican border (maquiladoras) create a cover for gendered violence. Specifically, they examine the ways in which the existence of these maquiladoras renders invisible domestic violence murders. Finally, the chapter by Hovsepian takes the reader beyond the United States and her contiguous neighbors to the conflict over the borders and territory on the West Bank in Israel. Specifically, she examines the ways in which border rules and crossing are navigated by Palestinian garment workers who travel in and out of segregated communities for work and to sell their wares. Taken together, these chapters address many of the most pressing issues facing U.S. immigration policy in the twenty-first century.

REFERENCES

Bonilla-Silva, E. 2001. *White Supremacy and Racism in the Post-Civil Rights Era.* Boulder: Lynne Rienner.

——2003. *Racism without Racists: Color-Blind Racism and the Persistence of Racial Inequality in the United States.* Lanham, Md.: Rowman & Littlefield.

Davis, A. Y. 1983. *Women, Race, and Class.* New York: Vintage Books.

Friedman, Thomas. 2006. *The World Is Flat: A Brief History of the 21st Century.* New York: Farrar, Straus & Giroux.

Hattery, Angela J., and Earl Smith. 2007. *African American Families.* Thousand Oaks, Calif.: Sage.

Kasarda, John D., and James H. Johnson Jr. 2006. *The Economic Impact of the Hispanic Population on North Carolina.* Chapel Hill, N.C.: Kenan Institute of Private Enterprise.

Kerber, L. K. 1997. "The Meanings of Citizenship." *Journal of American History* 84: 833–54.

Mills, Doug. 2007. "Senate Votes to Keep Temporary Worker Program." *New York Times,* May 23.

Schoen, J. 2001. "Between Choice and Coercion: Women and the Politics of Sterilization in North Carolina, 1929–1975." *Journal of Women's History* 13: 132–56.

7

Immigrant Rights as Human Rights[1]

Tanya Golash-Boza and Douglas A. Parker

Current global policies and immigration regulations of the United States result in violations of the human rights of migrants. These policies and regulations are designed to maximize profits for corporations and minimize the price of consumer goods for customers in the global North with little if any consideration of the human costs inside and outside U.S. borders. Multinational corporations increasingly are globalizing their operations, moving their factories from the United States to Mexico, to China, and to other countries, constantly in search of the cheapest source of labor. This corporate border hopping creates displaced worker populations that are often forced to emigrate to survive. Yet, while current international laws often allow for the free movement of capital, they do not allow for the free movement of labor. This leads to high levels of undocumented migrants and temporary workers in the global North who are frequently separated from their families that have been left behind.

This chapter explains how temporary worker programs prevent immigrants from becoming full and equal members of the communities in which they work and live and how the criminalization of undocumented immigrants transforms these migrants into dehumanized individuals. From a human rights perspective, all human beings should have rights to jobs, to safe working conditions, to food security, to decent health care, to education, to a family, and to a cultural identity. Temporary worker programs that permit workers to come to a country only to work for low wages with no benefits and that do not permit them to bring their families, to send their children to school, and to form communities are a violation of these workers' human rights.

Globalization is a set of social processes that is bringing the world closer together. One of the central processes of globalization involves the international trade in and movement of human labor. This includes both transnational corporations setting up production facilities as well as sending out recruiters around the world in pursuit of cheaper labor and immigrants leaving their countries of origin in pursuit of employment in other countries and thus better lives. These processes are intimately linked and are a fundamental part of what we might call the human face of globalization in the contemporary era. Recognizing the interconnectedness between corporate migration and recruitment on the one hand and human migration on the other is the key for thinking about the rights of migrants.

From a human rights perspective, all men and women, both those who live in their countries of origin and those who reside in other countries, share a common human dignity and deserve certain human rights. As Blau and Moncada (2005) point out, these rights apply to all persons, not just to citizens of certain nation-states. Human rights also involve the recognition of the rights of others and generally require states or other organizations to do something to ensure that rights are realized. Article 23 of the UN Universal Declaration of Human Rights specifies that "everyone has the right to work, to free choice of employment, to just and favorable conditions of work and to protection against unemployment," and Article 25 stipulates that "everyone has the right to a standard of living adequate for the health and well-being of himself and of his family, including food, clothing, housing and medical care and necessary social services" (Blau and Moncada 2005, 39). These statements seem hard to disagree with, yet they raise the question of who is responsible for providing these fundamental rights. More specifically, in a globalizing world, as the actions of states and private corporations often adversely affect the globe's population, whose responsibility is it to ensure that human rights are ensured?

THE GREAT WALL AROUND THE UNITED STATES

Political leaders in the United States have been reluctant to recognize human rights for all men, women, and children. For example, in Rome in 2002, the United Nations called on countries to recognize the human right to food security. Although delegates from 182 countries affirmed the right to food, the United States objected. American delegates stated that they had no problem with the principle of food security but also indicated that they did not want to endorse food security in a way that was legally binding for governments.[2]

Inasmuch as the rights discourse in the United States has revolved primarily around negative rights that limit the powers of the state, such as the freedom from search and seizure or the freedom of the press, it should come as no surprise that the current debates over immigration do not usually involve much discussion about the rights of migrants. Instead, these debates focus primarily on border security and the threats posed by illegal immigrants as well as terrorists. It could be useful, then, to consider how we plan to protect the borders from illegal immigrants and terrorists, as these two groups are frequently referred to by some U.S. political leaders and the media in general.

During 2005 and 2006 and up to mid-2007, a number of bills dealing with immigration were introduced in the Congress, some of which were endorsed by President George W. Bush. Although their strategies differed, all the proposed bills attempted to regulate the flow of immigrants into the United States. The only bill dealing with immigration that was passed in 2006, the Secure Fence Act, had as its main goal a reduction in the number of undocumented immigrants entering the United States. This act authorized but did not appropriate funds for a 700-mile barrier (sometimes involving double or triple fences) along the U.S. border with Mexico. Congress did provide the Department of Homeland Security with $1.5 billion for upgrading technology at the border, but no funds were allocated specifically for the 700 miles of fence that the nonpartisan Congressional Research Service (CRS) estimated would cost as much as $49 billion over the expected twenty-five-year life span of the fence (the CRS estimate did not include the costs of acquiring private land along the border or the labor if the construction were to be done by private contractors). The CRS questioned the effectiveness of the fence in preventing illegal entry into the United States, particularly if the fence was not extended to cover the entire 1,952-mile border.[3] Others have asked whether some of the construction might not be feasible, as the fence would have to climb rugged rocks and plunge into deep ravines. The partial fence's primary effect may be to force people from the global South to use more dangerous ways of crossing the border, such as through the treacherous desert in southern Arizona.[4]

Reducing undocumented immigration might be possible only through an aggressive militarization of all the borders or through a comprehensive immigration reform that took into account the global processes that produce migration flows. The military approach would be difficult given that we have two extensive borders to the north and south as well as a large number of ports and sandy beaches where boats could dock or land. Currently, the northern border is largely unprotected, with the exception of a few Border Patrol stations at certain key junctures, and there are not enough Border Patrol agents or National Guards to patrol either the northern or the southern border. Decreasing undocumented immigration by use of the regular military would involve deploying tens of thousands of troops along the borders, and this possibility appears unlikely given the current shortage of troops. This shortage is exacerbated by the increasing practice since World War II of positioning and maintaining units of the U.S. Army and Marine Corps in Europe, Asia, and other locations abroad for possible conflicts with foreign countries and, more recently, terrorist groups in some of those countries.[5]

In the Middle East and elsewhere, the United States has resorted to using private contractors for various military services. According to Source Watch, private military contractors are the second-largest force in Iraq with more than 20,000 active personnel in the country.[6] A recent Democracy Now! report affirms that 48,000 people work for private security firms in Iraq.[7] But the use of private military contractors does not seem to be a viable strategy for securing substantial parts of the borders unless an enormous amount of money is poured into the effort, and this would likely require recruiting workers from abroad, as is currently being done to rebuild New Orleans.[8] Placing either regular or private military forces along the southern border may be appropriate and feasible only in areas where the drug cartels and their paramilitary forces are creating problems, such as around Nuevo Laredo, Mexico, which resembles "a Sunni town in Anbar Province," according to one conservative analyst.[9]

Every time the U.S. government has implemented a plan to deter immigration through enforcement, the efforts have been costly and ineffective. In 1993, the Clinton administration made a decision to get serious about border enforcement. This meant building more fences and increasing the number of Border Patrol agents along the border. The tripling of the amount of resources spent on border enforcement led to a temporary decline in the rate of success of would-be border crossers. However, it did not take too long for migrants and people smugglers to figure out new ways to cross the border. These new ways tended to be more dangerous and more clandestine than previous ways. Organized groups dug tunnels under fences to smuggle people and drugs. Between 2001 and 2004, fourteen such transborder tunnels were found along the California–Mexico border (Cornelius 2005). Between 1995 and 2005, there were reports of 3,218 migrants who died trying to cross the border. The actual number is probably much higher because this number includes only those people whose bodies were found by the Border Patrol or the Mexican police. The peak year for deaths was 2000, with 491, up from fifty-nine in 1996 (Cornelius 2005).

Migrants seeking employment or reunification with their families increasingly risk their lives in attempting to cross the border. Of those who died trying to cross the border in 2002 and 2003, approximately 75 percent died of heat exposure (Sapkota et al. 2006). Prior to 1994, heat-related deaths were almost never reported along the border (Cornelius 2001). And some of the migrants from Central or South American countries have been robbed, raped, injured, or even killed during their journey through Mexico.[10] Their absences from their families have had adverse economic and psychological effects on their relatives and children. In Ecuador, for example, suicides by children left behind have been increasing.[11]

The difficulties in crossing borders have also meant that undocumented migrants are more likely to stay longer in the United States. In the case of Mexican migrants, in 1992, about 20 percent returned home from the United States after six months; by 1997, this figure had gone down to 15 percent, and by 2000, only 7 percent of Mexican migrants went home after six months (Cornelius 2005). Circular migration between the United States and Mexico has been common since the border lines were drawn up in the nineteenth century (Massey, Durand, and Malone 2002). Efforts to increase security along the border have not stopped this migration; they simply have made it more dangerous for people to cross the border and more likely for people to prolong their stays once they are inside the United States. Attempts to further secure the border will result only in a more dangerous and deadly crossing for migrants. Efforts such as the Secure Fence Act can thus be characterized as inhumane.

MIGRANTS AND THE AMERICAN DREAM

Do we really want a physical or military wall between ourselves and the rest of the world? Pat Buchanan does. Buchanan (2006) argues that the United States is being invaded by immigrants, legal and illegal, primarily from Mexico, Central America, and the Caribbean. He claims that these migrants come with considerably less education than European, Iranian, and Asian immigrants and bring with them an array of diseases, such as malaria, polio, and the type of tuberculosis that is resistant to multiple drugs. Buchanan states that Mexicans substantially outnumber all other immigrant groups so that "the core of the crisis is Mexico" (45) and insists that we must halt the Third World invasion by building twin fences "along the entire 2,000-mile border with Mexico, defining, sealing and securing it forever" (254).

Buchanan (2006) claims that inasmuch as immigrants work for lower wages than Americans, they drive down the wages of American workers, particularly unskilled or low-skilled black, Hispanic, and white Americans, and recommends that employers who break the law by hiring illegal aliens be severely punished. Some demographers, though, have found that the presence of undocumented workers does not affect the wages of native workers (Bean, Lowell, and Taylor 1988).

Lou Dobbs, another critic, emphasizes the importance of penalizing those who do not provide adequate wages to immigrant as well as American workers. Dobbs, who also calls for heavy penalties for employers of illegal aliens, argues that "the exploitation of illegal workers must end" and that any employer "who does not pay workers at least a minimum wage should be subjected to additional fines." He adds, "And this would be a good time to raise the minimum wage to a living wage and to establish heavy penalties for those who violate that standard" (Dobbs 2006, 207).

Another analyst contends that the most important issue is whether the world economy should continue to be regulated by corporations that are answerable only to the rich and powerful or whether it should be managed by national governments built to assess risk and to be answerable to all citizens.[12] But Buchanan (2006) maintains that in the United States, the corporations and their lobbyists have captured the American government and that the proposals of Republicans like President Bush, Arizona Senator John McCain, and many liberal Democrats to grant amnesty to 12 million illegal workers and to give pardons to businesses that hired the illegal workers constitute "economic treason" against American workers. According to Buchanan, immigration, for Bush, is all about "America as a giant job mart" (74) for corporations that want to roam the world and hire foreign workers at the lowest possible wages in order to de-Americanize the better-paid U.S. labor force. A minimum wage, preferably a living one, which is enforced, as Dobbs has urged, is one response that would be helpful.

Dobbs (2006) agrees that the government is directed by the corporations and lobbyists but believes that it is possible to "take back America" by having us register as independents, by financing elections completely from public funds, by using initiatives and referendums, by extending the period of time between completion of government service and the commencement of service as lobbyists, by making our trade agreements with other nations reciprocal and fair, by placing tariff duties and fees on any product or service that corporations produce overseas for U.S. consumption, and in general by reinvigorating participatory democracy. Others suggest that it might be more effective to develop international agreements in organizations such as the United Nations and to work toward collective goals with nongovernmental organizations or associations such as the World Social Forum (Blau and Moncada 2005).

Buchanan (2006), who wants to seal the borders, acknowledges that by 2050, the portion of the U.S. population of European descent will be "aging, shrinking, and dying" (37). But he does not call for American women to have more babies, as has been asked of Russian women by President Vladimir Putin, who has been worried about the rapidly declining Russian population and has pledged payments to mothers who elect to have a second child.[13] Buchanan points out that Russia and almost all other European nations are not reproducing their populations and are also "aging, shrinking, and dying," and he argues that to maintain economic growth and tax revenues to fund health care and pensions for increasing numbers of the retired and elderly, these European countries will need millions of new workers, which they can find only in the Third World. But Buchanan does not use the same argument when discussing the graying American population of European descent.

The United States has a higher fertility rate than other industrialized countries only because the hundreds of thousands who migrate have comparatively large families. White Americans have not had enough children to replace themselves since 1971, with their greater education being the best predictor of decreased childbearing (Longman 2004). The U.S. population is aging rapidly, and very soon the federal government will have serious problems funding its three senior benefit programs. By 2030, Social Security, Medicare, and Medicaid, in addition to the interest on the national debt, may consume 24 percent of the gross domestic product (GDP), and by 2050 these programs and the interest could consume 47 percent of the GDP (Longman 2004). The United States will also need millions of new workers to pay taxes that can be used for its programs for the retired and the elderly.

Continued immigration from Mexico and other countries in the global South will help, although it is not a complete solution to the aging U.S. population. Mexico is the largest source of immigration to the United States; in 2002, of 32.5 million foreign born, 9.8 million, or 30 percent, were from Mexico, and 5.3 million of these Mexicans were undocumented immigrants.[14] In 2004, the foreign-born population in the United States was 35.7 million persons, with 32 percent naturalized citizens, 29 percent legal permanent residents, and 29 percent undocumented migrants (7 percent were refugees and 3 percent were temporary legal residents). The undocumented migrants were predominantly younger than the native born, with 34 percent of the undocumented migrants between the ages of eighteen and twenty-nine compared to 16 percent of the native population.[15]

Birthrates, which have already fallen below replacement levels in Europe as well as in Asia, are now falling in Latin America, raising the definite possibility that the last major source of workers from abroad will yield a declining group of workers. In addition, the United States will face increasing competition from Europe for new immigrants from Latin America (Longman 2004). Given that population growth, together with productivity, is the engine of economic growth and thus of potential tax revenues for the three major senior benefit programs as well as educational and scientific programs, is it reasonable to continue to make it so difficult for Mexicans and others to migrate to the United States? For at least graying Americans if not also for others in the United States, migrants may prolong the American dream.

A NATION OF IMMIGRANTS

We often hear that we are a nation of immigrants, but it will be useful to briefly consider the extent to which this is true, especially with regard to Mexican immigration into the United States. The first Mexicans who came to be part of the United States never crossed any border. Instead, the border crossed them. Native Americans had been living in the southwestern region of the United States for thousands of years prior to the arrival of any Europeans in the Americas. Some of these Native Americans (or American Indians) were referred to as Mexicans and others as Americans, depending on which side of the border they were on when the lines were drawn. Spaniards arrived in present-day New Mexico in 1598 and founded the city of Santa Fe in 1610, ten years before the Pilgrims landed at Plymouth Rock. Mexico acquired New Mexico and other northern territories, such as California and Texas, when it gained its independence from Spain in 1821. After American immigrants legally and illegally entered the Mexican territory of Texas and eventually defeated a Mexican army that attempted to expel them, the United States and Mexico fought each other in a war, and once again Mexico experienced defeat. In 1848, the Treaty of Guadalupe Hidalgo was negotiated, resulting in Mexico's loss of almost half its territory. Mexico gave the United States control over California, Nevada, Utah, Texas, and parts of Arizona, New Mexico, Colorado, and Wyoming in exchange for $15 million.[16] In 1854, with the Gadsden Purchase, the United States bought what are now southern Arizona and southwestern New Mexico. Along with these lands, 50,000 Mexicans, both descendants of Native Americans and descendants of Spaniards, became residents of the United States (Massey et al. 2002).

After that substantial mid-century increase in the Mexican-origin population, in-migration and out-migration remained relatively stable. However, in the early twentieth century, a revolution in Mexico brought a large increase in immigration from Mexico, and the Mexican immigrant population tripled between 1910 and 1930, from 200,000 to 600,000. With the onset of the Great Depression and the very high rates of unemployment in the United States, many of these Mexican immigrants as well as U.S. citizens of Mexican descent were deported to Mexico. World War II produced labor shortages in the United States, and Mexicans were permitted to come in to meet that labor need. A seasonal worker program, the "Bracero Program," was established that brought in temporary Mexican workers to work in agriculture from 1942 to 1964, although in 1954 the Eisenhower administration carried out another deportation campaign called "Operation Wetback," which sent more than a million Mexicans back to Mexico. The third great surge in Mexican immigration came after the passage in 1965 of the U.S. Immigration and Nationality Act, which removed the preferential national origin quotas from Europeans. Immigration from Mexico as well as from other non-European countries of the global South increased dramatically as a consequence of that legislation. Immigration was further accelerated by the passage of the North American Free Trade Agreement (NAFTA) in 1994.[17]

Until the 1970s, over 80 percent of Mexican immigrants were temporary workers who came to the United States to work in the agricultural sector for a few months and returned to Mexico with their savings. By 1997, only 40 percent of Mexican migration was for temporary work in the agricultural sector.[18] Massey et al. (2002) argue that the changes in U.S. immigration law, in combination with the economic integration between the United States and Mexico, is responsible for the dramatic changes in the character of Mexico–U.S. migration since the 1970s. Prior to the passage of NAFTA, Mexican immigrants came almost exclusively from Mexican states in what are known as the "traditional region" of migration and the northern states that are close to the border. The states in the traditional region include Aguascalientes, Colima, Durango, Guanajuato, Michoacán, Naryarit, San Luis Potosí, and Zacatecas. The northern border states include Baja California, Baja California Sur, Coahuila, Chihuahua, Nuevo León, Sinaloa, Sonora, and Tamaulipas. In 1993, 80 percent of Mexican migrants to the United States came from these states; by 1997, 25 percent came from other states, and by 2002, 31 percent came from other states of Mexico.[19] In three of these states, Veracruz-Llave, Hidalgo, and Tlaxcala, the number of emigrants tripled between 1990 and 2003.[20]

Just as emigration has spread across Mexico, immigration has spread across the United States. Whereas Mexican immigrants were previously concentrated in a few states, today Mexican immigrants can be found in every state of the United States. In 1970, 85 percent of Mexican immigrants lived in the traditional receiving region, which includes Arizona, California, New Mexico, and Texas. By 2000, only 69 percent of Mexican immigrants lived in those states, and Mexicans were the most predominant immigrant group in over half the states in the United States.[21]

The presence of people of Mexican origin in the United States is largely a result of labor needs in the United States and political and economic circumstances in Mexico, some of which the U.S. government played a role in creating. NAFTA is only the most recent example of this. Although NAFTA purportedly was designed to reduce immigration, it has caused large increases in the number of Mexican immigrants in the United State for a variety of reasons. First, NAFTA has had a devastating effect on the profitability of agriculture in Mexico. The entry of heavily subsidized U.S. corn and other products into the Mexican market has made it unprofitable to grow corn in Mexico, and around 2 million Mexicans have been forced out of agriculture. These former peasants often move to cities to work and, from there, often migrate to the United States. Second, NAFTA created favorable conditions for large transnational retail corporations, such as Wal-Mart, that pushed smaller businesses out of business. These former small-business owners are also often potential migrants. Finally, NAFTA has resulted in the reduction of wages along the Mexican border. When workers are earning lower than the subsistence level, they are also more likely to send a family member abroad to work or to migrate themselves in order to survive.[22]

WHY DO WE HAVE IMMIGRATION INTO THE UNITED STATES?

The current flow of immigration into the United States is strongly affected by the actions of the U.S. government and U.S.-based corporations. Migration has become an unstoppable global response, as Jenni Russell points out: "Just as capital restlessly hunts the globe, opening a plant here and closing a factory there as it searches for the highest returns, so people follow in its wake, looking for jobs they no longer have at home."[23] Blau and Moncada (2005) note that "multinationals such as Wal-Mart, Sears, and Tarrant Apparel Group first set up operations in Mexico, where workers are paid $1.00 per hour, then moved to China, where workers make $.50 an hour, and then to Bangladesh, where workers make $.30 an hour, and then to Mozambique, where they make even less" (102). Each time a transnational corporation moves its factories from one country to another, a displaced worker population is created, and this population is more likely to become transnational itself.

Another prominent reason for increased emigration from the global South has to do with structural adjustment programs imposed by the International Monetary Fund (IMF) and the World Trade Organization (WTO). While these are transnational organizations, the U.S. government plays a significant role in the decisions made by the IMF and the WTO. Structural adjustment programs fuel migration from rural areas to urban areas and pull workers into the global economy. One example of this is the fact that structural adjustment often means cutting back basic social services such as education or health care. This has led to increased migration of young people from rural areas. Young women often leave their villages to work as domestics or in factories in the capital city in order to send money home to pay for school supplies and medicine for their younger siblings—basic services that were once supplied by the state. Once these women find themselves in the capital city, they are more likely to migrate to countries such as the United States, often lured by potential employers and stories of riches there. Some of these women who are promised well-paying jobs in the

United States are forced to work as prostitutes, others are treated as slaves and forced to work long hours as domestic servants, and most have to struggle to survive and maintain their dignity.[24]

Over half of the immigrants who legally entered the United States in 2003 came from just ten countries: Mexico, India, the Philippines, China, El Salvador, the Dominican Republic, Vietnam, Colombia, Guatemala, and Russia.[25] These are all countries with which the United States has had important relationships through either direct foreign investment or military intervention. The top four countries sending unauthorized immigrants were Mexico, El Salvador, Colombia, and the Dominican Republic, accounting for 65 percent of all undocumented immigrants.[26] These flows are also due to U.S. military intervention, direct foreign investment by U.S. corporations, and the presence of people from those countries already residing in the United States (Sassen 1989).

In order to understand better how U.S. involvement produces immigration into the United States, let's examine the case of another migrant-sending country: El Salvador. American-based multinational companies began to invest heavily in manufacturing in El Salvador in the 1960s and 1970s. These companies set up factories primarily in large urban centers, such as San Salvador, La Libertad, and Sonsonate. This industrialization attracted peasants to the large cities, as it became increasingly difficult to make a living off farming, especially in light of the fluctuations in coffee prices and the turbulence generated by increases in foreign investment. These changes to the Salvadoran economy led to increased emigration, both legal and illegal, to the United States during the 1970s (Hamilton and Chinchilla 1991).

In the 1980s, immigration to the United States from El Salvador and other Central American countries increased rapidly as a result of the political violence in Central America. In Nicaragua, the U.S. Central Intelligence Agency financed and organized a counterrevolution against the Sandinista government. In El Salvador, the U.S. government supplied military equipment to the government in the 1980s that was used to kill thousands of civilians (Hamilton and Chinchilla 1991). As part of the Cold War strategy, the U.S. government supplied the Salvadoran government with more than $6 billion in military and economic aid between 1980 and 1992 (Quan 2003). The civil war in El Salvador caused massive population displacements, and many of those displaced came to the United States. Interference by the U.S. government and U.S. corporations in El Salvador helped to create the conditions that caused the displacement of Salvadorans.

Dobbs (2006) insists that illegal immigration occurs because there are employers in the United States who "want the cheapest labor possible" (135), and to get it, they break laws about who can be hired. But Dobbs does not acknowledge the long history of U.S. government and corporate complicity in creating migration flows. There are many employers willing to hire undocumented workers because there are millions of immigrants working in the United States without proper documentation. The presence of these workers can be attributed largely to the historical relations between the U.S. government and corporations and the countries of Latin America.

UNDOCUMENTED IMMIGRANTS AND OUR COMMUNITIES

The presence of undocumented workers creates a large-scale societal problem. People who do not have proper documentation are subject to employer abuses; they are often forced to work overtime or are not paid well or at all for their work. In addition, undocumented workers pay taxes for services for which they do not reap benefits. The Social Security Administration estimates that about 75 percent of undocumented workers pay payroll taxes as well as taxes for Social Security and Medicare benefits. Nearly all undocumented workers pay other taxes, such as state, real estate, sales, and automobile taxes. However, they do not have the right to collect Social Security or Medicare benefits. Undocumented workers contribute approximately $7 billion to the Social Security fund each year, and it is possible that the vast majority will never have access to those benefits.[27]

It should be noted, however, that in 2004 the Bush administration reached an agreement with Mexico that could require the payment of Social Security benefits to Mexicans who paid U.S. payroll taxes. As of early 2008, Bush had not signed the agreement, nor had he submitted it to Congress. If he does submit it prior to leaving office, Congress would have sixty days to vote against it, or it would become law. Bush may not sign and submit the agreement with Mexico given that Congress in 2007 reconsidered and rejected a somewhat different version of a defeated 2006 bill that would have allowed undocumented workers to apply for temporary visas and to complete a number of tasks (e.g., obtaining some level of fluency in English) in order to get citizenship. If the agreement with Mexico is not disapproved by Congress, undocumented workers could qualify for Social Security benefits for their work in the United States. The agreement would permit these workers to pool their retirement credits in both countries so that they could qualify for Social Security benefits for the period of time they worked in the United States.[28]

However, the quarter of the undocumented workers in the United States who do not pay taxes may never be eligible for many benefits or services. It is important to remember that payment of taxes is primarily up to employers, and some employers may not declare employees and pay their part of the payroll taxes. Employers are in a much better position to make sure that employees pay taxes than vice versa, and those employers who get away with not paying the costs associated with having employees create a problem for the communities in which their employees work and live. Tax revenues that could be used for facilities and services in numerous communities are not collected.

Another problem with immigration in its current form is that in many ways it creates a group of dehumanized individuals. The guest-worker programs exemplify this, as they have a long record of violations of labor rights and standards, including blacklists and deportations of workers who protest. Guest-worker programs create a vulnerable workforce. This allows companies to keep wages low and to break union-organizing efforts. Guest-worker programs are designed to extract labor from temporary workers while they are needed and to send them back home when they are not. However, history has taught us that in the Unites States and also in Sweden, Germany, and France, guest workers, after working a few years in their host countries, often have little desire to return home.

This situation creates two distinct problems: 1) while guest workers are working, they are prevented from putting down roots and becoming full and equal members of our communities, and 2) when guest workers finish their contracts or their visas expire, they are forced to leave communities in which they may have lived for years. The first problem becomes a problem for the worker's family and for the other families that live in the community. An ideal community is not one in which only some people have the right to have families, to send their children to school, and to lay down roots while others are denied these rights. In addition, guest workers have to pay taxes for schools their children may never attend and for Social Security programs and Medicare they may never benefit from. The second problem becomes an issue when guest workers do not wish to leave. In the past, guest workers who did not wish to return have simply stayed in the United States and continued to work, usually without proper documentation. There has never been a viable way to ensure that guest workers leave, and there are numerous reasons to believe that many guest workers will not wish to leave. This problem seems to be an inherent flaw in the guest-worker programs. People are asked to come to the United States only to work. However, workers are also human beings and are likely to seek social interaction and participation in the communities in which they live. What guest-worker programs are missing is recognition of the human rights of migrants to form families and to be parts of the communities in which they live. Anti-immigration activists may claim that undocumented or guest workers should have no rights, but from a human rights perspective, such a claim is a denial of our common dignity and thus inhumane.

A particularly vulnerable segment of the immigrant population includes those people who work as household employees. Many domestic workers in the United States do not have proper documentation. In California, for example, around two-thirds of domestic workers are undocumented. Their vulnerable legal status means that they are more subject to employer abuses than workers with proper documentation. However, abuses are also prevalent among immigrants who are brought legally to the United States to work as household employees. Over 4,000 domestic workers are brought into the United States legally each year on special visas issued to three sets of people—diplomats, employees of international agencies, and foreign nationals. Despite the legal status of these domestic workers, many are abused by their employers. Although the special visas could potentially benefit both the employees and the employers, the lack of protection for the employees often entails various abuses. Zarembka (2002) recounts several cases where domestic workers were unpaid; physically, sexually, and mentally abused; made to work around the clock; and effectively held hostage by their employers. These sorts of abuses can be attributed to the fact that the employers, not the employees, are the ones in control of the employees' migration and status. If the employee leaves the employer, she (most are female) is automatically out of status and thus subject to deportation. By contrast, another category of visas, the "au pair," or J-1, visas, give much more control and many more rights to the employee, and abuses are much less rampant. Notably, the majority of au pairs are from the global North, while the majority of the employees who come on the special visa programs are from the global South.

CONCLUSION: THE HUMAN RIGHT OF MIGRATION

From a human rights perspective, all human beings should have the right to a job, to a living wage, to safe working conditions, to food security, to decent health care, to education, to a family, to a cultural identity, and to a community. The creation of guest-worker and special visa programs that permit workers to come to the United States only to work for low wages and no benefits and that do not permit them to bring their families, to send their children to school, and to form communities will negatively impact both the workers and the communities in which they live. Building a fence across the southern border will be ineffective at preventing illegal immigration and terrorism and will only endanger the lives of migrants and potential migrants. What, then, is a more humane solution to the current humanitarian crisis?

Blau and Moncada (2006) comment that "American leaders have always drawn on the exceptionalist argument, which is rooted in the idea that

America has a unique mission to inspire and transform the world" (61). We need to advance another exceptionalist argument: that immigration to the United States and other countries should be facilitated for those people who are without rights in their own countries in part because of the economic and military interventionist policies and practices of countries in the global North. These practices were designed to extract money, cheap labor, and cheap raw materials from the global South. The consequences have been devastating for these countries. American corporate and government complicity in the impoverishment of countries in the global South must be a part of the immigration debate. This new kind of "exceptionalism" would mean that national sovereignty, in terms of setting rules about borders, should be limited given the history of the United States, France, Spain, Portugal, and other countries in the global North. The United States, for example, has a history of slavery, genocide, and internment where African Americans, Native Americans, and Asian Americans are concerned, in addition to its history of colonial acquisitions in the Pacific Ocean and its long history of interventions in Latin America.

All this is not to say that there is not an issue of border security. There is. As much as the United States and other countries in the global North are responsible for the hatred that Islamic terrorists have for us because of the ongoing efforts to maintain some control over oil in the Middle East and for other reasons, the terrorist groups are sending their warriors to countries in the global North to inflict harm on civilians. New York, Madrid, and other locations have already been attacked by terrorists. There is a need for defense systems against those who would smuggle in, through ports or land borders, chemical or biological weapons or nuclear bombs. These defense systems will have to be more elaborate than fences across an entire border. Fences will not keep terrorists or other well-organized groups out; they can fly planes over them or dig tunnels under them.

But migrants from Mexico, Central and South America, or other countries in the global South who walk across deserts, swim across rivers, or climb over fences in search of better employment prospects make up a different population. They have families, they need jobs, and they do not want to steal. Very few of them, if any, are terrorists. We do ourselves as well as the immigrants an incredible disservice if we allow governments in the global North and their corporate sponsors to portray them as inferior and inhuman.

Jenni Russell concludes about migration in Western Europe that "either we will have to consider an amnesty, alongside many more work permits for others abroad, or accept that we intend to do nothing about this situation because it suits the majority of us to have large numbers of unofficial workers available." She comments that "if we choose the latter, we are making it even harder for recent arrivals and their host communities to adjust and trust one another."[29]

Indeed, the second and later generations of these immigrants who experience discrimination and exclusion may be at elevated risk for identifying themselves as those who are different from persons who are native citizens and for not being assimilated into the host society. A recent analysis of survey data in the United States found that some children of Latin American immigrants who have experienced discrimination are self-identifying themselves as Latino and Latina Americans rather than as simply Americans. Golash-Boza (2006) argues that these analyses show that discrimination against the children of immigrants teaches them that they are not seen as Americans by others in the United States. A recent study by Alejandro Portes (2007) has revealed that 20 percent of the male children of low-income Mexican immigrants in San Diego spent time in prison by the age of twenty-four. This number is strikingly high, given that it is higher than that for African American men of that same age range. It also shows that these children, raised in the United States, are finding it difficult to attain the American dream and are suffering the consequences of the marginalization of their parents. In addition, this figure reveals that, while employers are benefiting from a low-wage workforce today, the costs of the exploitation of these workers will be socialized. A society that treated immigrants with dignity and respect would be much less likely to witness the large-scale incarceration of their children.

A society in which everyone's human rights are recognized is a better society for everyone. The United States has a long history of hate and xenophobia toward immigrants, and it is time to make a change for everyone's benefit. In this chapter, we have argued that immigrants deserve full recognition of their human rights, as immigrants, too, are human beings. We have also argued that any attempts to close the U.S. border will be unsuccessful. This is because we have immigration into the United States not because the border is unprotected but because of a long history of military and corporate involvement in other countries. Finally, the current rhetoric and practices involved in closing the border create an environment in which immigrants in the United States are consistently denied basic human rights. This is not the sort of society we want to live in.

Migration is a phenomenon that affects people both in sending and receiving states and therefore must be part of an international forum. Consequently, discussions about immigration should be restricted or controlled not by the states of individual countries but by civil societies where "membership" would mean different kinds of transnational solidarities as found in networks of global social movements (and not in networks of multinational corporations and international agencies and banks). These discussions could lead to the adoption and promotion of the position that there should be a human right to migrate in addition to other human rights, such as to a job, to a living wage, to safe working conditions, to education, to food security, and to decent health care. Another world is possible only once these sorts of discussions take place and our common human dignity is realized, regardless of our history as citizens or immigrants.

NOTES

1. The authors of this chapter began working together on immigration rights when they prepared a policy statement for Sociologists without Borders that was posted May 15, 2006, on Counterpunch.org at www.counterpunch.org/golash05152006.html.

2. www.silentkillerfilm.org/right_food.html.

3. Tyche Hendricks, "Study: Price for Border Fence up to $49 Billion: Study Says Fence Cost Could Reach $49 Billion," *San Francisco Chronicle*, January 8, 2007, www.sfgate.com/cgi-bin/article.cgi?f=/c/a/2007/01/08/BAG6RNEJJG1.DTL (accessed May 2007).

4. Michael A. Fletcher and Jonathan Weisman, "Bush Signs Bill Authorizing 700-Mile Fence for Border," *Washington Post*, October 26, 2006, www.washingtonpost.com/wpdyn/content/article/2006/10/26/AR2006102600120.html (accessed February 4, 2007); María Eugenia Anguiano Téllez, "Desviados al Desierto de Sonora-Arizona: Nuevas Rutas de la Emigración Mexicana a los Estados Unidos" (paper presented at the Third *Cumbre* of the Great Plains, Omaha, Nebraska, April 26–29, 2007).

5. The use of the military for the purpose of reducing undocumented immigration appears to be precluded if President Bush and other political leaders such as Senator John McCain of Arizona continue to insist on the deployment of additional soldiers and marines in Iraq as they did in early 2007. The military is stretched as it is and has had to relax its standards in order to increase its numbers, in addition to outsourcing many of its operations to private contractors. Congressman Martin Meehan recently pointed out that "the data is crystal clear; our armed forces are under incredible strain, and the only way that they can fill their recruiting quotas is by lowering their standards" (www.democracynow.org/article.pl?sid=07/02/14/1646210&mode=thread&tid=25) (accessed February 14, 2007).

6. "Private Military Corporations," www.sourcewatch.org/index.php?title=Private_Military_Corporations (accessed February 5, 2007).

7. www.democracynow.org/article.pl?sid=07/02/08/1611238 (accessed February 8, 2007).

8. www.democracynow.org/article.pl?sid=07/01/25/153210&mode=thread&tid=25 (accessed January 25, 2007).

9. Buchanan (2006, 115); see also Geri Smith, "Mexico's Drug Wars Heat Up," *BusinessWeek*, August 2006, www.businessweek.com/bwdaily/dnflash/content/aug2006/db20060829_272510.htm?chan=top+news_top+news+index (accessed February 2, 2007).

10. James McKinley, "Migrants Stream into South Mexico," *New York Times*, January 28, 2007.

11. Chris Kraul, "Youth Suicides Soar in Wake of Ecuador's Exodus, *Los Angeles Times*, January 28, 2007, latimes.com/news/nationworld/world/la-fg-suicides28jan28,1,1797386.story?coll=la-headlines-world (accessed January 28, 2007).

12. Barry Lynn, "Globalization Must Be Saved from the Radical Global Utopians," *Financial Times*, May 30, 2006, 13, available at www.newamerica.net/publications/articles/2006/globalisation_must_be_saved_from_the_radical_global_utopians.

13. Kim Murphy, "A Dying Population," *Los Angeles Times*, October 8, 2006.

14. Jeffrey Passel, "Mexican Immigration to the US: The Latest Estimates," www.migrationinformation.org/usfocus/display.cfm?ID=208 (accessed February 16, 2007).

15. Jennifer Van Hook, Frank D. Bean, and Jeffrey Passel, "Unauthorized Migrants Living in the United States," www.migrationinformation.org/Feature/display.cfm?ID=329 (accessed February 17, 2007).

16. Zinn (1997); "Mexican-American War," en.wikipedia.org/wiki/Mexican-American_War (accessed February 11, 2007).

17. "Bracero Program,"en.wikipedia.org/wiki/Bracero_Program; "Mexico; The North American Free Trade Agreement (NAFTA): Effects on Human Rights," www.fidh.org/IMG/pdf/Mexique448-ang2006.pdf (accessed February 15, 2007).

18. Avila, Fuentes, and Tuirán (2000).

19. Avila et al. (2000); Elena Zúñiga Herrera, "Tendencias y características de la migración mexicana a los estados unidos," www.conapo.gob.mx/publicaciones/migra2006_01/01.pdf, 2004 (accessed February 8, 2007). Zúñiga Herrera provides another measure: there are 2,443 municipalities in Mexico, and in 2000, 96 percent of these municipalities sent migrants to the United States.

20. Statistical Report of Consejo Nacional de Población, "Población nacida en México residente en Estados Unidos por entidad federativa de nacimiento, 1990, 2000 y 2003,"www.conapo.gob.mx/mig_int/series/070103.xls (accessed May 2007).

21. Zúñiga Herrera et al., "Origen y destino de la migración reciente de mexicanos a los estados unidos," www.conapo.gob.mx/publicaciones/migra2006_01/02.pdf, 2005 (accessed February 8, 2007).

22. Blau and Moncada (2006, 115); www.commondreams.org/views06/0425-30.htm (accessed February 17, 2007).

23. "Barricades Won't Stop Migration: We Have to Learn How to Manage It," *The Guardian*, July 10, 2006, 25, available at www.guardian.co.uk/commentisfree/story/0,1816888,00.html.

24. David Shirk and Alexandra Webber, "Slavery without Borders: Human Trafficking in the U.S. Mexico Context," *Hemisphere Focus*, 12, no. 5 (January 23, 2004): 1–2; Basav Sen, "Legalizing Human Trafficking," *Dollars & Sense: The Magazine of Economic Justice*, www.dollarsandsense.org/archives/2006/0506sen.html (accessed January 29, 2007).

25. www.migrationinformation.org/USfocus/display.cfm?id=263#2 (accessed February 20, 2007).

26. www.migrationinformation.org/Feature/display.cfm?id=329 (accessed February 20, 2007).

27. Eduardo Porter, "Illegal Immigrants Are Bolstering Social Security with Billions," *New York Times*, April 5, 2005. Porter reports that Angel Martinez has harvested asparagus, pruned grapevines and picked fruit, and washed trucks, earning $8.50 to $12.75 per hour, and that in the last year (2004) he paid about $2,000 in Social Security taxes and about $450 in Medicare taxes but that, when he turns sixty-five, he will not be eligible for benefits that most Americans will be able to collect

at the same age. Because of his status as an undocumented immigrant, his taxes will go into a Social Security surplus—the difference between what is being collected and what is being paid out in benefits—a surplus provided in part by the millions of undocumented workers who pay taxes.

28. Stephen Dinan, "Social Security for Illegal Aliens," *Washington Times*, January 4, 2007, www.washtimes.com/national/20070104-120950-4277r.html; "Agreement on Social Security between the United States and the United Mexican States," www.tscl.org/newcontent/totalization_agreement.pdf (accessed February 16, 2007).

29. "Barricades Won't Stop Migration."

REFERENCES

Avila, José Luis, Carlos Fuentes, and Rodolfo Tuirán. 2000. "Tiempos de estancia de los trabajadores temporales en los Estados Unidos: Situación actual y perspectivas." In *La Situación Demográfica de México, 2000*. Mexico City: Consejo Nacional de Población. Available at www.conapo.gob.mx/publicaciones/2000/pdf/13 Migracion.pdf.

Bean, Frank D., B. Lindsay Lowell, and Lowell J. Taylor. 1998. "Undocumented Mexican Immigrants and the Earnings of Other Workers in the United States." *Demography* 25, no. 1: 35–52.

Blau, Judith, and Alberto Moncada. 2005. *Human Rights: Beyond the Liberal Vision.* Lanham, Md.: Rowman & Littlefield.

———. 2006. *Justice in the United States: Human Rights and the U.S. Constitution.* Lanham, Md.: Rowman & Littlefield.

Buchanan, Pat. 2006. *State of Emergency: Third World Invasion and Conquest of America.* New York: St. Martin's Press.

Cornelius, Wayne. 2001. "Death at the Border: Efficacy and Unintended Consequences of US Immigration Policy." *Population and Development Review* 24, no. 4: 661–85.

———. 2005. "Controlling 'Unwanted' Immigration: Lessons from the United States, 1993–2004." *Journal of Ethnic and Migration Studies* 31, no. 4: 775–94.

Dobbs, Lou. 2006. *War on the Middle Class.* New York: Viking.

Golash-Boza, Tanya. 2006. "Dropping the Hyphen? Becoming Latino(a)-American through Racialized Assimilation." *Social Forces* 85, no. 1: 27–55.

Hamilton, Nora, and Norma Stoltz Chinchilla. 1991. "Central American Migration: A Framework for Analysis." *Latin American Research Review* 26, no. 1: 75–110.

Longman, Phillip. 2004. *The Empty Cradle.* New York: Basic Books.

Massey, Douglas S., Jorge Durand, and Nolan J. Malone. 2002. *Beyond Smoke and Mirrors: Mexican Immigration in an Era of Free Trade.* New York: Russell Sage Foundation.

Portes, Alejandro. 2007. "No Margin for Error: Determinants of Achievement among Disadvantaged Children of Immigrants." Paper presented at the Third *Cumbre* of the Great Plains, Omaha, Nebraska, April.

Quan, Adán. 2003. "Through the Looking Glass: US Aid to El Salvador and the Politics of National Identity." *American Ethnologist* 32, no. 2: 276–93.

Sapkota, Sanjeeb, Harold Kohl, Julie Gilchrist, Bruce Parks, Tim Flood, Mack Sewell, Dennis Perrotta, Miguel Escobedo, Corrine Stern, David Zane, and Kurt Noite. 2006. "Unauthorized Border Crossings and Migrant Deaths: Arizona, New Mexico, and El Paso, Texas, 2002–2003." *American Journal of Public Health* 96, no. 7 (July): 1282–87.

Sassen, Saskia. 1989. "America's Immigration 'Problem.'" *World Policy Journal* 6, no. 4 (fall): 811–32.

Zarembka, Joy. 2002. "America's Dirty Work: Migrant Maids and Modern-Day Slavery." In *Global Woman: Nannies, Maids, and Sex Workers in the New Economy*, edited by Arlie R. Hochschild and Barbara Ehrenreich. New York: Henry Holt & Co.

Zinn, Howard. 1997. *A People's History of the United States*. New York: New Press.

8

"Aliens," "Illegals," and Other Types of "Mexicanness": Examination of Racial Profiling in Border Policing

Pat Rubio Goldsmith and Mary Romero

In their study of recovered unauthorized border-crosser deaths in Arizona between 1990 and 2005, the Binational Migration Institute at the University of Arizona's Mexican American Studies and Research Center found "a major public health and humanitarian crisis in the deserts of Arizona" (Rubio-Goldsmith et al. 2006). The twentyfold increase of deaths in the area is attributed to the "funnel effect" created by immigration policy that forces migrants to cross through the most desolate and isolated desert Arizona landscapes. Ignoring reports of human rights violation, President Bush moved forward with his plan to place 3,100 agents in the Tucson sector in 2008 and to build a national force of 14,000 agents. Governor Napolitano of Arizona supported enforcement measures by requesting the deployment of National Guard units to the border. Federal authorities responded with a plan to create a network of police agencies throughout the state. While growing anti-immigration sentiment proliferates in the state legislature, radio talk shows, and everyday conversation, the vigilante group the Minute Men increases its number of recruits and the children of immigrants are targeted as the reason for the lack of public education, welfare, and medical care.

Violation of human rights is evident in current immigration policies that force migrants to endure life-threatening conditions in order to enter the country, and they are denied basic access to food, housing, and health care. In addition, U.S. immigration policy and enforcement is—and historically has been—racially defined. The nondiscrimination ideal embedded in the UN Charter, the Universal Declaration of Human Rights, the International

Human Rights Covenants, and the International Convention on the Emanation of All Forms of Racial Discrimination is clearly lacking in U.S. immigration law and policy. In addressing the racialized pattern of U.S. immigration law and enforcement, Article 7 of the Universal Declaration of Human Rights, which specifically pertains to discrimination, and the International Convention on the Elimination of All Forms of Racial Discrimination are particularly noteworthy. While scholars such as Berta Esperanza Hernández-Truyol (1997) have identified international rights strategy for incorporating a human rights perspective into immigration policies, many legal scholars have explored civil rights as a more strategic position since the United States has refused to endorse many of these international human rights documents. Nevertheless, both advocate for justice based on human rights.

This chapter examines the impact of the growing anti-immigration sentiment from the standpoint of the racialized population being policed on a daily basis in their neighborhoods in the U.S.–Mexico border region. Since the majority of interaction between local and state law enforcement agents and racialized "others" occur outside the public view, glimpses into the everyday practices of law enforcement usually occur from inquiries resulting from scandals or protests. However, even in these cases, documented accounts are almost overwhelmingly framed from the perspective of law enforcement with the goal of exonerating agents or soldiers involved (Romero 2001). Our study investigates the mistreatment of Mexican immigrants and Mexican Americans from their standpoint rather than from that of the justice system. In doing so, we attempt to identify the degree to which mistreatment is integrated within everyday immigration law enforcement practices in low-income Mexican American neighborhoods. Our study explores the relevance and significance of racialized social labels of the "other" and state-sanctioned violence. While most of the mistreatment of racialized others documented in the press and researched by social scientists has focused exclusively on African Americans, our study will demonstrate the importance of framing the analysis of Immigration and Naturalization Service (INS), Border Patrol, and police interaction with Latinas/os within a human rights discourse as well as critical race theory. Critical race theorists contend that the victim's perspective of discriminatory practices in immigration law enforcement is not officially documented and remains invisible (Johnson 2004; Romero 2006; Romero and Serag 2005; Vargas 2001). In order to position our study from the perspective of persons identified by the state as suspected illegal aliens, we use survey data collected in 1993 and 2003 from persons of South Tucson, Arizona, a predominantly Latino/Latina town near the U.S.–Mexico border. We investigate the characteristics shared by persons stopped for citizenship inspection by the Border Patrol and police and the degree of mistreatment reported in these encounters. In order to analyze the survey findings on mistreatment, we discuss the significance of framing immigration as a human rights issue and analyze racialized policing by the Border Patrol in predominantly Latina/o public and private spaces in urban areas.

CONSTRUCTING RACIALIZED IMMIGRATION AND LAW ENFORCEMENT PRACTICES

Controlling people's movement, including the right to leave or return to one's homeland and the ability to move within one's country, was formalized through designing identification documents, such as passports. In addition, various forms of citizenship status, ranging from property rights, access of welfare, and freedom to move across nation-states, could also be regulated (Torpey 2000). Racialized immigration laws and citizenship distinctions allowed physical appearance to be used as a proxy and functioned to control specific racial and ethnic groups. In the United States, race has been a significant criterion in determining immigration laws; cases and trials and immigration law enforcement have had serious implications for racialized minority citizens (Chang 1999; Hing 1997; Johnson 2004; Moran 1997). Chinese exclusion laws, the Gentleman's Agreement between the United States and Japan, *United States v. Thind* (ruling immigrants from India were ineligible for naturalization because Indians were not classified as white), the 1924 national origins quota system, and the Immigration Act of 1965 (limiting the number of migrants from the Western Hemisphere) constitute the most widely cited evidence of the significance of race in constructing immigration status in the United States. As legal scholar Kevin Johnson (2004) reminds us,

> Fabricated out of whole cloth, the "alien" represents a body of rules passed by Congress and reinforced by popular culture. It is society, with the assistance of the law, that defines who is an "alien," an institutionalized "other," and who is not. It is a society, through Congress and the courts, that determines which rights to afford "aliens." . . . Like the social construction of race, which helps to legitimize racial subordination, the construction of the "alien" has helped justify the limitation on noncitizen rights imposed by our legal system (154).

Anti-immigrant hysteria, fueled by the war on terrorism and the Patriot Act, reinforces the legal and social construction of "aliens" and perpetuates the scapegoating of Mexican-origin people as responsible for the lack of social services, economic downturns, and U.S. failure in Iraq.

Law institutionalizes the identified "alien," but the social construction of immigrant status is not complete without policing and surveillance. Through the practice of singling out particular racialized groups for increased citizenship inspection of passports and other types of identification documents, nation-states can control immigrants' access to social services and movement (Caplan and Torpey 2001). While the forms of "writing on the body," such as branding and tattooing, are not used to identify "aliens" from citizens, racial profiling is widely used in immigration law enforcement and is evidence that distinctions are prescribed to the body. Johnson (2000) points out that in 1975, the Supreme Court officially legitimated racial profiling in their decision that "Mexican appearance" "constitutes a legitimate consideration under the Fourth Amendment for making an immigration stop" (675). Consequently, Latinos are stigmatized as "aliens," and surveillance and citizenship inspection rely on racial profiling of their "Mexicanness" rather than specific behavior (Benitez 1994; Johnson 1996–1997, 2000; Lugo 2000; Rodríguez 1997; Romero 2006; Rosenbaum 1994).

Research on racialized law enforcement practices has established the use of micro- and macroaggressions as well as petit apartheid occurring in the racial profiling of African Americans and Latinos. Katheryn Russell (1998) identified microaggressions as racial assaults on a personal level, whereas macroaggressions are "face group affronts" and are "not directed toward a particular Black person, but at Blackness in general" and may be made "by a private individual or official authority" (139). In the case of immigration, macroaggressions reinforce the idea that Mexicans are foreigners, criminals, and inferiors. Repeated micro- and macroaggressions against a particular group of people not only routinize demeaning treatment but also reinforce a racial hierarchy and minimize the extent to which injuries are experienced. Offended parties are denied their achieved status, and they experience "limit[ed] access to equal opportunities and fair dealings before the law" (Milovanovic and Russell 2001, xvi).

The process of racialized law enforcement captures the use of petit apartheid, which relies on "discretional decision-making by both criminal justice agents and criminal justice agencies" (Georges-Abeyie 2001, x). Milovanovic and Russell (2001) construct a continuum of petit apartheid practices from a range of discriminatory practices from the more covert and informal forms to the more covert, formal forms. Nonverbal gestures, postures, and mannerisms are the most hidden covert and informal forms of discrimination. Racial profiling, legitimated by the courts or official immigration campaigns, is an example of an overt and formal form of discrimination under petit apartheid.

Russell (2004) further develops the concept of petit apartheid by identifying four distinctive aspects in policing that are relevant to immigration law enforcement: "they occur largely outside of public view," and "even when they take place within plain view, they are typically minimized or ignored"; petit apartheid practices "proliferate where criminal justice personnel have high levels of unchecked discretion," and "these practices reflect and reinforce the racialized images of deviance that exist within society at large" (13). The selection for citizen inspection of persons based on perceived "Mexicanness" reinforces the notion of Latinos as foreign and alien to the United States. The "funnel effect" that forces migrants to cross in desolate areas of the desert ensures that human rights violations are hidden from the public view and provides agents the opportunity to act with a high level of secrecy. Inspection of the general public at border crossings and the growing airport security checkpoints assist in minimizing the different levels of inspection and mistreatment of racialized Latinos.

In the case of citizenship inspection of specific racialized bodies, petit apartheid is further explicated by the police and Border Patrol targeting Mexican American neighborhoods for heavy surveillance. Gary Marx's (2001) reference to the "police practice known as 'field investigations' in which police interrogate persons who appear not to 'belong' to a given place" (323) is synonymous with immigration surveillance that identifies suspected aliens on the basis of their appearance as not belonging. Consequently, law enforcement reinforces the exclusionary use of urban spaces and limits freedom of movement (Heyman 1995; Weissinger 1996). As a result, working-class Latinos are frequently the victims of racially motivated stops and searches and are more likely to encounter INS abuse (Arriola 1996–1997; Benitez 1994; Lazos Vargas 2002; Pabón-López 2001; Vargas 2001). The likelihood of mistreatment of Mexican immigrants and Mexican Americans increases with the routine use of racial profiling in citizenship inspections. As Kevin Johnson (2003) cautions, "Alien terminology helps rationalize harsh, perhaps inhumane, treatment of persons from other countries" (154).

This chapter analyzes comparative survey data collected in 1993 and 2004 on community experiences and perceptions of micro- and macroaggressions as well as policing and surveillance practices consistent with petit apartheid. There are three major questions to be explored in the following analysis: 1) What are the specific practices that make up the petit apartheid system in regard to border enforcement? 2) Do urban areas with the highest concentration of Latinos experience heavy immigration inspection and surveillance and, as a consequence, also become locations for high levels of secrecy and mistreatment by law enforcement agents? 3) Are Latinos, especially those who are Spanish speaking, transnational, and noncitizens, more likely to be profiled by immigration authorities for surveillance and mistreatment?

METHODOLOGY

To answer these questions, we use survey data collected using identical instruments in 1993 and 2003 from two independent random samples of the household population of South Tucson, Arizona. South Tucson is a small, incorporated place completely surrounded by the city of Tucson. The 5,000 residents are about 80 percent Latino, 35 percent foreign born, and 40 percent under the poverty threshold. A sixty-five-mile interstate highway connects South Tucson to the U.S.–Mexico border (at Nogales). The sample size is 346 persons, of which 165 were obtained in 1993 and 181 in 2003.

The characteristics of the samples were compared to those obtained for South Tucson in the 1990 and 2000 censuses. These comparisons reveal that the samples and the population parameters are very similar as to ethnicity, language use, and place of birth. However, the samples contain noticeably higher proportions of females, married persons, and unemployed persons than the population. Presumably, this bias resulted from minimal follow-ups for households not home at the time of contact. These biases can be adjusted for with controls in regression analyses, but they are likely to result in an underestimation of mistreatment rates because the people overrepresented in the sample are slightly less likely to be mistreated than their counterparts. Further discussion of the methodology is available elsewhere (Koulish 1995; Koulish et al. 1994).

Our primary interests are to determine the amount and nature of mistreatment and surveillance as well as the patterning of these across South Tucson's residents. Mistreatment episodes were measured through a series of questions, beginning with a general question about whether the respondent or someone they know had ever had face-to-face interactions with immigration authorities. Respondents who could recall having one or more such interactions were then asked whether any of these were less than cordial, whether they felt "wronged" in any of them, and whether any of the interactions contained one or more negative elements read from a list. The list included such things as being insulted, being detained, or some "other" act. If they answered yes to any of these questions, they were asked to describe each incident separately. The interviewers recorded these descriptions.

Interviewers also asked an extensive list of questions about each episode, including their date, the agency involved, the location, whether a complaint was filed, the nature of the mistreatment, and who the victim was. Legal precedent and official guidelines pertaining to appropriate behavior of immigration authorities were used by the researchers to define which reports were, on their face, credible claims of mistreatment and which were not. Information on sixty-eight mistreatment episodes was gathered from the 346 respondents. We use these data to see if the patterning of mistreatment is consistent with the theory of petit apartheid (Koulish 1995; Koulish et al. 1994).

We also calculate regression models to see who is mistreated and who perceives an oppressive atmosphere of surveillance. We use a bivariate indicator of who has been a victim of mistreatment and who has not to analyze in logistic regression models. To see which respondents report high levels of surveillance, we use a question asking respondents how many times they have seen the Border Patrol in their "neighborhood" or in "South Tucson" in the past year. This variable is transformed by taking its natural log to reduce the influence of respondents who report very high levels of surveillance (which are presumably less accurate) and to normalize error terms in the models.

To predict who reports being under greater surveillance and who is most at risk of mistreatment, we use survey questions about respondents' demographic characteristics to develop independent variables capturing respondents' ethnicity, language, transnationalism, and residency status as well as a set of control variables. Definitions and descriptive statistics for variables are described in table 8.1.

Table 8.1.   Definitions, Means, and Standard deviations for Independent Variables

Variable		Mean	St. D.
Latino/Latina	1 = yes, 0 = other	0.82	
Spanish Primary Language	Only Spanish = 1 More Spanish than English = 1 Spanish and English = 1 Else = 0	0.71	
Transnational Status	Sum of: 1) has a close relative living in Mexico/ S.C. America? 2) would like to bring relative to the U.S.? 3) would like to go to Mexico/S.C. America? (1 = yes, else = 0 for all). Alpha = 068	1.77	1.15
Naturalized citizen	1 = yes, 0 = no	0.16	
Lawful permanent resident	1 = yes, 0 = no	0.17	
Undocumented	1 = yes, 0 = no	0.04	
Residency status missing	1 = yes, 0 = no	0.07	
Other status	Temporary resident, border crossing card, employment authorization, asylee/refugee, other (1 = yes, 0 = no)	0.04	
Native born citizen	Comparison group	0.53	
Year	0 = 1993, 1 = 2003	0.52	
Employed last year	1 = yes, 0 = no	0.49	
Age	Years of age	42.2	15.9
Female	1 = yes, 0 = no	0.58	
Education	Years of education	10.3	3.3

N = 322

PETIT APARTHEID IN THE BORDER REGION

Table 8.2 shows characteristics of sixty-eight mistreatment episodes that are relayed from the 346 respondents. These episodes include first- and secondhand descriptions of events. According to the theory of petit apartheid, mistreatment is likely to occur outside the view of Anglo society. The data show the percentage of mistreatment episodes that occurred in five different locations. Two of these locations are largely Latino areas: South Tucson and Nogales. Combined, they account for 64.2 percent of all the episodes of mistreatment, clearly indicating a pattern of mistreatment in Latino areas. The number of mistreatment episodes reported in Tucson is remarkably low. Tucson has an area of 226 square miles, completely surrounding and dwarfing South Tucson's one-square-mile area. Nogales, on the other hand, is much smaller than Tucson and sixty-five miles to the south. South Tucson's residents undoubtedly spend more time in Tucson than in Nogales. Nevertheless, the percentage of mistreatment episodes in Nogales is more than twice as high as in Tucson, further suggesting a concentration of mistreatment episodes in Latino areas.

Petit apartheid also suggests that agents with more discretion do the bulk of mistreating. In our case, this suggests that Border Patrol agents would most likely be responsible for mistreatment because their behavior is less scrutinized than that of local law enforcement agents (Johnson 2004). As seen in table 8.2, 64.7 percent of the mistreatment episodes involved Border Patrol agents. Officials of the INS and the Customs Service and the local police were responsible for only 19.1, 14.7, and 1.5 percent of the mistreatment episodes, respectively.

Table 8.2 also provides information on the types of mistreatment suffered by respondents. Theoretically, these acts represent the discriminatory customs and norms that officials practice in their day-to-day interactions with people in the border region and fit into the overall petit apartheid system articulated by Milovanovic and Russell (2001).

The most common types of mistreatment are being rude (44.1 percent), insulting (22.1 percent), detaining without cause (19.1 percent), and threatening or coercing (13.2 percent). Physical mistreatment, although not as common as other forms, is present in more than one in ten mistreatment episodes. This table illustrates the uncivil and sometimes brutal manner in which immigration authorities treat South Tucson residents, but the descriptions of the events told by the respondents show an even darker side of the mistreatment. Many of the insults were racial slurs directed toward Mexicans and are the kinds of microaggressions that Georges-Abeyie (1990) has argued result in petit apartheid. The episodes involving detainment often last up to twelve hours, and some include the separation of children from

Table 8.2. Characteristics of 68 Mistreatment Episodes

Location	Percent of Episodes
South Tucson	28.4
Tucson	16.4
Nogales	35.8
Other	16.4
Phoenix	3.0

Agency	
Mistreatment by INS	19.1
Mistreatment by Border Patrol	64.7
Mistreatment by Customs	14.7
Mistreatment by Local Police	1.5

Official record of mistreatment	
Complaints filed	8.8

Physical mistreatment	
Handcuffs	10.3
Hands/fists	8.8
Beaten in other ways	7.4
Sexual assault	4.4
Used firearms	1.5

Verbal mistreatment	
Rude language	44.1
Insults	22.1
Threats or coercion	13.2
Unlawful interrogation	8.8
Sexual harassment	2.9

Legal mistreatment	
Detained without cause	19.1
Not advised rights	11.8
Unlawful deportation	8.8
False arrest	5.9
Questioned appearance	5.9
Fabricated evidence	4.4
Not understand papers	4.4
Seized documents	4.4
Denied Counsel	2.9
Denied phone call	2.9
Not told benefits	2.9
Denied food/water	2.9
Seized items	2.9

Table 8.3. Regression of Surveillance and Mistreatment onto Selected
Independent Variables

Ethnicity	Seen Border Patrol Log of Times	Mistreated
Latino/Latina (1 = yes)	−0.050	−0.404
Other race/ethnicity (comparison)	—	—
Language		
Spanish is primary language (1=yes)	-0.776	1.742***
Other language is primary (comparison)	—	—
Transnationalism		
No. of transnational characteristics	0.572***	0.399*
Residency Status		
Naturalized citizen	0.018	−0.322
Lawful permanent resident	0.615	−0.395
Undocumented	0.784	−0.014
Residency status missing	−0.508	0.101
Other status	1.055	−1.162
Native born citizen (comparison)	—	—
Control Variables		
Wave (2003 = 1; 1993 = 0)	−1.038***	−0.395
Employed (1 = yes)	1.027***	0.049
Years of age	0.007	−0.011
Female (1 = yes)	−0.512	−0.557
Years of education	−0.094	0.118**
Intercept	2.311**	−4.164***

***, **, * indicate $p < .01$ and .05 on a two-tailed test and .05 on a one-tailed test. One tailed tests are used
   when significance is not reached on a two-tailed test and the direction is predicted.

their parents. Sexual assaults are committed by agents searching women's
bodies.

In addition, table 8.3 shows evidence supporting critical race theorists
who have noted that the victim's perspective of discriminatory practices in
immigration law enforcement is not officially documented and remains invisible (Johnson 2004; Romero 2006; Romero and Serag 2005; Vargas
2001). Our data indicate that of the sixty-eight mistreatment episodes, only
six, or 8.8 percent, resulted in a complaint being filed.

VICTIMS OF MISTREATMENT AND SURVEILLANCE

In all, 10.7 percent of the 346 respondents reported being a victim of mistreatment. Analyses of victimization rates in the three most recent years cor-

responding to each survey suggest that 2.14 percent of South Tucson's residents are mistreated each year. In a city the size of South Tucson (5,000 people), this translates to 2.06 mistreatment episodes per week.

The measure of surveillance suggests that respondents saw the Border Patrol in "South Tucson" or their "neighborhood" frequently in the last year. The median number of sightings reported was ten, but many people reported seeing them over a hundred times. Taken together, the evidence shows a pattern of heavy surveillance and mistreatment in barrios in the border region. It occurs largely outside of Anglos' view and appears highly related to the discretionary actions of law enforcement found in the informal stages of the criminal justice system.

We now turn to the multiple regression models, shown in table 8.3, to further investigate patterns of surveillance and mistreatment across residents of barrios. The first model predicts reports of surveillance (i.e., the natural log of the number of times having seen the Border Patrol in the past year), and the second model predicts mistreatment (i.e., the respondent is a victim of mistreatment).

Surprisingly, the effect of being Latino rather than some other ethnicity is not significant in either model, and the coefficients actually have a negative sign. Thus, there is no evidence that immigration officials target Latinos/as *within* barrios, even though it is known from the previous analyses that they target Latino/a areas.

The models do show that immigration authorities profile on the basis of language. Although Spanish speakers do not observe the Border Patrol more often than English speakers, the odds of being mistreated are (exp = 1.742) 5.7 times greater for Spanish speakers than their counterparts, all else being equal.

The models also show that having more transnational characteristics is related to both outcomes. The first model shows that each additional transnational characteristic is associated with a 57 percent increase in Border Patrol sightings. The second model shows that the odds of being mistreated are 1.5 times greater for each additional transnational characteristic.

The significant effects of transnational characteristics on surveillance and mistreatment can be reasonably interpreted in two ways. First, people with more transnational characteristics, like those who speak Spanish, may appear more "Mexican" to immigration officials, making them a target for inspection, and, second, people with more transnational characteristics may have routines (like crossing the border more often) that bring them into more frequent contact with immigration officials.

The most surprising findings are in relation to residency status. We test for different rates of mistreatment for various immigration statuses using dummy variables. The results for these tests show no differences between any immigrant status and any other, including those who report being undocumented.

Thus, the data indicate that native-born U.S. citizens in South Tucson are as likely to be mistreated as people with any other residency status when controlling for transnational characteristics.

Among the control variables, there are three interesting findings. First, Border Patrol sightings vary considerably between the two survey waves. Respondents report 103 percent more sightings in 1993 than in 2003. This is consistent with changing immigration policies and law enforcement tactics that emphasize patrolling barren areas in the deserts for persons crossing the border illegally and combating drug smuggling rather than monitoring urban areas (Massey, Durand, and Malone 2002). Unfortunately, the declining presence of the Border Patrol in South Tucson did not result in a decline in mistreatment in South Tucson, as seen by the lack of significant effects for this variable in the latter model.

Second, the models show that having a job is associated with greater risk. Employed people report 103 percent more sightings of the Border Patrol than the unemployed. South Tucson's residents therefore risk having face-to-face interactions with the Border Patrol if they are employed. Third, people of lower social class (as indicated by years of education) may be less likely than people of higher social class to suffer mistreatment.

DISCUSSION

This study examines the prevalence and nature of mistreatment that residents of poor, Latino neighborhoods in the border region experience in their interactions with immigration officials. Unlike official reports of mistreatment, which are often biased by an ideological stance that criminalizes immigrants and justifies state action, our information is based on reports from a random sample of barrio residents and provides an alternative view of state action.

Barrio residents' reports indicate that mistreatment by immigration officials is exceedingly common. Our data suggest that one in ten people in South Tucson has been mistreated by immigration officials. While this rate is high, it is also likely that this estimate is too low. Our sample contains more women, elderly, unemployed, and married persons than would be expected in a random sample of South Tucson residents, and all these characteristics of individuals are associated with a slightly reduced risk of mistreatment. Moreover, undocumented people who are mistreated are likely to be deported, suggesting a process wherein mistreated individuals are being systematically driven out of South Tucson and into Mexico or farther south.

Mistreatment is most likely to occur outside the view of Anglo society, being concentrated in barrio areas themselves or in border towns with high proportions of Latino residents. Mistreatment is being carried out by the portions of law enforcement with the greatest unchecked discretion, the Border Patrol, which accounts for two-thirds of mistreatment episodes. The contrast between official reports of mistreatment and barrio residents' view of mistreatment is seen most vividly in the lack of official complaints filed by residents who suffer mistreatment. A scant 7 percent of mistreatment episodes are followed by an official complaint.

Over one in ten of the episodes of mistreatment reported by South Tucson's residents involved physical force. More common yet are rude, insulting, and coercing verbal mistreatment that occurs in over half the mistreatment episodes. Another common practice of immigration officials is to detain residents without cause for long time periods, which is seen in about one in five episodes of mistreatment. While rarer, practices like illegal deportation and sexual assault are also reported. These practices represent an informal yet institutionalized pattern of subordinating and criminalizing all barrio residents.

While many might perceive—or wish—that mistreatment is doled out primarily to people without documents, there is little evidence here that this is the case. More than half the mistreatment episodes reported are by native-born U.S. citizens. Their rate of mistreatment is at least as high as it is for people with another form of residency status, including the undocumented. Instead of targeting the undocumented for mistreatment, immigration officials target people who display "Mexicanness." Barrio residents who speak primarily Spanish and who have social ties to people in Mexico are much more likely to be mistreated than other people in barrios, even net of their residency status. Mistreatment is thus likely to result in a deculturalization of the Mexican/Mexican American/Latino and Latina population, robbing them of a basic human right of maintaining their culture.

CONCLUSION

National security has been one of the major reasons that the United States has given for not signing human rights documents. Increased security is also used to condone inhumane immigration policies that result in hundreds of migrant deaths every year in the Sonoran Desert. Our study documents the less life-threatening human right violations experienced by Latinos, including citizens, racially stigmatized as "alien," "foreign," and "illegal." While much attention has been given to racial profiling in law enforcement practices used in communities of color and in selective highway stops of blacks and Latinos, little attention has been given to similar tactics used in immigration law enforcement. Immigration law enforcement, framed as a national security concern, has made racial profiling publicly acceptable. The significance of Article 7 of the Universal Declaration of Human Rights, which prohibits the unequal protection of the law or discrimination, is clearly relevant to the human violations found in our study. Racial and cultural construction of citizenship places Mexican Americans at risk before the law through the targeting of barrio neighborhoods, discretionary stops, use of intimidation, reinforced stereotypes, and limited access to fair and impartial treatment before the law. Overt and covert discriminatory immigration law enforcement practices found in this study establish, maintain, and reinforce second-class citizenship while limiting the civil, political, economic, and cultural rights and opportunities for Mexican Americans and legal residents.

Furthermore, overt and covert discriminatory immigration law enforcement practices establish, maintain, and reinforce second-class citizenship while limiting the civil, political, economic, and cultural rights and opportunities for Mexican Americans and legal residents. Immigration law enforcement along the border is probably the most obvious example of petit apartheid in the United States, specifically as a result of the increasing militarization in desolate desert areas and the presence of petit apartheid. Heavy policing and surveillance by immigration officials in low-income Latino urban communities are largely outside public view, and Border Patrol officers are permitted high levels of unchecked discretion. Under the Patriot Act and the increased security in airports and the request of identification, any previous concerns of civil and human rights violations resulting from racial profiling have largely disappeared from public discourse. Under the current concerns of national security and anti-immigrant sentiment, evidence of racial profiling and the use of force or mistreatment may actually serve to reinforce racialized images of illegal status among persons of Mexican ancestry.

Our findings point to the need to center the field of immigration research on human rights concerns, particularly in analyzing immigration policy and law enforcement. Critical race theorists suggest useful frameworks for thinking about the relationship between racial discrimination and human, as well as civil, rights discourse. Highlighting the use of racial profiling and mistreatment by immigration law enforcement agents reminds us how inseparable immigration restrictions and domestic race relations are. Anti-immigrant sentiment has an immediate impact on communities of color, and they are most affected in immigration raids and field investigations. Centering the sociology of immigration into a human rights framework may shed new understandings on the exclusion of race, color, descent, or national or ethnic origin underlying the decisions of assimilation and intergenerational conflicts within immigrant communities and the price of human rights violations.

REFERENCES

Arriola, Elvia R. 1996–1997. "LatCrit Theory, International Human rights, Popular Culture, and the Faces of Despair in INS Raids." *University of Miami Inter-American Law Review* 28: 245–62.

Benitez, Humberto. 1994. "Flawed Strategies: The INS Shift from Border Interdiction to Internal Enforcement Actions." *La Raza Law Journal* 7: 154–79.

Caplan, Jane, and John Torpey. 2001. *Documenting Individual Identity: The Development of State Practices in the Modern World.* Princeton, N.J.: Princeton University Press.

Chang, Robert. 1999. *Disoriented: Asian Americans, Law, and the Nation-State.* New York: New York University Press.

Georges-Abeyie, Daniel E. 1990. "Criminal Justice Processing of Non-White Minorities." In *Racism, Empiricism and Criminal Justice*, edited by Brian D. MacLean and Dragan Milovanovic. Vancouver: The Collective Press.

———. 2001. "Foreword." In *Petit Apartheid in the U.S. Criminal Justice System: The Dark Figure of Racism*, edited by Dragan Milovanovic and Katheryn Russell. Durham, N.C.: Carolina Academic Press.

Hernández-Truyol, Berta Esperanza. 1997. "Reconciling Rights in Collision: An International Human Rights Strategy." In *Immigrants Out!: The New Nativism and the Anti-Immigrant Impulse in the United States*, edited by Juan F. Perea. New York: New York University Press.

Heyman, Josiah. 1995. "Putting Power in the Anthropology of Bureaucracy: The Immigration and Naturalization Service at the Mexico-United States Border." *Current Anthropology* 36, no. 2: 261–87.

Hing, Bill Ong. 1997. *To Be an American.* New York: New York University Press.

Johnson, Kevin. 1996–1997. "Aliens and the U.S. Immigration Laws: The Social and Legal Construction of Nonpersons." *University of Miami InterAmerican Law Review* 28: 263–92.

———. 2000. "The Case against Race Profiling in Immigration Enforcement." *Washington University Law Quarterly* 78, no. 3: 676–736.

———. 2003. "The Struggle for Civil Rights: The Need for, and Impediments to, Political Coalitions among and within Minority Groups." *Louisiana Law Review* 63, no. 3: 759–83.

———. 2004. *The "Huddled Masses" Myth: Immigration and Civil Rights.* Philadelphia: Temple University Press.

Koulish, Robert E. 1995. "US Immigration Authorities and Victims of Human and Civil Rights Abuses in Two Border Communities." The Border Interaction Project and Study of South Tucson, Arizona. Tucson: Mexican-American Studies Research Center, University of Arizona.

Koulish, Robert E., Manual Escobedo, Raquel Rubio-Goldsmith, and John Robert Warren. 1994. "Final Report of the Tucson's Border Interaction Project: A Study of Immigration Authorities and South Tucson, Arizona." Working paper no. 20. Tucson: Mexican-American Studies Research Center, University of Arizona.

Lazos Vargas, Sylvia R. 2002. "'Latina/o-ization' of the Midwest: *Cambio de Colores* (Change of Colors) as *Agromaquilas* Expand into the Heartland." *Berkeley la Raza Law Journal* 13, no. 113: 343–68.

Lugo, Alejandro. 2000. "Theorizing Border Inspections." *Cultural Dynamics* 12, no. 3: 353–73.

Marx, Gary. 2001. "Identity and Anonymity: Some Conceptual Distinctions and Issues for Research." In *Documenting Individual Identity: The Development of State Practices in the Modern World,* edited by Jane Caplan and John Torpey. Princeton, N.J.: Princeton University Press.

Massey, S. Douglas, Jorge Durand, and Nolan J. Malone. 2002. *Beyond Smoke and Mirrors: Mexican Immigration in an Era of Economic Integration.* New York: Russell Sage Foundation.

Milovanovic, Dragan, and Katheryn Russell, eds. 2001. *Petit Apartheid in the U.S. Criminal Justice System: The Dark Figure of Racism.* Durham, N.C.: Carolina Academic Press.

Moran, Rachel. 1997. "Neither Black nor White." *Harvard Latino Law Review* 2: 61–99.

Pabón-López, María. 2001. "The Phoenix Rises from El Cenizo: A Community Creates and Affirms a Latino/a Border Cultural Citizenship through Its Language and Safe Haven Ordinances." *Denver University Law Review* 78, no. 4: 1017–48.

Rodríguez, Néstor P. 1997. "The Social Construction of the U.S.-Mexico Border." In *Immigrants Out!: The New Nativism and the Anti-Immigrant Impulse in the United States,* edited by Juan F. Perea. New York: New York University Press.

Romero, Mary, and Marwah Serag. 2005. "Violation of Latino Civil Rights Resulting from INS and Local Police's Use of Race, Culture and Class Profiling: The Case of the Chandler Roundup in Arizona." *Cleveland State Law Review* 52, no. 1–2: 75–96.

Romero, Mary. 2001. "State Violence, and the Social and Legal Construction of Latino Criminality: From El Bandido to Gang Member." *Denver University Law Review* 78, no. 2: 1089–1127.

———. 2006. "Racial Profiling and Immigration Law Enforcement: Rounding Up of Usual Suspects in the Latino Community," *Critical Sociology* 32, no. 2–3: 449–75.

Rosenbaum, Stephen A. 1994. "Keeping an Eye on the I.N.S.: A Case of Civilian Review of Uncivil Conduct." *La Raza Law Journal* 7, no. 1: 1–49.

Rubio-Goldsmith, Raquel, M. Melissa McCormick, Daniel Martinez, and Inez Magdalena Duarte. 2006. "The 'Funnel Effect' and Recovered Bodies of Unauthorized Migrants Processed by the Pima County Office of the Medical Examiner, 1990–2005." Binational Migration Institute, Mexican American Studies and Research Center, University of Arizona, Tucson.

Russell, Katheryn K. 1998. *The Color of Crime: Racial Hoaxes, White Fear, Black Protectionism, Police Harassment and Other Macroaggressions.* New York: New York University Press.

———. 2004. *Underground Codes: Race, Crime and Related Fires.* New York: New York University Press.

Torpey, John. 2000. *The Invention of the Passport: Surveillance, Citizenship and the State.* Cambridge: Cambridge University Press.

Vargas, Jorge A. 2001. "U.S. Border Patrol Abuses, Undocumented Mexican Workers, and International Human Rights." *San Diego International Law Review* 2, no. 1: 1–92.

Weissinger, George. 1996. *Law Enforcement and the INS: A Participant Observation Study of Control Agents.* New York: University Press of America.

9

El Sueño Americano? Barriers to Home Ownership for Mexican-Origin Populations[1]

Mercedes Rubio and Linda Lopez

Having a secure place to live has been defined, in 2003, by the United Nations as a fundamental human right (www.ohchr.org/english/issues/housing/index .htm). In the United States, home ownership is seldom viewed as a human right; rather, it is widely regarded as an important element to achieving the American dream. Historically, home ownership has been linked to economic security, inheritance, and intergenerational mobility (Saunders 1990). Prior research on home ownership suggests that for immigrants, home ownership may signify a desire to settle and become Americans (Alba and Logan 1992). In fact, empirical studies reveal that home ownership is a key indicator for immigrant groups to assimilate in a host society (Alba and Logan 1993; Balakrishnan and Wu 1992). Related research also suggests that high socioeconomic status translates into residential mobility (Massey and Fong 1990). However, table 9.1 highlights disparities with an average of 68 percent of all U.S. households owning homes, compared to 47 percent of Latino households (U.S. Census Bureau 2002).

Research on Latino[2] home ownership is sparse with only three national studies conducted exclusively on Latino home ownership (Alba and Logan 1992; Krivo 1986; Lee, Tornatzky, and Torres 2004). As the Latino population grows numerically in the United States and expected median income increases, this ethnic group will be faced with choices about whether to rent or purchase a home. The significance of a growing Latino population cannot be underestimated, particularly given future demographic projections. According to Census Bureau data, Latinos composed 12 percent of the total U.S. population in 2000 and are now the largest minority group in the

Table 9.1.   Home ownership Rates by Race & Ethnicity, 1980–2002

		Percent of Head of Household			
Year	*All*	*White*	*Black*	*Asian*	*Latino*
1980	64.4	67.8	44.4	52.5	43.4
1990	64.2	68.2	43.4	52.2	42.2
2000	66.2	71.3	46.3	53.3	45.7
2002	68.0	71.8	48.2	52.6	47.3

Note: Latino head of household can be of any race.
Source: *U.S. Census Bureau (2002). Housing and Household Economic Statistics Division*

United States. It is estimated that Latinos may constitute up to 25 percent of the U.S. population by 2050. These changes are driven not just by immigration but also by fertility. In 2002, fertility rates in the United States were estimated at 1.8 for non-Hispanic whites, 2.1 for blacks, and 3.0 for Hispanics (Population Resource Center 2002). Population growth in Latino communities coincides with a growing Latino middle class (Lee et al. 2004), yet home-ownership rates among Latinos still lag behind non-Hispanic whites. What accounts for this disparity in home-ownership rates?

Prior research provides some explanations for low levels of home ownership among Latinos, including language, sociodemographic factors such as age and income (Coulson 1999; Wachter and Megbolugbe 1992), the absence of well-established relationships with financial institutions, and concerns with residency status and documentation. However, little research examines comparatively the extent to which Latino immigrant groups are different than their native counterparts. Are there significant differences in home-ownership patterns between foreign-born and native-born Latinos? This research contributes to our understanding of the cultural and socioeconomic dynamics present among recent immigrants and the native born in several ways. First, we explore individual-level characteristics, such as owning a bank account, occupational status, educational attainment, minors in the household, and English-language proficiency, as factors that estimate home ownership. Second, we examine the effects of these factors on the likelihood of owning a home and its intersection with sociodemographic variables, such as age, gender, and marital status. We focus our study exclusively on the Mexican ancestry population given their size in the United States, their expected growth in the nation's demographic landscape, and their potential entry into the housing market.

We first begin by introducing the theoretical constructs that are relevant to consider in developing a proper understanding of the complex interactions between race, ethnicity, socioeconomic status, and home ownership. We then use logistic regressions to identify variations between U.S.-born Mexicans and foreign-born Mexicans. Finally, we provide a full discussion of the findings, a discussion of current housing trends, and implications for public policy.

IMMIGRANTS, ETHNICITY, AND RACE IN HOUSING

Early research on housing and residential segregation offers some important insights into the process of assimilation for immigrants and the factors linked to residential outcomes for minority groups. Studies show that socioeconomic status is a strong determinant of home ownership (Jackman and Jackman 1980). For a long time, social scientists have been preoccupied with comparing racial and ethnic residential access between minorities and whites. Immigrant groups have been central in this analysis of neighborhood change, choice, and exit, with several studies reporting lower homeownership rates among immigrants as compared to their native counterparts (Pitkin et al. 1997). Research studies on immigrant assimilation into American society suggest a "process of assimilation" whereby immigrants perform low-wage tasks in the labor market, live in city centers, and eventually obtain the skills and income required to leave ethnic enclaves and move to majority white neighborhoods (Burgess 1925; Gordon 1964; Massey 1985).

Often two types of assimilation are discussed to better understand this process—spatial assimilation and acculturation. The *spatial assimilation model* posits that as members of a minority group achieve higher levels of education, enter the labor market, and reach higher income levels, minority groups move away from ethnic enclaves into residential locations that are predominantly majority (Massey and Denton 1985). This process of dispersion is driven by socioeconomic mobility and increased acculturation in the host society (Borjas 1990). *Acculturation* can be defined as the acquisition of the dominant language (cultural patterns), and adoption of the values and behavior of the host society (Gans 1992; Gordon 1964) by recent immigrants, and this theoretical explanation figures prominently in the sociological literature explaining access to material benefits and social capital.

However, contrary to what is expected in acculturation models, empirical tests show that immigrants seek ethnically based residential enclaves, which provide immigrants access to social networks and resources (Painter, Yang, and Yu 2003; Rogers and Henning 1999). Immigrants who move to ethnic enclaves often do so because these neighborhoods provide a net advantage to their well-being and the potential for integration in the host society. Research by Logan, Alba, and Zhang (2002) confirms that the pattern of residential location for immigrants may not be a springboard away from ethnic neighborhoods but perhaps a destination. Based on these theoretical

models discussed previously, we can postulate that among Latino immigrants who have a higher educational attainment and higher income, coupled with greater knowledge of the host society, they are more likely to own
a home regardless of the residential location. To better understand the mul-
tidimensional explanations for home ownership, we turn our attention to
the factors related to Latino access to home ownership.

DETERMINANTS OF LATINO HOME OWNERSHIP

Among Latino immigrants, Alba and Logan (1993) find that rates of home
ownership increase with the passage of time as immigrants acculturate into
the host society and learn English. One predictor of home ownership is
English-language proficiency and the extent to which immigrants entering
the United States learn how to communicate in the host society (Alba and
Logan 1992). In some cases, however, language disappears as a predictor of
home ownership among immigrant groups, particularly among Asian immigrants (Painter et al. 2003). Other research reinforces the role of race and
ethnicity in structuring household outcomes. For instance, Rosenblaum
(1986) finds that even after controlling for socioeconomic status and family composition, blacks and Latinos are less likely to own a home. Research
by Krivo (1986) that compares Latinos and whites shows that even after
controlling for socioeconomic, life cycle, and geographic factors, Latinos are
less likely to own a home. Some of the reasons cited for lower Latino home
ownership are family composition and age. Hispanic households are more
likely to have children and be married, and they tend to be relatively
younger households, limiting the probability of owning a home (Krivo
1986). Additionally, Jones-Correa (2006) suggests that Latinos are not often heavily concentrated in one geographic location within cities like blacks
but rather are spread throughout metropolitan areas.

Theories of acculturation provide a prism to understand how Latino immigrants enter majority neighborhoods, leaving culturally distinctive ethnic
enclaves to move from urban areas to the suburbs (Alba et al. 1999). Newcomers to the United States are more likely to rent than to own because it
may take longer for immigrants to understand the housing market or fa-
miliarize themselves with how to invest in a neighborhood (Painter,
Gabriel, and Myers 2000). In addition, immigrants generally experience
lower earning potential, which has direct consequences on their ability to
purchase a home. Length of time in the United States becomes an important predictor of home ownership, providing individuals greater exposure
and experience to equity investment than recently arrived migrants. Thus, it
is not surprising that among Mexican immigrant groups, less experience
with financial institutions, coupled with lower levels of income and educa-

tion, has been shown to dampen the rate of home ownership (Painter et al. 2000). Higher education levels have consistently been shown to be positively associated with a higher propensity to earn greater income and have been linked to steady employment patterns enabling prospective home owners to meet the financial burdens associated with home ownership (e.g., making a down payment, qualifying for a loan, and ability to make mortgage payments). Alba and Logan (1993), in their study of twelve racial and ethnic groups, found that household income predicted home ownership for the groups studied.

Access to credit is typically considered a necessary component for successful home purchasing. Within the immigrant population, research shows that there are some attitudinal differences in perception and beliefs about the banking and financial institutions (Bendixen and Associates 2004). Mexican immigrants often have a distrust of financial institutions, such as banks, and some of this can be partially explained by socialization in the home country, where prior experiences with financial institutions have not been positive. In addition, there is a perception that there are bad business practices in foreign banks and fraudulent practices in Latin America (Bendixen and Associates 2004), and these beliefs are possible barriers to opening a bank account in U.S. banks.

Moreover, in the United States, Latinos often report that banks are not welcoming institutions and that their inability to speak English prevents them from receiving equal treatment by bank personnel and to understand the intricacies of opening a bank account (Bendixen and Associates 2004). Thus, immigrants often import old financial values and beliefs from their home country to the United States. The challenge is to demystify these beliefs in order for Latinos to become a part of the American financial sector. As documented in the research by Kotkin, Tseng, and Ozuna (2002), foreign-born Latinos face greater challenges in finding a home and understanding the home-buying process (e.g., application, down payment, and finding a good real estate agent and a reputable mortgage company), including language barriers that make negotiating these types of business transactions difficult (Krivo 1986).

METHODS

Data from the *Kaiser/Pew 2002 Latino Survey* are used to conduct the analyses (International Communications Research 2002). The primary advantage of these data includes a sufficient number of cases to understand homeownership patterns of Mexican-origin individuals by analyzing social and economic indicators. The primary shortcoming of the *Kaiser/Pew 2002 Latino Survey*, however, is that the survey questions do not offer in-depth measures for understanding the home-owner phenomenon in its entirety. For example, the *Kaiser/Pew 2002 Latino Survey* provides only a handful of questions regarding structural variables related to home ownership but does not provide key questions on important variables (e.g., neighborhood characteristics such as suburban–urban settings, loan type, and so on). Additionally, the sample size for specific Latinos groups besides Mexican-origin individuals is rather small; therefore, we have limited our analysis to Mexican-origin respondents.

The *Kaiser/Pew 2002 Latino Survey* was conducted by telephone from April 4 to June 11, 2002, among a nationally representative sample of 4,213 adults eighteen years and older, including 2,929 Latinos and 1,284 non-Latinos. Among the non-Latinos were 1,008 non-Latino white adults and 171 non-Latino black adults. The survey includes interviews of a representative number of Latinos in six ethnic groups with the largest sample size of Mexican-origin individuals ($N = 1,059$). International Communications Research in Media, Pennsylvania, conducted all interviews using the Computer Assisted Telephone Interviewing system and employed a highly stratified random-digit dialing telephone sample in an effort to segregate Latino respondents by geography and ensure a representative Latino sample.

Independent Variables

Socioeconomic Status

The major focus of our analysis is to explore how a variety of sociodemographic variables relate to home ownership. In the multivariate analysis, we consider the role of socioeconomic status (SES) as measured by owning a bank account, education attainment, occupation, and household income. For each of these variables, we constructed dummy variables. For example, individuals with a bank account are assigned a value of 1, and those without a bank account are given a value of 0.

We measure education with four dummy variables: 1) 0 to 8 years of education; 2) completed some high school education (9 to 11 years of education completed); 3) high school graduate, general equivalency diploma, or vocational training; and 4) those with some college. Individuals with postcollege education represent the reference category.

Occupation was dummy coded to reflect blue-collar occupations (assigned a value of 1) and white-collar occupations (assigned a value of 0). Blue-collar occupations consist of those whose work includes clerical, retail (sales/clerks), service worker, craftsman, unskilled laborer, and farmer. White-collar occupations consist of those whose work can be categorized as self-employed/owner, professional/technical, management/administrator, executive sales/service, and federal/state/local government. Individuals with a blue-collar occupation serve as the reference category.

The last SES measure considered is household income. We measure income with three dummy variables: 1) less than $20,000, 2) $20,000 to $39,999, and 3) $40,000 to $74,999. Individuals with a household income exceeding $75,000 represent the reference category.

Cultural Retention

Given that measures related to cultural retention have been found to also play an important role in the domain of life chances, we explore nativity, length of time in the United States, and language proficiency. Nativity is dummy coded to reflect foreign-born individuals as the reference category. We measure length of time in the United States with four dummy variables: 1) 0 to 10 years, 2) 11 to 20 years, 3) 21 to 30 years, and 4) 31 to 40 years. Individuals who have been in the United States longer than forty years represent the reference category. Language proficiency was measured with two dummy variables: Spanish dominant and bilingual. English-dominant individuals are the reference category.

Dependent Variable

Home Ownership

Our interest in this study is to examine the possible impact that socioeconomic status and cultural retention plays on the likelihood that Mexicans can own a home. Home ownership is dummy coded, with persons who are home owners coded as 1 and renters as 0.

Control Variables

In an effort to more accurately assess the relationship between the independent and dependent variables, we include four control variables (age, sex, marital status, and number of individuals living in the household under the age of eighteen) in the multivariate analysis. We measure age as a continuous variable. Sex is coded as a dummy variable with male as the reference category. Marital status is measured as a categorical variable with married individuals as the reference category. And households with individuals under the age of eighteen years are coded as 1 and those without as 0.

Analytical Plan and Statistical Procedure

The analysis is carried out in two stages. First, we provide a descriptive analysis of key variables. Second, we use logistic regression to examine the relationship between the dependent, independent, and control variables.

The analyses are first presented for the entire sample and then conducted separately for native-born and foreign-born Mexican individuals.

RESULTS

Descriptive Overview

Table 9.2 provides summary statistics for the variables in the study. These data document that foreign-born Mexican-origin individuals are at a disadvantage when it comes to home ownership. Native-born Mexicans own homes in greater proportions than foreign-born Mexicans with 48.9 percent owning homes compared to 31.4 percent of foreign born; however, both are largely renters. Over 50 percent of native-born and foreign-born Mexicans do not own a home.

First, we will highlight some of the findings for the SES measures: bank account, educational attainment, occupation, and annual household income. Almost 60 percent of the Mexican-origin respondents have a bank account. When the sample was stratified by nativity, three out of four native-born Mexican individuals have a bank account compared to 48 percent of their foreign-born counterparts. At least three out of four respondents have a high school degree or less. However, the education disparity is best highlighted when nativity is considered. An overwhelming percentage (86.9 percent) of the foreign-born Mexicans have a high school degree or less; this is in contrast to a rate of slightly over 50 percent for their native-born counterparts. Educational attainment is linked to occupational status and annual household income, and these data show preliminary evidence of the correlation among these sociodemographic variables. The descriptive statistics for occupation illustrate a significant difference in occupation with 75 percent of all Mexicans as blue-collar workers compared to 25 percent in white-collar occupations. After disaggregating the variable occupation by nativity, we observe that 59 percent of all native-born Mexicans are in blue-collar occupations compared to 86 percent of the foreign born. Roughly 30 percent of the sample has a middle-class household income (a household annual income of at least $40,000). The data further show that 15 percent of foreign-born annual household income is $40,000 or more as compared to 37.8 percent of native born.

In considering the cultural retention factors—length of time in the United States and language proficiency—the data suggest that roughly half of those sampled are Spanish dominant and that among the immigrants roughly one out of two have been in the United States less than ten years. Not surprisingly, only 1.9 percent of foreign-born Mexicans are English dominant, and this has severe consequences in the extent to which an immigrant is incorporated into the host society.

Table 9.2.   Summary Statistics on Selected Characteristics (N=1059)

Variables	ALL N	ALL %	NATIVE BORN N	NATIVE BORN %	FOREIGN BORN N	FOREIGN BORN %
Variables	*1059*		*423*	*39.9*	*636*	*60.1*
Dependent Variable						
Home ownership						
Own	407	38.4	207	48.9	200	31.4
Rent	652	61.6	216	51.1	436	68.6
Independent Variables						
Bank Account						
Yes	629	59.4	321	75.9	308	48.4
No	430	40.6	102	24.1	328	51.6
Education in years						
0 to 8 years	202	19.2	12	2.8	190	29.9
9 to 11 years	233	22.2	61	14.4	172	27.0
High School, GED, or Vocational	342	32.6	147	34.8	195	30.7
Some College	167	15.9	126	29.8	41	6.4
College Grad	74	7.0	53	12.5	21	3.3
Post-Graduate	32	3.0	23	5.4	9	1.4
Occupation						
Blue Collar	462	43.6	127	30.0	335	52.7
White Collar	597	56.4	296	70.0	301	47.3
Annual Household Income						
Less than $20K	250	29.0	76	18.0	174	27.4
$20K to $39.9K	356	41.3	120	28.4	236	37.1
$40K to $74.9K	180	20.9	105	24.8	75	11.8
$75K or more	75	8.7	55	13.0	20	3.1
Time in the U.S.						
10 years or less	N/A	N/A	N/A	N/A	295	46.4
11 to 20 years	N/A	N/A	N/A	N/A	206	32.4
21 to 30 years	N/A	N/A	N/A	N/A	91	14.3
31 to 40 years	N/A	N/A	N/A	N/A	27	4.2
41 years or more	N/A	N/A	N/A	N/A	17	2.7
Language Proficiency						
Spanish Dominant	515	48.6	18	4.3	497	78.1
Bilingual	284	26.8	157	37.1	127	20.0
English Dominant	260	24.6	248	58.6	12	1.9
Control Variables						
Age in years						
18–25	276	26.1	141	33.3	135	21.2
26–35	335	31.6	100	23.6	235	36.9

(continued)

Table 9.2. (*continued*)

Variables	ALL		NATIVE BORN		FOREIGN BORN	
	N	%	N	%	N	%
Variables	*1059*		*423*	*39.9*	*636*	*60.1*
Control Variables						
Age in years						
36–45	241	22.8	87	20.6	154	24.2
46–55	117	11.0	49	11.6	68	10.7
56–65	41	3.9	25	5.9	16	2.5
66+	49	4.6	21	5.0	28	4.4
Sex						
Male	512	48.3	191	45.2	321	50.5
Female	547	51.7	232	54.8	315	49.5
Marital Status						
Married or Living with Partner	692	65.6	233	55.1	459	72.2
Other	363	34.4	189	44.7	174	27.4
Individuals < 18 yrs in the household						
No Minors	237	24.2	122	32.8	115	18.9
1 Minor or More	744	75.8	250	67.2	494	81.1

Finally, we highlight the major findings for the control variables: age, sex, marital status, and number of individuals in the household under the age of eighteen years. Overall, the Mexican-origin respondents are young. Approximately 60 percent are less than thirty-five years of age, and less than 5 percent are over the age of sixty-five. And both native-born and foreign-born tend to be younger with over 50 percent located in the range of eighteen to thirty-five. The sex distribution of the respondents is similar with 48.3 percent male and 51.7 percent female. Roughly 65 percent of those surveyed live in partnerships, but the foreign born are more likely to be in a partnership (72.2 percent) than the native born (55.1 percent). As expected, we find that about three out of four respondents stated that there was at least one individual under the age of eighteen in the household. However, when we examine this variable by nativity, we find that 81.1 percent foreign-born Mexicans have at least one individual under the age of eighteen in the household compared to 67.2 percent for their native-born counterparts.

In an effort to begin to understand the variables influencing home-ownership rates among Mexican-origin populations, we next turn to relevant factors that may affect these outcomes.

Multivariate Analysis

We analyze the results of the logistic regressions to assess the relationship between predictors of home ownership and the selected independent variables. Table 9.3 provides the odds ratios associated with predictors of home ownership by selected socioeconomic (annual household income) and selected cultural retention characteristics (nativity and length of time in the United States for the foreign born) and controls (age, sex, and marital status). These analyses include the entire sample of Mexican-origin individuals.

Table 9.3. Logistic Regressions (Odds Ratio) of Selected Demographic Characteristics on Annual Household Income, Cultural Retention, and Control Variables

Selected Predictors	A Bank Account	Blue Collar Occupation	Some College	Individuals <18y in house	English Dominant
Measures of SES					
Income: $20K to $39.9K	0.58**	1.63+	0.32***	1.65*	0.83
Income: $40K to $74.9K	1.30	1.12	0.44***	1.65*	0.54*
Income: $75K and over	3.26***	1.30	1.47+	1.43	1.14
Cultural Retention					
US Born	2.39*	0.92	2.22	0.98	21.81**
Time in US: Less than 10y	0.40***	2.57	0.32+	1.51	0.05+
Time in US: 11y to 20y	0.90**	2.83+	0.33+	4.17*	0.16
Time in US: 21y to 30y	1.59	2.83	0.39	1.71	1.03
Time in US: 31y to 40y	2.08	1.44	0.36	0.79	2.45
Control Variables					
Age in years	1.11+	0.82**	1.06	0.71***	0.91
Male	1.11	5.77***	0.94	0.54***	1.37
Married	1.70**	1.05	1.02	2.08***	0.73
Chi-Square Likelihood Ratio	225.39***	243.86***	234.61***	111.89***	522.57***
df	11	11	11	11	11
N	1059	1059	1059	1059	1059

+ p < 0.10, * p < 0.05, ** p < 0.01, *** p < .000

We focus our discussion across each of the posited intervening variables to home ownership: bank account, occupation, educational attainment, number of individuals under the age of eighteen years in the household, and English-language acquisition.

First, we consider bank account. These data show that Mexican-origin individuals who earn $75,000 or more are twenty times more likely to have a bank account than those who earn less than $20,000. Age is positively associated with having a bank account. As expected, those with a partner are 1.56 more likely to have a bank account than their noncoupled counterparts.

Second, we consider the effect of selected predictors of occupation. We find that the demographic variables are most salient. For instance, those who are younger are 18 percent less likely to be blue-collar workers. Men are 5.77 times more likely to be in blue-collar occupations than women.

Third, we consider education attainment with a particular interest in those with some college education and above. As expected, there is a positive association between income and education. Mexican-origin individuals who earn from $40,000 to $74,900 are four times more likely to have some college education. And for the highest income, $75,000 and above, this income group is almost eleven times more likely to be college educated. This finding indicates a significant gap in earnings by educational attainment. Further, U.S.-born Mexicans are more likely to obtain a college education than foreign-born Mexicans. In fact, the former are almost six times more likely to have some college education compared to their immigrant counterparts.

Fourth, we consider the association between the predictors and number of individuals under the age of eighteen years in the household. Income is inversely related to having minors in the household. The data show that Mexican-origin individuals whose household income is above $75,000 are 60 percent less likely to have minors in the household. There appears to be no substantial difference between U.S.-born Mexicans and immigrants and the likelihood of having minors in the household. Recent immigrants (those who have been in the United States less than five years) are 50 percent more likely to have minors in the household than their counterparts who have been in the United States longer.

Finally, we consider the association between measures of SES and cultural retention with English-language acquisition. Individuals who have an annual household income between $40,000 and $74,999 are 46 percent less likely to be English dominant compared to their counterparts whose annual family income is less than $20,000. We also find that U.S.-born Mexicans are twenty-six times more likely to be proficient in English than their foreign-born counterparts.

We now turn our attention to the multivariate analyses for home ownership. We stratify the data by nativity to better examine how sociodemographic variables and measures of cultural retention relate to home ownership. We present two models for each group (U.S.-born versus foreign-born Mexicans), as shown in table 9.4. In model I, we present the association between the basic sociodemographic characteristics and home ownership. For U.S.-born Mexicans, the data show that age is positively associated with home ownership and that marriage increases the likelihood of owning a home by 2.37 times. In model II, we add the measures of SES and English proficiency and find that income is the main predictor of home ownership. Specifically, middle-class income increases the odds of home ownership. More striking, the data show that if one lives in a household income of $75,000 or more, the prospects for home ownership are significantly higher (12.26 times more likely).

Model I, for the foreign-born Mexicans, highlights some similarities between the two groups of Mexicans. For example for both groups, age is

Table 9.4. Logistic Regressions (Odds Ratio) of Home ownership by Socioeconomic Status, Immigration and Controls for Mexican-Origin Individuals, by Nativity

	U.S. BORN		FOREIGN BORN	
	Model I	Model II	Model I	Model II
Sociodemographic Variables				
Age in years	1.97***	1.83***	1.57***	1.46**
Male	1.08	0.93	0.59*	0.50*
Married	2.81**	2.12*	2.22**	2.16*
Individuals under 18 yrs in the household	1.50	2.5	11.34	1.13
Measures of SES				
Bank Account		1.41		3.32***
Education in years		1.22		0.95
Blue Collar Occupation		0.68		0.97
Income: Less than $20K		1.8		1.55
Income: $20K to $39.9K		2.72*		4.62**
Income: $40K to $74.9K		16.10***		7.26***
Cultural Retention				
Time in U.S.: Less than 10y		N/A		1.38
Time in U.S.: 11y to 20y		N/A		1.47
Time in U.S.: 21y to 30y		N/A		1.58
Time in U.S.: 31y to 40y		N/A		1.43
English Proficient		0.70		2.13
Chi-Square Likelihood Ratio	49.12***	87.38***	39.26***	101.92***
df	4	11	4	15
N	423	423	636	636

+ $p < 0.10$, * $p < 0.05$, ** $p < 0.01$, *** $p < .000$

positively associated with home ownership, and married individuals are more likely to own a home. However, we find some notable differences in model II, where it is clear that having a bank account is a significant predictor of home ownership for foreign-born Mexicans. By comparison, access to a bank account is not a predictor of home ownership for U.S.-born Mexicans. This finding provides strong evidence that achieving the American dream, in this case owning a home, necessitates the interface between immigrants and financial institutions such as banks. The influence of household income cannot be minimized. Model II shows that a middle-class household income is also an important predictor for foreign-born immigrants to obtain a home. Finally, time "in country" is important; among immigrants, we find that those who have been in the United States five years or less are 65 percent less likely to own a home than those who have lived in the United States longer.

CONCLUSION

President George W. Bush, in his January 2005 inaugural address, coined the phrase "ownership society." Bush offered the following statement to reinforce the importance of home ownership in achieving the American dream:

> To give every American a stake in the promise and future of our country, we will bring the highest standards to our schools, and build an ownership society. We will widen the ownership of homes and businesses, retirement savings and health insurance preparing our people for the challenges of life in a free society (www.whitehouse.gov/inaugural).

Our study suggests that there are still some important changes necessary to narrow the gap between those who are owners and renters and that several factors affect the likelihood of attaining the "ownership society." While some progress has been made over time, we do observe continued disparities in home ownership, particularly for Latinos.

This chapter set out to answer two questions. First, are there differential rates of home-ownership patterns among Mexican ancestry populations in the United States (native born or foreign born)? Second, if there is a difference, what are the factors (bank account, education, occupation, annual household income, length of time in the United States, and language proficiency) that influence the likelihood of home ownership? With regard to the first question, our results suggest that there are differences in home ownership and that these patterns differ by nativity. While the descriptive analysis shows that in general Mexicans tend to be renters versus home owners, a more in-depth analysis by nativity shows that the native born are more likely to own homes than their foreign-born counterparts. This is an important contribution of this research since prior researchers focus minimally on ethnic heterogeneity within Mexican populations. Further, the multivariate analysis illustrates a more complex picture of salient factors that influence home ownership.

Two variables emerge as significant predictors of home ownership. Consistent with prior research (Alba and Logan 1993), we find that income is an important predictor of home ownership. For example, for both native-born and foreign-born Mexicans, a middle-class standing is paramount to home ownership (Lee et al. 2004), but a bank account is critical to home ownership for the foreign born. We suspect that, for immigrants, bank accounts suggest a tangible form of socialization to U.S. customs and values and a move away from a cash-only existence, a practice common among immigrants (Kochhar 2004; Lee et al. 2004).

In contrast to Alba and Logan (1992), who argue that English proficiency is a predictor of home ownership, we find that for Mexicans, regardless of immigration status, English proficiency is not associated with home ownership (Painter, Yang, and Yu 2003). Economic vitality to purchase a home trumps language deficiency.

We recognize that an "ownership society" has both tangible and intangible benefits but is not immune from negative consequences. On the positive side, home ownership has measurable outcomes, such as the appreciation of the home, the accumulation of wealth, and financial security. Home ownership can also provide individuals with privacy, adequate space, security, and an opportunity for community building. Often community building, for Latinos, means purchasing a home in areas where people look like them and where they have access to social networks and resources (Rogers and Henning 1999). Yet it is unclear whether these neighborhoods provide individuals a sense of security, a sense of stability and durability, and a sense of access to good public services (e.g., sanitation and waste management facilities, policing, fire services, recreational areas, and so on). If Latinos in general and Mexicans specifically live in areas where the basic infrastructure and environmental qualities are questionable, then these can have long-term implications for other aspects of their day-to-day existence, such as educational opportunity, ability to earn a livable wage, and physical and mental well-being (Bonnefoy et al. 2004).

Potential negative consequences of home ownership are illuminated by recent housing trends related to predatory lending practices. Socially, racially, and economically marginalized groups often do not understand the intricacies of financial institutions and are more likely to be at greater risk for predatory lending practices (U.S. Department of Housing and Urban Development 2000). For instance, subprime loans have recently been the subject of controversy since it is argued that these types of loans create a scenario whereby home owners are unable to make their mortgage payments as a result of adjustable interest rates, which in turn place many home owners at risk for foreclosure. In the long run, these lending practices may exacerbate the gap in home ownership by racial/ethnic, immigrant status, and SES. Achieving the "ownership society" becomes somewhat more complicated by these processes and practices, raising fundamental questions with regard to human rights.

Basic human rights call for a family's ability to own a home; they also include sound lending practices. Future investments in human and social capital (e.g., education and income) are necessary as suggested by our research findings. Yet, in order to reduce disparities and barriers to home ownership, it is equally salient to educate consumers about financial institutions and home loan standards so that those living within U.S. geopolitical borders are able to achieve *el sueño americano*.

NOTES

1. This research was performed while Dr. Rubio was at the American Sociological Association and prior to joining the National Institute of Mental Health. The opinions expressed in the chapter are those of the authors and do not necessarily represent those of the National Institute of Mental Health or National Institutes of Health or the National Science Foundation or the U.S. government.

2. We use "Latino" and "Hispanic" interchangeably. U.S. Census Bureau figures are based on the term "Hispanic," and we report these estimates accordingly.

REFERENCES

Alba, Richard, and John R. Logan. 1992. "Assimilation and Stratification in the Homeownership Patterns of Racial and Ethnic Groups." *International Migration Review* 26, no. 4: 1314–41.

———. 1993. "Minority Proximity to Whites in Suburbs: An Individual-Level Analysis of Segregation." *American Journal of Sociology* 98, no. 6: 1388–1427.

Alba, Richard, John Logan, Brian Stults, Gilbert Marzan, and Wenquan Zhang. 1999. "Immigrant Groups in the Suburbs: A Re-Examination of Suburbanization and Spatial Assimilation." *American Sociological Review* 64, no. 3 (June): 446–60.

Balakrishnan, T. R., and Zheng Wu. 1992. "Home Ownership Patterns and Ethnicity in Selected Canadian Cities." *Canadian Journal of Sociology* 17, no. 4 (autumn): 389–403.

Bendixen and Associates. 2004. "The Barriers to Banking and Building Credit History for Latin Americans: A Focus Group Study of Un-Banked Hispanics in Mobile, Alabama and Las Vegas, Nevada." Washington, D.C., June 16. www.bendixenandassociates.com/studies/Homeownership%20Alliance%20Presentation%202004.pdf.

Bonnefoy, Xavier R., Isabella Annesi-Maesano, Luis Moreno Aznar, Matthias Braubach, Ben Croxford, Maggie Davidson, Véronique Ezratty, Jérôme Fredouille, Marcela Gonzalez-Gross, Irene van Kamp, Christian Maschke, Mounir Mesbah, Brigitte Moissonnier, Kubanychbek Monolbaev, Richard Moore, Simon Nicol, Hildegard Niemann, Carita Nygren, David Ormandy, Nathalie Röbbel, and Peter Rudna. 2004. "Review of Evidence on Housing and Health." World Health Organization, Fourth Ministerial Conference on Environment and Health, Budapest, Hungary, June 23–25. www.euro.who.int/document/ HOH/ebackdoc01.pdf.

Borjas, George J. 1990. *Friends or Strangers: The Impact of Immigrants on the U.S. Economy.* New York: Basic Books.

Burgess, Ernest. 1925. "The Growth of the City: An Introduction to a Research Project." In *The City,* edited by R. E. Park, E. W. Burgess, and R. D. McKenzie. Chicago: University of Chicago Press.

Coulson, N. Edward. 1999. "Why Are Hispanics and Asian American Homeownership Rates So Low? Immigration and Other Factors." *Journal of Urban Economics* 45, no. 2: 209–27.

Gans, H. J. 1992. "Second Generation Decline: Scenarios for the Economic and Ethnic Futures of the Post-1965 American Immigrants." *Ethnic and Racial Studies* 15, no. 2: 173–92.

Gordon, Milton. 1964. *Assimilation in American Life: The Role of Race, Religion, and National Origins.* New York: Oxford University Press.

International Communications Research. 2002. *Kaiser/Pew 2002 Latino Survey.* Washington, D.C.: Kaiser Family Foundation/Pew Hispanic Center.

Jackman, Mary R., and Robert W. Jackman.1980. "Racial Inequalities in Home Ownership." *Social Forces* 58, no. 4 (June): 1221–34.

Jones-Correa, Michael. 2006. "Reshaping the American Dream: Immigrants and the Politics of the New Suburbs." In *The New Suburban History,* edited by Thomas Sugrue and Kevin Kruse. Chicago: University of Chicago Press.

Kochhar, Rakesh. 2004. *The Wealth of Hispanic Households: 1996–2002.* Washington, D.C.: Pew Hispanic Center.

Kotkin, Joel, Thomas Tseng, and Erika Ozuna. 2002. *Rewarding Ambition: Latinos, Housing and the Future of California.* La Jolla, Calif,: Pepperdine University, School of Public Policy, Davenport Institute, La Jolla Institute, and Cultural Access Group, Inc.

Krivo, Lauren. 1986. "Homeownership Differences between Hispanics and Anglos in the United States." *Social Problems* 33, no. 4 (April): 319–34.

Lee, Jongho, Louis Tornatzky, and Celina Torres. 2004. *El Sueno de Su Casa: The Homeownership Potential of Mexican-Heritage Families.* Los Angeles: Tomas Rivera Policy Institute.

Logan, John, Richard D. Alba, and Wenquan Zhang. 2002. "Immigrant Enclaves and Ethnic Communities in New York and Los Angeles." *American Sociological Review* 67, no. 2 (April): 299–322.

Massey, Douglas. 1985. "Ethnic Residential Segregation: A Theoretical Synthesis and Empirical Review." *Sociology and Social Research* 69: 315–50.

Massey, Douglas, and Nancy A. Denton. 1985. "Spatial Assimilation as a Socio-Economic Outcome." *American Sociological Review* 50 (February): 94–105.

Massey, Douglas, and Eric Fong. 1990. "Segregation and Neighborhood Quality: Blacks, Hispanics and Asians in the San Francisco Metropolitan Area." *Social Forces* 69, no. 1 (September): 15–32.

Painter, Gary, Stuart Gabriel, and Dowell Myers. 2000. *The Decision to Own: The Impact of Race, Ethnicity, and Immigrant Status.* Working paper no. 00-02. Washington, D.C.: Research Institute for Housing America. www.housingamerica.org/docs/RIHAwp00-02.pdf.

Painter, Gary, Lihong Yang, and Zhou Yu. 2003. "Why Are Chinese Homeownership Rates So High? Assimilation, Ethnic Concentration, and Nativity." Lusk Center for Real Estate, University of Southern California, Los Angeles. www.usc.edu/schools/sppd/lusk/research/pdf/wp_2003_1001.pdf.

Pitkin, John, Dowell Myers, Patrick A. Simmons, and Isaac F. Megbolugbe. 1997. *Immigration and Housing in the United States: Trends and Prospects.* Washington, D.C.: Fannie Mae Foundation.

Population Resource Center. 2002. www.prcdc.org. (accessed January 31, 2008)

Rogers, Andrei, and Sabine Henning. 1999. "The Internal Migration Patterns of Foreign-Born and Native Born Populations in the United States: 1975–80 and 1985–90." *International Migration Review* 33, no. 2 (summer): 403–29.

Rosenblaum, Emily. 1986. "Racial and Ethnic Differences in Home Ownership and Housing Quality, 1991." *Social Problems* 43, no. 4 (November): 403–26.

Saunders, P. 1990. *A Nation of Home Owners.* London: Unwin Hyman.

U.S. Census Bureau. 2002. *Housing and Household Economic Statistics Division, 2002.* Washington, D.C.: U.S. Census Bureau.

U.S. Department of Housing and Urban Development. 2000. "Unequal Burden: Income and Racial Disparities in Subprime Lending in America." Washington, D.C., April. www.huduser.org/publications/fairhsg/unequal.html.

Wachter, Susan M., and Isaac F. Megbolugbe. 1992. "Racial and Ethnic Disparities in Homeownership." *Housing Policy Debate* 3: 333–70.

10

No Phone, No Vehicle, No English, and No Citizenship: The Vulnerability of Mexican Immigrants in the United States

Karen M. Douglas and Rogelio Saenz

Immigrants have historically occupied the bottom rungs of American society. Indeed, they have toiled for low wages in jobs that are shunned by many Americans. Commonly isolated from the mainstream population and from the opportunity structure of American society, immigrants have also experienced significant discrimination and violation of their human rights. A particularly vulnerable segment of immigrants—Mexicans (the largest segment of immigrants)—are the focus of this chapter. In particular, we examine four hypotheses based on the relationship between the lack of basic human and related forms of capital (telephone, automobile, English fluency, and citizenship status) and labor market conditions (employment and hourly wages). Data from the 2000 5% Public Use Microdata Sample are used to conduct the analysis. The results provide support for the hypotheses. The results illustrate the costs that the most vulnerable segment of Mexican immigrants pays in the labor market for their lack of resources. These findings are placed within the context of the significant shifts that have occurred in employer–employee relations in which employers increasingly seek workers with few resources and connections.

In general, the past three decades have witnessed significant shifts in employer–employee relations in the United States with employers increasingly seeking workers with few resources and connections. The shifts in the patterns of the American economy are part of a larger globalization process that has also witnessed the increasing transfer of societal risks (health insurance, financial risk, and so on previously born in larger portions by both government and/or employers onto individuals, rendering everyone more vulnerable to risk although not proportionately so. Those who are the least socially advantaged are placed in more precarious situations because their marginality increases their risk for exploitation, discrimination, and abuse of human rights. Further, these shifts in the American economy—which in various sectors has witnessed both the outsourcing of jobs abroad and the replacement of native workers with immigrants—coincides with a steady erosion of basic human rights for U.S. citizens in general and further marginalizing the conditions (and rights) of noncitizens.

As detailed by Sjoberg, Gill, and Williams (2001), there are ongoing and long-standing debates regarding the nature of human rights, including one such divide between "ethicists" and "rights" orientations, the former emphasizing duties and the performance of duties in the acquisition of rights and the latter assuming basic human rights at the outset before the performance of duties (civic, social, and so on). For our purposes here, we accept Sjoberg et al.'s conceptualization of rights as something that humans possess simply because of their human status and their definition of human rights as "social claims made by individuals (or groups) upon organized power arrangements for purposes of enhancing human dignity" (42).

While there has been an erosion of human rights in general in the United States, the vulnerability and marginalization of Mexican immigrants have been exacerbated by the rabid xenophobia and anti-immigrant hysteria and Mexican bashing of the early part of the twenty-first century fomented by groups such as the Ku Klux Klan, the Minutemen, Friends of the Border Patrol, America in Danger, and Secured Borders U.S.A., to name a few. Mexican immigrants have historically occupied the bottom rungs of American society, where they have toiled for low wages in jobs that are shunned by many Americans. Because many lack basic resources that most U.S. citizens take for granted, they are at increased risk of exploitation, discrimination, and the violation of their human rights. Mexican immigrants who lack such basic resources are particularly vulnerable and isolated from the opportunity structures of American society.

This chapter examines the costs that Mexican immigrants who lack selected basic resources bear in the labor market. In particular, we examine the relationship between the lack of four basic resources (telephone, vehicle, English-language proficiency, and U.S. naturalization status) and employment status and hourly wages among Mexican immigrants. As expected, our results show that workers with the fewest human and other forms of capital investments fare the worst in the labor market.

We follow with a discussion about the vulnerabilities of Mexican immigrants to employer exploitation as a result of several transformations, including changes in the structure of existing immigration law that increased the desirability among U.S. employers for immigrant labor; the restructuring of the American workplace over the past several decades that has seen an increase in the use of private contractors, part-time employees, and somewhat stagnant wages (and, in some sectors, declining wages); and the resultant wholesale replacement of primarily domestic workers (and, in many cases, African American workers) with Latino immigrants. We end on an urgent note pointing to recent and alarming trends that have continued the erosion of human rights in general and the exploitation of the most vulnerable segments of society—with seemingly little public attention and much less public outcry.

COMMENTS FROM THE LITERATURE

Social scientists have compiled evidence showing the degree to which persons who make greater investments in the acquisition of human capital and related forms of capital (e.g., social capital and technology) reap more favorable labor market outcomes (see Becker 1993; Saenz 2000; Stolzenberg and Tienda 1997). For example, communication (e.g., telephone and access to the Internet and e-mail) and transportation technologies allow people to tap a variety of information and social networks that facilitate more favorable labor market outcomes. Access to the Internet has been shown to be useful to unemployed workers, especially those in rural areas (McQuaid, Lindsay, and Greig 2004).

In addition, research has demonstrated the importance of the availability of personal transformation for the attainment of more favorable labor market outcomes. For example, research has shown that African Americans have longer commutes to their places of employment compared to whites, with the automobile essential for linking African Americans to jobs in more distant suburban areas (Johnston-Anumonwo 2001). Similarly, immigrants tend to commute longer distances than do their native-born counterparts (Preston, McLafferty, and Liu 1998). Moreover, in their study of the employment patterns of former welfare recipients, Crew and Eyerman (2001) observe that a vehicle is important not only for securing employment but especially for keeping a job two years later. Longer commutes place workers, especially those with limited socioeconomic resources, at risk of low wages, costly job searches, and unemployment (Preston et al. 1998).

There is also a well-developed body of scholarship that shows the relationship between more traditional forms of human capital and labor market outcomes. Two forms of human capital that are especially relevant to immigrants include English fluency and naturalization status. Research has observed linkages between English proficiency and labor market outcomes (Enchautegui 1992). For instance, research demonstrates that immigrants with greater English fluency tend to be more successful in locating employment (Waldinger 1996). In addition, Davila and Mora (2001) found that

Latinos would have higher hourly wages if they had higher levels of English proficiency, all else being equal. Furthermore, Stolzenberg and Tienda (1997) discovered that penalties for the lack of English fluency among minority-group members are greater for those with low levels of education.

Research has also suggested that naturalization status has an impact on labor market outcomes. For example, Aguilera (2004) observes that citizenship status became a more important predictor of labor market wages after the passage of the Immigration Reform and Control Act (1986).

These more traditional social and cultural capital studies have been supplemented with a more recent literature that suggests that for a sizable sector of the labor force—that characterized by immigrant labor—social and cultural capital do little to advance their workplace experiences. In contrast with much of the social capital literature, which focuses on the positive outcomes of a person's social capital, Cranford (2005) argues for the need to "decouple the concepts of "social capital" and "social networks" (380). In particular, decentralized employment relations in which firms outsource (subcontract) many of their recruitment, training, and management functions have resulted in exploitative relations for immigrants regardless of whether their network ties are weak or strong. Further, as Cranford illustrates, social capital need not always result in better working conditions, negotiating position, or any positive aspects at all. "In some contexts immigrants may be piling up at the bottom rather than moving upward" (382).

On the basis of the literature, we develop four hypotheses linking the presence or absence of basic human and related forms of capital to labor market outcomes:

1. Mexican immigrants who lack a phone in their households are more likely to be unemployed and to have lower hourly wages than their peers who have a phone in their households.
2. Mexican immigrants who lack an automobile in their households are more likely to be unemployed and to have lower hourly wages than their counterparts who have an automobile in their households.
3. Mexican immigrants who lack English fluency are more likely to be unemployed and to have lower hourly wages than their peers who are fluent in English.
4. Mexican immigrants who are not naturalized citizens are more likely to be unemployed and to have lower hourly wages than their counterparts who are naturalized citizens.

METHODS

Data from the 2000 5% Public Use Microdata Sample (PUMS) are used to conduct the analysis. The PUMS represents an ideal data source on the demographic and socioeconomic patterns of specific racial and ethnic groups, including immigrants, because of its large sample size, approximately 14.1 million persons. The primary sample used in this analysis consists of foreign-born persons of Mexican origin. The first part of the analysis is based on 224,181 foreign-born Mexicans sixteen years of age and older who were part of the civilian labor force (i.e., they were either employed or unemployed but actively seeking employment in the civilian sector of the economy) at the time of the census in 2000. The second part of the analysis is based on 195,234 foreign-born Mexicans sixteen years of age and older who had earnings in 1999 and who worked at least 1,040 hours that year (i.e., roughly equivalent to full-time employment over half the year or half-time employment for the entire year) (see Saenz and Morales 2005). The restriction related to hours worked during the year ensures that the analysis is limited to workers who are significantly attached to the labor market.

Dependent Variables

The analysis includes two dependent variables: unemployment and the logged hourly wage. First, *unemployment* is a dichotomous variable with a value of 1 assigned to those persons who are unemployed and a value of 0 to those who hold a job. Second, the *logged hourly wage* represents the logged form of the hourly wage, which is computed by dividing the earnings of workers in 1999 by the estimated total number of hours that they worked during the year (i.e., hours usually worked in 1999 multiplied by the number of weeks worked in 1999). We log the hourly wage in order to minimize outliers at both (lower and higher) ends of the distribution of the hourly wage. The logged form of the variable allows us to interpret the regression coefficients as the percentage difference in hourly wages between different categories of the independent variables.

Independent Variables

The analysis includes four primary independent variables that we related to the two dependent variables. First, *lack of a telephone* is a dummy variable with a value of 1 assigned to persons who do not have a telephone in their households and a value of 0 to those with a telephone. Second, *lack of an automobile* is a dummy variable with a value of 1 assigned to people who do not have an automobile in their households and a value of 0 to those who have access to a vehicle in their households. Third, *lack of English fluency* is a dummy variable with a value of 1 assigned to individuals who do not speak English well and a value of 0 to those who speak English well. Fourth, *lack of citizenship* is a dummy variable with a value of 1 assigned to persons who are not naturalized citizens and a value of 0 to those who are naturalized citizens. In each of the four variables, the category of individuals with a value of 0 represents the reference group.

Control Variables

In order to more accurately assess the relationships between the independent and dependent variables, we introduce a series of control variables into the analysis because they tend to be related to each of the two sets of variables. The control variables for each of the two parts of the analysis (unemployment and hourly wages) include age, period of immigration to the United States, educational attainment level, marital status, disability status, metropolitan/nonmetropolitan residence, and region. The second part of the analysis (hourly wages) includes four additional control variables: occupation; self-employment status; "experience" measured as age minus years of education minus 6, which is a commonly used proxy for labor force experience; and "experience" squared. Finally, because the analysis is carried out separately for females, the presence and age of children is included as a control variable for the analysis involving females. Note that this information was collected only for females age sixteen years and older in the census.

Statistical Procedures and Analytical Plan

The first part of the analysis related to unemployment is conducted through the use of logistic regression because of the categorical nature of the unemployment variable. The second part of the analysis involving the logged hourly wages is carried out through the use of ordinary least squares multiple regression because of the interval-level form of the logged hourly wage. The analysis for each part of the analysis is carried out separately for males and females to determine the extent to which the relationships between the independent and dependent variables differ or are consistent across gender groups.

RESULTS

We begin the analysis with a descriptive overview of the bivariate relationship between the four independent variables (lack of a telephone, lack of an automobile, lack of English fluency, and lack of citizenship) and the two dependent variables (unemployment and hourly wages). Across gender groups, people who lack any one of the four basic human and related forms of capital are more likely to be unemployed and to have lower hourly wages compared to those who hold such resources (table 10.1). The differences across groups are especially noticeable with respect to unemployment

Table 10.1.   Unemployment Rates and Median Hourly Wages of Mexican Immigrants by the Availability of Selective Resources and Sex, 2000

Selected Resources and Availability	Unemployment Rate		Median Hourly Wage	
	Male	Female	Male	Female
No Telephone	8.3%	20.1%	$7.21	$6.41
Telephone	7.3%	13.2%	$9.13	$7.50
No automobile	9.7%	20.1%	$7.21	$7.50
Automobile	7.0%	12.6%	$9.23	$7.65
No English Fluency	7.9%	16.7%	$7.81	$6.67
English Fluency	6.8%	10.5%	$10.26	$8.61
No Citizenship	7.7%	15.4%	$8.33	$6.92
Citizenship	6.0%	8.8%	$11.60	$9.09
N	151,279	72,902	139,529	55,379

among females. Indeed, women who lack any of these resources are about one-half (no phone) to three-fourths (no citizenship) more likely to be unemployed compared to women who have a given resource. Among both males and females, the lack of access to an automobile and the lack of citizenship tend to be most detrimental to the securing of employment.

Among males, overall, those who lack any specific human or related form of capital have median hourly wages that are between 21 percent (no phone) and 27 percent (no citizenship) lower than those of their counterparts who have such endowments. Similar patterns exist for females with the earnings gap being between 15 percent (no phone) and 23 percent (no English or no citizenship).

We now turn our attention to the results from the multivariate analysis. The left-hand side of table 10.2 provides highlights based on odds ratios for the four independent variables drawn from the logistic regression analysis (the complete table showing the results including for the control variables is available from the authors). With only one exception, the hypotheses related to unemployment are supported. The only exception is for the lack of a telephone among males. In this case, lack of a telephone does not affect the odds of one's employment status. Men who lack the other three resources (automobile, English fluency, and citizenship) are significantly more likely to be unemployed. In particular, those who do not have an automobile in their households are 36 percent more likely to be unemployed, those who lack citizenship are 22 percent more likely to not have a job, and those who lack English fluency are 7 percent more likely to be jobless than their respective counterparts.

Table 10.2. Multivariate Results Examining the Relationship Between the Lack of Selected Resources and Unemployment and Logged Hourly Wages among Mexican Immigrants by Sex, 2000

COEFS	ODDS RATIOS		UNSTANDARDIZED REGRESSION	
Selected Resources	Unemployed		Logged Hourly Wage	
and Availability	Male	Female	Male	Female
No Telephone	1.071	1.351**	−0.085**	−0.065**
No Automobile	1.356**	1.490**	−0.089**	−0.056**
No English Fluency	1.070**	1.284**	−0.089**	−0.070**
No Citizenship	1.223**	1.317**	−0.098**	−0.066**

**Statistically significant at the 0.01 level.
NOTE: These results are based on the inclusion of the series of control variables described in the text.

All four resources are significantly related to the employment conditions of women. In this case, those who do not have a vehicle in the household are 49 percent more likely to be unemployed, those who do not have a telephone are 35 percent more likely to be jobless, those who are not citizens are 32 percent more likely to be unemployed, and those who do not speak English fluently are 28 percent more likely to be without a job. Overall, it appears that women are hurt more in finding employment if they lack the four human and related forms of capital than are men. This may reflect their less dense social networks compared to those of their immigrant male counterparts (Hagan 1994) as well as the greater limitations that gender roles place on women in securing employment (Boyd 1992).

We now examine the four hypotheses associated with the logged hourly wages. All four hypotheses are supported across gender groups (table 10.2, right-hand side). The effect of the lack of each of the four basic resources on the logged hourly wages is consistent with men who lack any of the four resources, having hourly wages that are about 9 percent lower than the wages of their counterparts who have a given resource. The relationships are also consistent across resources among women. In this case, women who lack any of the four resources have hourly wages that are about 6 percent lower than those of their counterparts who have a given resource.

Mexican Immigrant Jobs and Lack of Resources

Mexican immigrants are concentrated in jobs that tend to be designated as "Mexican immigrant jobs" and are characterized as low-wage, dead-end, and dangerous jobs where workers face tremendous levels of exploitation. It is these sectors of the economy, where Mexican immigrants are appealing to employers because of their low skills, desperate economic situation, and the presence of a large labor pool of coethnics (the reserved labor army), that can easily replace workers who demand higher wages and better working conditions. This is particularly the case among Mexican immigrants who lack the basic resources discussed previously.

Our data show that it is this specific segment of the Mexican immigrant workforce that is clustered in "Mexican immigrant jobs." We draw on the work of Waldinger (1996; see also Model 1993) to identify the occupations where Mexican immigrants are disproportionately represented relative to their presence in the overall workforce. Thus, we obtain two sex-specific percentages: 1) the percentage of workers in a given occupation who are Mexican immigrants (p_i) and 2) the percentage of all workers—regardless of occupation—who are Mexican immigrants (p_t). We then compute the ratio of the percentage of workers who are Mexican immigrants in a given industry to the percentage of all workers who are Mexican immigrants using the following formula for each sex:

$$\text{Ratio} = p_i / p_t$$

We then use two criteria to identify Mexican immigrant jobs: 1) the ratio is 1.5 or higher, and 2) there are a minimum number of workers in a given occupation (25,000 for males and 10,000 for females). This procedure results in twenty-five Mexican immigrant occupations among men and twenty-three Mexican immigrant occupations among women. More than half of all currently employed Mexican immigrant men (54.3 percent) and women (53.5 percent) worked in these occupations in 2000. Our analysis confirms that the occupations making up the "Mexican immigrant jobs" are typically those associated with Mexican immigrants, such as agriculture labor; meat, poultry, and seafood processing; construction; waiters/waitresses; cooks; maids and housekeeping cleaners; and janitors and building cleaners (see this chapter's appendix).

Workers, men and women alike, who lack any of the four basic resources examined here are concentrated in "Mexican immigrant jobs" (table 10.3). In particular, men and women are clustered in such jobs when they do not speak English or are not naturalized citizens. Moreover, there is a positive relationship between the number of basic resources lacked and the prevalence of workers employed in "Mexican immigrant jobs." Indeed, while nearly 70 percent of workers who lack all four basic resources are working in "Mexican immigrant jobs," far fewer of those who possess all four resources are toiling in such jobs (men, 33.6 percent; women, 31.8 percent).

Table 10.3. Percentage of Currently Employed Workers in Mexican Immigrant Jobs by the Availability of Selected Resources and Sex, 2000

Selected Resources and Availability	Percent Mexican Immigrant Jobs	
	Males	Females
No Telephone	65.4	60.9
Telephone	53.4	53.2
No Automobile	61.6	61.0
Automobile	53.2	52.5
No English Fluency	63.8	68.6
English Fluency	44.2	38.4
No Citizenship	58.1	58.2
Citizenship	40.4	41.7
Number of Resources Lacked:		
0	33.6	31.8
1	48.4	46.3
2	63.1	67.3
3	66.8	68.1
4	69.4	67.4
N	187,113	102,622

Further analyses document the vulnerable employment conditions of Mexican immigrants who lack any of the four basic resources and who make their livelihood in "Mexican immigrant jobs" (data available on request from the authors). For example, these workers tend to have the highest unemployment rates compared to three other groups of workers (lack of a given resource and working in a "Mexican immigrant job," presence of a given resource and working in a "Mexican immigrant job," and presence of a given resources and not working in a "Mexican immigrant job"). However, interestingly, the differences across the four groups of workers are relatively minor among Mexican immigrant men, as this segment of the population has relatively low unemployment rates (5.1 percent overall). Nonetheless, consistently, workers who lack any of the four basic resources and who are working in "Mexican immigrant jobs" have the lowest median hourly wages.

These supplementary analyses highlight the vulnerable position of workers who lack basic resources that are commonly taken for granted and who are isolated from societal opportunity structures. It is these workers who are increasingly appealing to employers in the new era of labor relations be-cause they can be easily manipulated, exploited, and disposed. We now pro-vide a discussion of the restructuring of the U.S. economy, the increasing use of workers such as those who lack the human and related resources noted previously, and the precarious position of such works, especially with respect to the violation of their basic human rights.

VULNERABILITY AND SHIFTING LABOR RELATIONS

That the U.S. economy has fundamentally restructured itself has been well documented by many scholars (Bernhardt et al. 2001; Danziger and Gottschalk 1993; Rubin 1995). For example, Rubin (1995), in her descrip-tion of the transformation of the American workplace, describes how the traditional relationship between employers and employees has fundamen-tally changed from one characterized by long-term contractual relations to more flexible arrangements coinciding with the increasing popularity of short-term, temporary employment arrangements. The 1970s saw a serious challenge to U.S. business hegemony as many domestic industries experi-enced increased international competition that resulted in an erosion of corporate profits and market share.

The domestic response was multipronged and included a reduction in employment levels; a lowering of wages and benefits; renegotiated and/or elimination of union contracts; increased use of nonunionized subcontrac-tors; employment of new technologies to reduce dependence on labor; re-location, when possible, of production overseas to take advantage of lower labor costs and/or, in the United States, to locales in the more business-friendly Sunbelt states; and availing themselves to tax incentives and abate-ments offered by localities seeking to attract industry to their areas. Further, as we document later, it is precisely workers who lack human and related resources (e.g., phone, vehicle, English, and citizenship) to whom employ-ers have turned to fill the positions for the relocated and restructured busi-nesses.

More recently, academic attention has focused on the relationship of this economic restructuring to the domestic labor force, race relations, and the increased demand and use by U.S. companies for immigrant (predomi-nantly Latino) labor. For example, Kandel and Parrado (2005) link eco-nomic restructuring of several industries to the increased presence of the Latino population in nonmetropolitan areas and to the so-called new des-tination areas. Economic restructuring further demarcated primary-sector employment (e.g., "good" jobs) from secondary-sector jobs, which they de-scribe as unstable, poorly paid, "dead-end" employment. For example, the deskilling and deunionization of the meat-processing industry has resulted in stagnant wages, high turnover rates, high injury rates, and a growing need and presence of foreign-born workers to fill these positions. According to Kandel and Parrado (2005), the transformation in the meat-processing industry was almost complete by the 1980s: "a formerly urban, unionized, and semiskilled workforce employed in production plants, supermarkets, and butcher shops in the 1950s was transformed into one with rural, mostly nonunion, and unskilled workers concentrated at the industrial processing end of the meat production chain by the end of the 1980s" (458).

According to Kandel (2006), the twenty-year period from 1980 to 2000 saw the transformation of the workforce of the meat-processing industry from white to brown. During the period, the white share of workers in this industry declined from 74 to 49 percent, while the Latino percentage increased from 9 to 29 percent. At the same time, the fraction of the foreign born among Latino meatpacking workers climbed from 50 percent in 1980 to 82 percent in 2000. As the complexion of workers darkened, overall wages declined. As Eric Schlosser (2005) points out, meatpacking paid upward of $18 per hour when it was unionized. Today, processing and packing plants are staffed by nonunion workers, primarily from Mexico and Guatemala, making approximately $6 an hour.

Like Kandel and Parrado (2005), Casanova and McDaniel (2005) document how the restructuring of the forest service industry in Alabama has reshaped the industry along the lines of a dual labor market, creating primary- and secondary-sector jobs. Core-sector unionized jobs have transferred to the periphery. Like the meat-processing industry, secondary-sector forest service jobs are characterized as seasonal, low paid, and dangerous (Casanova and McDaniel 2005; McDaniel and Casanova 2003). Similarly, the forestry service industry has experienced difficulty in recruiting native workers to these low-paying, dangerous, and dead-end jobs. Here too, the industry has turned to foreign labor, particularly temporary guest workers from Mexico and Central America, to meet their needs. Unlike for domestic workers where a job brings both income and status, temporary guest workers "have no interest in improving their status or standing in the host society, and the jobs offer potential for substantially more cash income than opportunities at home" (Casanova and McDaniel 2005, 53–54), making them ideal for the jobs.

As Casanova and McDaniel (2005) document, historically many of the jobs in the timber services industry, including those defined as secondary-sector jobs such as tree planting, herbicide application, and thinning, were performed by native male workers earning decent wages. Indeed, rather than engage in a race to the bottom in a no-win competition against each other in terms of the fees charged to industry for performance of these tasks, native laborers instead formed cooperatives. However, using tactics similar to those that companies employed in their importation of African American labor as scabs to break union strikes, industrial landowners recruited undocumented migrants to weaken the stronghold of these cooperatives. As a result of their success, forest management workers today earn less than they did doing the same work during the 1980s.

Despite heavy subsidization and recruiting of the timber service industry in Alabama, rural development has never materialized. Instead, according to Casanova and McDaniel (2005),

> "Timber dependency" has helped maintain racially based social inequities and segmented labor markets, inadequately funded public schools, and inequitable land concentrations that can be traced back to slave-based agriculture in the pre-Civil war era. The shift to guest workers to fill jobs previously performed by local workers represents a continued marginalization of local labor, and evidence that the linchpin of local economic activity is effectively divorced from the lives of people in rural Alabama. (51)

Similar themes are documented by David Griffith (2006). He reinforces the cases previously documented, including the displacement of domestic workers by foreign workers, illustrating this trend in three industrial sectors: blue crab processing and the replacement of African American female workers with Mexican female employees, North Carolina and Virginia tobacco and the erosion of African American labor with primarily Mexican laborers legalized under the SAW provision of the 1986 Immigration Reform and Control Act, and the New York apple-harvesting industry, which has similarly overseen the wholesale replacement of African American crews with Mexican crews.

Schlosser (2004) details some historical transformations to California's agricultural industry, concentrating heaviest on the strawberry industry. By now, the refrain should be familiar. Like the industries already described, California farmworkers (and farmworkers throughout the United States) have seen their real wages drop more than half since the 1980s. This drop in earnings has coincided with the increased use of sharecroppers (subcontractors who assume responsibility for hiring and overseeing workers to plant, tend, and harvest the crop) to minimize these costs for growers. According to Schlosser (2004), "By relying on poor migrants from Mexico, California growers established a wage structure that discouraged American citizens from seeking farmwork. The wages offered at harvest were too low to sustain a family in the United States" (95). He continues,

> Farm labor is more physically demanding and less financially rewarding than almost any other kind of work. A migrant who finds a job in a factory can triple his or her income. As a result, the whole system now depends upon a steady supply of illegal immigrants to keep farm wages low and to replace migrants who have either retired to Mexico or found better jobs in California. (96)

Cranford (2005) documents a similar story but for the janitorial industry in Los Angeles. Like the meat-processing, blue crab, tobacco, and timber industries, the janitorial industry has restructured itself 1) from a direct relationship between an employer and employee to indirect subcontracting relationships and 2) from union to nonunion workers. And, similar to several of the industries already described, displaced janitorial workers were largely African Americans, their replacements being almost exclusively Latino (Salvadorans, Guatemalans, and Mexicans). Deunionization has resulted in a decline in janitorial wages for both union and nonunion employees. For example, in the three-year period from 1983 to 1986, average hourly wages of janitors fell from $10 to $7 (Cranford 2005). Cranford also illustrates multiple ways in which Latino janitorial workers are exploited, including 1) violations of labor laws, 2) limited rights as a result of their undocumented status, and 3) a division of labor enforced by the worker's supervisor, often a family member or close friend.

Janitorial services, agricultural industry, seafood processing, and the timber industry are a few of the industries that have grown increasingly reliant on the use of subcontracts in many of its operations. Indeed, according to Cranford (2005), "Immigrant workers were recruited into this job because they were more easily exploited" (395).

As industries have transferred many of their jobs from the core to the periphery, charges of worker exploitation have begun to resound. For example, Hemmelgarn (2006) documents that in the recent past, the nation's largest meat producer and processor, Tyson Foods, has done the following:

- Been sued for violating child labor laws, smuggling illegal immigrants, worker injuries, and environmental abuses
- Pled guilty to twenty felony violations of the Clean Water Act for discharges from its poultry processing plant near Sedalia
- Had thirty-one of its facilities classified by the Occupational Safety and Health Administration in 2004 as workplaces with the highest injury and illness rates in the United States
- Been cited for five willful and twelve serious violations after an inspection at the company's facility in Texarkana, Arkansas, in which an employee died
- Been rated the eighth-worst polluter by the Political Economy Research Institute
- Provided many workers with far less than a living wage (www.columbia tribune.com/2006/Sep/20060906Life001.asp)

The literature cited here along with a recently published report by the Southern Poverty Law Center (2007) on the near slavelike conditions in which U.S. guest workers (a significant number of whom are Mexican) are employed paints a bleak cycle of entrapment, low wages, and little opportunity for advancement. This chapter only briefly touches on the still-growing volume of social science literature documenting these abuses. Yet employers, citing labor shortages despite high levels of unemployment in certain sectors, clamor for increased guest-worker quotas. It is these kinds of work conditions and abuses to basic human rights that workers lacking basic human and related resources (e.g., phone, vehicle, English, and citizenship) often encounter.

CONCLUSION

The restructuring of the U.S. economy has had significant consequences for American workers, both documented and undocumented. "The gilded age" is how *New York Times* editorialist Bob Herbert (2007) describes the wealth imbalance of the current era in the United States, also characterized by increasing rates of workers without health insurance or other company benefits, stagnant or declining wages, and rising poverty levels. The wealth and income inequalities have become so extreme as to challenge individual explanations of poverty and misfortune. However, an equally irrational explanation for the worsening plight of many American workers has emerged. Immigrants in general and Mexican immigrants more particularly are scapegoated as the cause for declining worker wages and job losses, again ignoring the governmental and corporate partnership that can be more directly implicated in the changing American workplace than can Mexican immigrants.

Mexicans represent the largest immigrant group in the United States today. Not unlike other Latino immigrants, Mexican immigrants often toil for low wages in jobs that many Americans, for a variety of reasons (including those delineated earlier), do not want. The consequences of the restructuring of selected industries in the American labor market (and confirmed by our own analysis presented here) show that those who lack basic resources are especially vulnerable to exploitation, discrimination, and the abuse of human rights. The vulnerability and exploitation that Latino workers face is reflected in a chilling statistic related to on-the-job deaths. A *USA Today* news report (Hopkins 2003) documented 6,800 Latino worker deaths (the largest segment of whom were Mexican immigrants) between 1992 and 2001—representing an increase in the workplace fatality rate of 15 percent—this during the same time period that also saw the workplace fatality rate decline by 15 percent for all other workers. The *USA Today* report explains these opposing trends as resulting from many Latino workers' lack of

English skills and the coercion to take any job regardless of bodily risk (www.usatoday.com/money/workplace/2003-03-12-hispanic-workers _x.htm)—precisely the kind of Mexican immigrant workers described in our empirical analysis in this chapter. The report continues,

> They died, in part, because they took some of the nation's most dangerous, thus hard-to-fill, jobs in construction and factories, government data show. They were often too scared of losing jobs to press for safer working conditions, advocates say. There weren't enough government inspectors to help ensure their safety, and lax penalties failed to discourage safety-law violators. Although lawmakers, regulators and prosecutors are stepping up efforts to reverse the trend, labor advocates worry it may take a major disaster—such as the 1911 Triangle Shirtwaist Factory fire that killed 146 immigrants, later spurring workplace reform—before real change is made.

And yet another shift in strategy by employers to seek out the cheapest sources of labor has emerged in the post-9/11 era. This era has seen a heightened border security and an increasing hostility toward Mexican immigrants. News reports document an increase in workplace raids by federal immigration officials, and communities are passing local ordinances (Farmers Branch and Friendswood, Texas, and Hazelton and Altoona, Pennsylvania, are just four examples that readily come to mind) intended to sniff out and deport undocumented immigrants. Courts have thus far ruled these measures unconstitutional, but they nevertheless reflect the hostile sentiment that many in the United States have toward Mexican immigrants. Facing acute labor shortages in this new environment, some employers are turning their gaze to even more vulnerable populations. For example, farmers in Colorado have begun to contract with the state for prisoners to work in agricultural fields. In true slavelike conditions, prisoners who work in this program will be paid sixty cents per day for their labor (Riccardi 2007). This is a trend that human rights advocates will need to contest and closely monitor.

Illustrated most dramatically by passage of the Personal Responsibility and Work Opportunity Reconciliation Act in 1996 (also known as welfare reform) is the fundamental shift in the United States away from basic human rights toward the notion that rights are engendered only through the performance of certain duties. For U.S. citizens, entitlement to welfare assistance is now tied to the performance of work-related activities. However, legal immigrants, working or not, are ineligible for federal assistance. With few safety nets, they are especially vulnerable to the vagaries of the labor market more broadly and to their employers more specifically. This shift away from entitlements is part of the shifting risk from employer to employee and away from government that has disproportionately impacted those whose rights were only negligibly recognized in the United States during the best of times.

Sjoberg et al. (2001) posit that in light of globalization and a general decline in the power of nation-states and a concomitant increase in the power of large-scale corporations and transnational organizations, a human rights perspective must be one that holds large-scale corporations accountable for human rights abuses. "Human rights principles cannot be advanced if we simply hold individuals accountable and leave intact powerful organizations that shape them," argue Sjoberg et al. (2001, 38), for individuals act as agents for organized power. In other words, holding one individual (or even two or three for that matter) responsible for the litany of human rights abuses uncovered at Tyson will do nothing to redress the corporate culture that allowed these types of abuses to flourish. Instead, Tyson and all other corporate entities have a moral obligation to respect the dignity and safety of *all* human beings—regardless of the human and related resources they possess—and not just to the protection of their bottom line. Only when human rights are more broadly conceptualized in this light can we begin to hope to right the serious wrongs wrought by the divorce of corporate accountability from the social and moral order that corporations mold and shape and on which they depend.

REFERENCES

Aguilera, Michael B. 2004. "The Effect of Legalization on the Labor Markets of Latin American Immigrants: A Gendered Comparison." *Sociological Focus* 37, no. 4: 351–71.

Becker, Gary S. 1993. *Human Capital: A Theoretical and Empirical Analysis, with Special Reference to Education.* 3rd ed. Chicago: University of Chicago Press.

Bernhardt, Annette D., Martina Morris, Mark S. Hancock, and Marc A. Scott. 2001. *Divergent Paths: Economic Mobility in the New American Labor Market.* New York: Russell Sage Foundation.

Boyd, Monica. 1992. "Gender, Visible Minority and Immigrant Earnings Inequality: Reassessing and Employment Equity Premise." In *Deconstructing a Nation: Immigration, Multiculturalism and Racism in 90's Canada,* edited by V. Satzewich. Toronto: Fernwood Press.

Casanova, Vanessa, and Josh McDaniel. 2005. "'No Sobra y No Falta': Recruitment Networks and Guest Workers in Southeastern U.S. Forest Industries." *Urban Anthropology and Studies of Cultural Systems and World Economic Development* 34, no. 1: 45–84.

Cranford, Cynthia J. 2005. "Networks of Exploitation: Immigrant Labor and the Restructuring of the Los Angeles Janitorial Industry." *Social Problems* 52, no. 3: 379–97.

Crew, Robert E., Jr., and Joe Eyerman. 2001. "Finding Employment and Staying Employed After Leaving Welfare." *Journal of Poverty* 5, no. 4: 67–91.

Danziger, Sheldon, and Peter Gottschalk. 1993. *Uneven Tides: Rising Inequality in America.* New York: Russell Sage Foundation.

Davila, Alberto, and Marie T. Mora. 2001. "Hispanic Ethnicity, English-Skill Investments, and Earnings." *Industrial Relations* 40, no. 1: 83–88.

Enchautegui, Maria E. 1992. "Geographic Differences in the Socioeconomic Status of Puerto Ricans: Human Capital Variations and Labor Market Characteristics." *International Migration Review* 26, no. 4: 1267–90.

Griffith, David. 2006. *American Guestworkers: Jamaicans and Mexicans in the U.S. Labor Market.* University Park: Pennsylvania State University Press.

Hagan, Jacqueline M. 1994. *Deciding to Be Legal.* Philadelphia: Temple University Press.

Hemmelgarn, Melinda. 2006. "Consider Companies' Labor Policies When Choosing Meats." *Columbia Daily Tribune,* September 6. Available at www.columbiatribune.com/2006/Sep/20060906Life001.asp.

Herbert, Bob. 2007. "American Cities and the Great Divide." *New York Times,* May 22.

Hopkins, Jim. 2003. "Fatality Rates Increase for Hispanic Workers." *USA Today,* March 13. Available at www.usatoday.com/money/workplace/2003-03-12-hispanic-workers_x.htm.

Johnston-Anumonwo, Ibipo. 2001. "Persistent Racial Differences in the Commutes of Kansas City Workers." *Journal of Black Studies* 31, no. 5: 651–70.

Kandel, William. 2006. "Meat-Processing Firms Attract Hispanic Workers to Rural America: Hispanics Increasingly Meet Labor Demand Arising from Industry Restructuring." In *Amber Waves,* U.S. Department of Agriculture, Washington, D.C., June. Available at www.ers.usda.gov/AmberWaves/June06/Features/MeatProcessing.htm.

Kandel, William, and Emilio A. Parrado. 2005. "Restructuring of the U.S. Meat Processing Industry and New Hispanic Migrant Destinations." *Population and Development Review* 31, no. 3: 447–71.

McDaniel, Josh M., and Vanessa Casanova. 2003. "Pines in Lines: Tree Planting, H-2B Guest Workers, and Rural Poverty in Alabama." *Southern Rural Sociology* 19, no. 1: 73–96.

McQuaid, Ronald W., Colin Lindsay, and Malcolm Greig. 2004. "'Reconnecting' the Unemployed: Information and Communication Technology and Services for Job Seekers in Rural Areas." *Information, Communication and Society* 7, no. 3: 364–88.

Model, Suzanne. 1993. "The Ethnic Niche and the Structure of Opportunity: Immigrants and Minorities in New York City." In *The Historical Origins of the Underclass,* edited by M. Katz. Princeton, N.J.: Princeton University Press.

Preston, Valerie, S. McLafferty, and X. F. Liu. 1998. "Geographical Barriers to Employment for American-Born and Immigrant Workers." *Urban Studies* 35, no. 3: 529–45.

Riccardi, Nicholas. 2007. "Going behind Bars for Laborers: After Colorado Passed Laws Targeting Illegal Immigrants, Field Hands Fled and Crops Rotted. Who Is Left to Work?" *Los Angeles Times,* March 1.

Rubin, Beth A. 1995. *Shifts in the Social Contract: Understanding Change in American Society.* Thousand Oaks, Calif.: Pine Forge Press.

Saenz, Rogelio. 2000. "Earning Patterns of Mexican Workers in the Southern Region: A Focus on Nonmetro/Metro Distinctions." *Southern Rural Sociology* 16, no. 1: 60–95.

Schlosser, Eric. 2004. *Reefer Madness: Sex, Drugs, and Cheap Labor in the American Black Market.* New York: Houghton Mifflin.

———. 2005. *Fast Food Nation: The Dark Side of the All-American Meal.* New York: HarperPerennial.

Sjoberg, Gideon, Elizabeth Gill, and Norma Williams. 2001. "A Sociology of Human Rights." *Social Problems* 48, no. 1: 11–47.

Southern Poverty Law Center. 2007. *Close to Slavery: Guestworker Programs in the United States.* Montgomery, Ala.: Southern Poverty Law Center.

Stolzenberg, Ross M., and Marta Tienda. 1997. "English Proficiency, Education, and the Conditional Economic Assimilation of Hispanic and Asian Origin Men." *Social Science Research* 26: 25–51.

Waldinger, Roger. 1996. *Still the Promised City? African-Americans and New Immigrants in Postindustrial New York.* Cambridge, Mass.: Harvard University Press.

APPENDIX: LIST OF OCCUPATIONS COMPRISING "MEXICAN IMMIGRANT JOBS" BY SEX

Men

Code	Occupation
402	Cooks
403	Food Preparation Workers
411	Waiters and Waitresses
413	Dining Room and Cafeteria Attendants, Bartender Helpers, and Miscellaneous Food Preparation and Serving-Related Workers
414	Dishwashers
422	Janitors and Building Cleaners
425	Grounds Miscellaneous Workers
605	Miscellaneous Agricultural Workers, including Animal Breeders
622	Brickmasons, Blockmasons, and Stonemasons
623	Carpenters
624	Carpet, Floor, and Tile Installers and Finishers
626	Construction Laborers
633	Drywall Installers, Ceiling Tile Installers, and Tapers
642	Painters, Construction, and Maintenance
651	Roofers
775	Miscellaneous Assemblers and Fabricators
781	Butchers and Other Meat, Poultry, and Fish Processing Workers
814	Welding, Soldering, and Brazing Workers
822	Other Metal Workers and Plastic Workers, including Milling, Planing, and Machine Tool Operators
832	Sewing Machine Operators
880	Packing and Filing Machine Operators and Tenders

896	Other Production Workers, including Semiconductor Processors and Cooling and Freezing Equipment Operators
960	Industrial Truck and Tractor Operators
961	Cleaners of Vehicles and Equipment
964	Hand Packers and Packagers

Women

Code	Occupation
402	Cooks
403	Food Preparation Workers
413	Dining Room and Cafeteria Attendants, Bartender Helpers, and Miscellaneous Food Preparation and Serving-Related Workers
422	Janitors and Building Cleaners
423	Maids and Housekeeping Cleaners
460	Chefs and Head Cooks
461	Personal and Home Care Aides
561	Shipping, Receiving, and Traffic Clerks
604	Agriculture Products Graders and Sorters
605	Miscellaneous Agricultural Workers, including Animal Breeders
770	First-Line Supervisors/Managers of Production and Operating Workers
772	Electrical, Electronics, and Electromechanical Assemblers
775	Miscellaneous Assemblers and Fabricators
781	Butchers and Other Meat, Poultry, and Fish Processing Workers
822	Other Metal Workers and Plastic Workers, including Milling, Planing, and Machine Tool Operators
830	Laundry and Dry-Cleaning Workers
831	Pressers, Textile, Garment and Related Materials
832	Sewing Machine Operators
874	Inspectors, Testers, Sorters, Samplers, and Weighters
880	Packing and Filing Machine Operators and Tenders
896	Other Production Workers, including Semiconductor Processors and Cooling and Freezing Equipment Operators
962	Hand Laborers and Freight, Stock and Material Movers
964	Hand Packers and Packagers

11

Border Sexual Conquest: A Framework for Gendered and Racial Sexual Violence

M. Cristina Morales and Cynthia Bejarano

Adriana, a young women laborer working six days a week in a foreign-owned maquiladora (export processing plant) making turn signals for the automobiles that you and I drive, risked being stalked and murdered by sexual predators (see Bowden 1996). One day, Adriana did not come home from work; she had been kidnapped, raped, and murdered. Her body was found at Chamizal Park, which links Ciudad Juárez, Mexico, and El Paso, Texas. This binational park on both sides of the Rio Grande represents globalized forces that shaped her work and to some degree even her death.

Since 1993, over 440 young women have been strangled, mutilated, dismembered, raped, stabbed, torched, disfigured, murdered, and disposed of in the desert of Ciudad Juárez. Not counted in those homicide estimates are the young women who are still missing in this same region. A report by the Special Commissioner to Eradicate and Prevent Violence against Women in Chihuahua reported that the statistics of missing women vary between 70 and 400, the Comisión Nacional de Derechos Humanos (Commission for National Human Rights) claims there are 4,587 reports of missing women, and La Fiscalia Mixta (Fiscal Mixed), a specially formed state and federal prosecution office assigned to investigate femicides, has recognized only forty cases (Comisión Para Prevenir y Eradicar la Violencia Contra Las Mujeres en Cuidad Juárez 2006). These inaccuracies in numbers reflect the decades-long impunity and cover-up of the hundreds of murders and disappearances by state authorities.

Esther Chávez Cano, one of the main activists of this cause, calls this struggle *feminicidio*, or femicide (Wright 2001). Diana E. H. Russell first coined the term *femicide*, and sociologist Julia Monárrez (2003) has expanded on this definition, asserting, "Femicide comprises a progression of violent acts that range from emotional, psychological, and verbal abuse through battery, torture, rape, prostitution, sexual assault, child abuse, female infanticide, genital mutilation, and domestic violence—as well as all policies that lead to the deaths of women, tolerated by the state" (3). The authors of a proposed book suggest that researchers and activists in Latin America prefer the term *feminicide* described by anthropologist Marcela Lagarde as the "politics of gender extermination." Fregoso and Bejarano argue that feminicide "stresses the intentional and *genocidal* character of gender-based violence and thus proposes remedies based on international human rights law."[1]

Too often, women's rights are dismissed as marginalized requests for recognition of human rights within UN and international treaties. Now recognized as a worldwide discourse, feminicides demand attention within the scope of international human rights treaties like the Convention on the Elimination of All Forms of Discrimination Against Women (CEDAW). "The [CEDAW] treaty calls for ratifying nations to overcome barriers of discrimination against women in the areas of legal rights, education, employment, health care, politics, and finance" (Rassekh Milani, Albert, and Purushotma 2004, 8). The disappearances and deaths of countless women, along with the mere thought of disappearance, bring a pause of concern as girls and women fear for their safety and security. Such occurrences also fit within the parameters of CEDAW and the UN treaty for human rights. The mantra of women's rights as human rights was, ironically, first demanded at the First World Conference on Women in Mexico City in 1975, and yet Mexico, along with the United States, continues to refuse enforcing CEDAW (in the case of Mexico) and of even ratifying CEDAW (in the case of the United States) (Rassekh Milani et al. 2004). The feminicides rhetoric has singularly been described as a women's rights issue; by failing to recognize women's rights as a human rights concern, women are further disempowered because their rights as humans are minimized and are viewed narrowly through their gender. Femicides fall within the rubric of human rights discourse as women are impacted by the infrastructures of politics, economy, and structural violence that draft the treaties that have most exploited them. Globalization and its accompanying arsenal of abusive and exploitive practitioners have assuaged the issue of violence against women and feminicides as an inconsequential necessity for advancement, modernization, and capitalism.

From a structural perspective, rather than asking who the perpetuators are of this sexual violence, it is perhaps more important to ask, How is sexual violence facilitated within these existing social, political, and economic conditions? Viewing the causes of sexual oppression from a structural perspective, one can see how sexual violence can be used as a weapon against a social group (see Jackson 1995; Scully and Marolla 1995) and how these victims are what Scully and Marolla (1995) refer to as a "collective liability" where women are seen as a class/category rather than individuals. Similarly, sexual violence can also be framed as sexual conquest used to collectively control women physically, psychologically, socially, and even economically.

Theoretical explanations for sexual violence against women have focused on the issues of masculinity, particularly male domination. For example, while referring to the sex industry, Brock and Thistlewaite (1987) identify hypermasculinity as an exaggerated form of masculinity that emphasizes dominance, control, and strength. This hypermasculinity then intimately links violence and sexuality. Similarly, Jackson (1995) explains that "sexual conquest becomes an acceptable way of validating masculinity, of demonstrating dominance of superiority over women" (19). In this sense, sexual violence is the result not of personal pathology but of the sexual scripts in our society. While a hypermasculinity framework would lead us to hypothesize that sexual violence in Juárez is a consequence of male dominance that links sexuality and power, it is critical to explain the structural context in which both men and women are disempowered. Specifically, in the process of globalization, women transferred their skills to the workplace, and men were redefined as nonworkers, lazy, and unreliable (Salzinger 1997).

In this chapter, we suggest an alternative framework to analyze the sexual victimization of women. We build on structural violence perspectives and elaborate on the political economic literature by incorporating the crucial role of regional context. We illustrate how the violence that women at the border are experiencing represents a form of corporate colonization that was supported by nation-states at the expense of women's lives. The political economy structurally and culturally transformed the border in a manner that has predisposed the region to one of border sexual conquest, exploitation, and the death of young women. Using Cuidad Juárez as an illustration, we devise the concept of border sexual conquest to establish how Western imperialism continues through the implementation of political economic treaties through which eroticized power is manifested as sexual conquest that resulted in feminicides and other forms of sexual violence at the Mexican–U.S. border.

THE FRONTIER AS GLOBAL ECONOMY: GENDER AND RACIAL INEQUALITY

The Mexico–U.S. border is situated at the frontier of the political global economy. People travel north to this border area in search of economic opportunities. It is along this Mexico–U.S. border that you find the "twin cities" of Ciudad Juárez, Mexico, and El Paso, Texas. As predicted by Wallerstein's world system theory, a series of unequal economic and political connections influence not only the flow of capital but also that of people. Juárez's multinational export-processing factories, or maquiladoras, offer a chance for employment in Mexico; conversely, El Paso represents a gateway to the United States. The lure of gaining employment in maquiladoras or of crossing to the north has consequently attracted tens of thousands of young women from southern Mexico and Central America (see Salzinger 2003).

The political economic agreements between Mexico and the United States have their strongest impact on the border region. Contemporary relationships began with the Emergency Farm Labor Program, also known as the Bracero Program (1942–1964). It established a temporary guest-worker program agreed on by the Mexican and U.S. governments to alleviate the labor shortages in the United States during World War II (see García y Griego 1996). When the program terminated, braceros were displaced and pushed out of the United States, creating social and economic turmoil for Mexico. Two hundred thousand braceros abruptly faced unemployment while simultaneously a growing number of workers continued to migrate to this region (Fernández-Kelly 1983). The resulting high unemployment rates in Mexico's northern border regions contributed to Mexico's industrialization (Cravey 1998).

This was the context for the birth of globalization in the border region. In 1965, the Border Industrial Program (BIP), known as the maquiladora program, was established, presumably to provide employment for those seasonal migrant laborers (almost all male) who had lost their livelihood when the Bracero Program terminated (Cravey 1998; Federación Internacional de los Derechos Humanos [FIDH] 2006; García y Griego 1996). These political-economic arrangements then continued under the guise of "free trade" with the North American Free Trade Agreement (NAFTA) in 1994. Through the 1980s and 1990s, the World Bank and International Monetary Fund encouraged further liberalization of Mexico that ultimately led to NAFTA, which initially influenced another "maquiladora boom" (FIDH 2006).

The maquiladoras, however, did not reduce unemployment because they did not employ members of the traditional workforce—*males* of working age. Similar to other free-trade zones around the world, maquiladoras had an image of export workers being young women from the Third World (see Cravey 1988; Fernández-Kelly 1983; Fuentes and Ehrenreich 1983; Salzinger 1997, 2003). It is widely known that transnational firms seek "docile" and "cheap" labor and rely on an extensive supply of young women for its profit (Wright 2001). There is little doubt that this form of production plays a crucial role in the latest phase of global capitalism (Sassen 1998). Even though there are more men and youth represented in this industry, it continues to be perceived as feminized labor (see FIDH 2006).

A question that arises is, What does the high number of unemployed men displaced by the global political economy (e.g., the termination of the Bracero Program and the implementation of BIP and NAFTA) in the border region have to do with sexual violence? A special prosecutor for crimes against women, a position created to investigate and prevent the murders of women in Juárez, speculates that the *perceived* economic empowerment of women, as the preferred laborers of the maquiladora industry, may have stirred up resentment from some of the unemployed men (see Kline and Reuters 1998). Therefore, economic development led to a devaluation of women's status.

Drawing some insights from Chasin's (1997) notion of the structural violence perspective, inequality can lead to interpersonal violence when the underprivileged react to their situation by engaging in street crime, or they may direct their anger at the unjust social order against scapegoats and more vulnerable members of society. As men questioned their role as heads of households and their unemployment rates increased, so did job competition; in addition, wages decreased, and working conditions worsened (Chasin 1997). These factors in turn lower the status of women and result in more rapes (Baron and Straus 1989; Chasin 1997).

Racialized Bodies and Globalization

These political-economic shifts not only reconfigure gender (see Beechey 1978; Fuentes and Ehrenreich 1983; Salzinger 2003; Tiano 1994; Wright 2001, 2003) but are based on racialized structures. It is well established that whiteness is socially constructed and varies situationally and historically. The search for "cheap" labor has led transnational corporations (TNCs) to developing countries populated mainly by nonwhites—"black," "brown," and "yellow"—inhabitants. Thus, on a global scale, the residents of Juárez are racially marked as "Third World," poor, and "nonwhite," and conquest is the next process in globalization with treaties as scripts on which women's value and labor is inscribed.

Global economic treaties are examples of the racial hierarchy that characterizes the global order and the presumptions of the underprivileged that go along with that. As Bhattacharyya, Gabriel, and Small (2002) argue, the power of whiteness in Western governments and TNCs on poor parts of the world comes through the capacity of governments and TNCs to impoverish, starve, contaminate, and murder all within the bounds of legality. This has led some to argue that the capitalists' world developments have reconfigured old patterns of ethnic relations (Bhat-tacharyya et al. 2002; Rodríguez 1995) and created new forms of racial privilege. Feminists of color and Third World or postcolonial feminists discuss the reconfiguration of multiple oppressions in the globalized context (Mohanty, Russo, and Torres 1991). Similarly, the devaluation of women's bodies is found in Kevin Bales's (1999) discussion of the plight of "disposable people" and the new slavery as a consequence of globalization, in which human labor has become plentiful and thus cheapened.

THE BORDER REGION AND CONTEXT OF SEXUAL VIOLENCE

While studies about the maquiladora industry have focused on the global division of labor and the economic importance of women's labor in the domestic and public spheres (see Fernández-Kelly 1983), limited attention has been brought to the possibility that these economic and political structures have increased the sexual victimization of women. Additionally, limited attention is given to the local context, particularly how the marginality of a region and not just race, class, and gender influence sexual violence. An exception is Vila (2000, 2003), who extends Brah's (1992) concept of "racialization of gender" to "regionalization of gender." We offer our concept of border sexual conquest as a starting point for building an alternative framework to explain sexual violence based not only on the marginality of being poor "Third" World women but also on being located on the marginality of region at the national level as a conquered nation and at the local level as the border region.

National Context of the Conquered Region

In these theoretical discussions about how global capitalists develop and reconfigure social inequality, it is also important to examine the regional context. Mexico's history is marked as a nation of conquered people. It is widely acknowledged that European colonization of Asia, Africa, and the Americas legitimized white superiority. The colonization literature describes how the domination of African and indigenous people by Europeans created racial hierarchies on skin color (Hunter 2002). As such, a system of colorism privileging whiteness over people of color prevails (see Bonilla-Silva et al. 2003; Bonilla-Silva and Glover 2004; Hunter 2002; Murguia and Saenz 2005; Murguia and Telles 1996).

At the center of the history of Mexico's colonization is the story of female treachery. According to the myth, Malintzín/la Malinche/la Chingada, Cortes's indigenous mistress, aided him in the conquest of her own people. Consequently, she has become the symbol of the rape of the indigenous people (Franco 1989) and is blamed for the "bastardization" of the indigenous people (Moraga 1986) and as the sellout to the white race (Moraga 1986). For instance, she is frequently referenced as La Chingada, or the "fucked one," symbolizing how she slept with the white man who conquered the indigenous people and thus executed cultural genocide (Moraga 1986). It is for this reason that when persons of Mexican descent are perceived to be transgressing boundaries that are against group interest, they are called *malinche* or *malinchista* (Alarcón 1983). Moreover, Norma Alarcón (1983) describes how the myth of Malintzín in aiding Cortes in the conquest has come to symbolize women's sexual weakness and openness to sexual exploitation. We believe that she is also portrayed as the woman who overstepped boundaries of sexual morality and is accused of using her sexuality to gain power. Regardless of either discourse, the female bodies are linked to national discourses about the role of "open female bodies" in Mexican history (see Vila 2003).

Conquest and the myth of the Malintzín are illustrations of eroticized forms of power used to control the inhabitants of the "brown" world, particularly women, through violence. Sexual violence has historically been used as a tool for imperialist expansion and is a powerful indicator of colonial control (see Bhattacharyya et al. 2002). The history of racism and imperialism illustrates how sexual conquest has permeated the cultures of European expansion—slavery and colonialism—as forms of eroticized power and scrutiny of bodies (Gill 1995; McClintock 1995). The history of these eroticized forms of power surfaces in today's globalized society in the form of sexualized violence.

Local Context of the Border as "Morally" Bankrupt

The historical context of the Mexico–U.S. border is one where U.S. citizens and others have engaged in vices for recreational use. Established through violence and colonization, the negative portrayal of the border is still marked by decades of illegal trade, vices, and the exploitation of the poor, especially women. It is constructed as a frontier where everything is "for sale" and little is sacred. Despite the wealth of two different cities, cultures, and people affirming their pride and heritage, little has stopped the appropriation of local economies and subjugated people. Many U.S. citizens have traditionally flocked to Mexico for prostitution, gambling, drug use, and underage drinking, even though the questions around people's morality typically scrutinize Mexicans rather than those seeking to engage in vices.

Northern Mexico has been described as a morally bankrupt region, a script used to justify the involvement of U.S. citizens in illegal or semilegal activity, according to Kirk Bowman (1994), who asserts, "It would be incorrect to assume that Mexican authorities are a morally-bankrupt homogenous group of sin-sellers who have always encouraged the sex and liquor business on the border" (56). Instead, he encourages the critical discussion of the clientele coming from the north and their perceptions of what is available and "for sale" to them. "Swelling populations of mobile university students augmented the client base [for prostitution]. Fraternity boys, military men, and the general population of the exploding U.S. border population frequented the adult playpens from Tijuana to Matamoros" (57).

The arguments we make about sexual border conquest and exploits are evident in these examples whether through the maquiladoras' highly sexualized work environment and exploitation of workers or the script of the Mexican woman as *malinche*, the whore, whose "open body" is sexualized to service the representative "colonizing" body of the U.S. citizen. In his book, Tom Miller (1985) describes the disturbing account of one man's depiction of Mexico:

> Something falls off of you when you cross the border into Mexico. You may be a faithfully married, church-going man in the United States but over here you can grope and paw and make a fool of yourself and no one says a word about it. If you want a temporary liaison, your whore takes you by the arm and parades you to the bar where you pay twenty-three dollars—twenty for the sex and three for a bed. . . . Indeed, the biggest attraction at the red-light district is not sexual at all. It is psychological. No man is ever rejected in Boys Town. (cited in Bowman 1994, 58)

Ultimately, border sexual conquest represents the expansion of contemporary imperialism through the routinization of sexual violence in everyday activity. Sexual border conquest has a well-established history that has been documented for a century, long before globalization set its tentacles at the Mexico–U.S. border. "Much of the problem with the discourse of globalism stems from its portrayal of sexual violence as primarily an effect of global capitalism without accounting for the ways in which global manifestations of power differ and also intensify earlier and more traditional forms of patriarchy within the nation-state" (Fregoso 2006, 132). In fact, globalization practices found at the Mexico–U.S. border were perpetuated by its wealthiest inhabitants and neocolonizers to continue the pattern of exploitation long practiced toward poor "brown" communities. Their complete disregard for the area illustrates the morally and culturally bankrupt script through corporate control over a transitional and desperate people, where little investment is made aside from the local context of globalization and multinational corporations.

BORDER SEXUAL CONQUEST

The experiences of colonization continue to resonate among the inhabitants of the border. We argue that at the Mexico–U.S. border, political economic policies (e.g., termination of the Bracero Program, BIP, and NAFTA) have reconfigured racial and gender privilege by intensifying neocolonial influences on this region. The color-caste system created in the quest of European expansion to maintain racial power (see Almaguer 1994) continues today through the global political economy. Racialization at the global level occurs when TNCs move their operations to this "nonwhite" "brown" region in search of "cheap" labor. Transnational corporations (about 320), mostly from the United States and Canada, are in Juárez exploiting their border residents by paying low wages and establishing control over trade unions (see FIDH 2006). Indeed, in Juárez, the average pay for a maquiladora worker is approximately U.S.$6 per day, or about U.S.$30 per week (FIDH 2006). This is not near a livable wage when considering that the average costs to feed a family of four is U.S.$50 per week (see FIDH 2006). As such, rather than reconfiguring old patterns of white and male privilege, TNCs exemplify contemporary imperialism with the exploitation of residents of this "brown" developing nation.

This border region has undergone several waves of globalization that intensified the racialized and sexualized violence that surfaces in Juárez as forms of sexual conquest. In Juárez, the elevated homicide rates were first documented in 1993 after the implementation of BIP or the maquiladora program and a year before NAFTA. However, women were not the only victims. Martinez Canizales and Howard (2006) find that as homicide rates skyrocketed, the male rates are almost sixteen times higher than female rates.

While the male homicides should not be easily dismissed, the violence associated with the female deaths is gendered because of the sexualized manner of the women's deaths (i.e., raped and/or dismembered feminine body parts). Western imperialism then continues to shape forms of sexual domination that have been historically woven into the social fabric of the border. Rape as a marker of conquest continues in the present day for the women of Juárez through both actual rapes and the threat of rape. Although not all the murder victims were raped, the manner in which the bodies are disposed of signals the sexualization of their bodies. Most of the bodies are found nude or seminude (see Washington Valdez 2005), and it is not uncommon to see illustrations of the female victim's legs, breasts, short skirts, and tight blouses (Salzinger 1997; Wright 1999, 2001). As such, the racial sexual violence against women in Juárez is exacerbated by the global economy that influenced the neocolonization of TNCs and resurrected the history of sexual conquest.

The violence is also gendered through its connection to the feminization of labor in the maquiladoras. When this pattern of feminicide began to be noticed, some of the victims were just en route to and from their work at mostly American-owned maquiladoras. In recent years, Monárrez, a professor at the

Colegio de la Frontera Norte, conducted an academic investigation that revealed that about one-fifth of the Juárez victims had worked in a maquiladora (Washington Valdez 2005). Fregoso (2006) further elaborates, "Rather than targeting 'actual' *maquiladora* workers, it is much more accurate to say that the mysoginist [*sic*]and racist killers are targeting members of the urban reserve of wage labor of the *maquiladora* industry, namely a pool of female workers migrating from Southern Mexico and Central America and living in the poor surrounding colonias of Juárez" (132). However, when AMAC (Asociación de Maquiladoras, A.C.), a trade organization representing American factories in Juárez, responded to the murders of women in an interview conducted for the news broadcast *20/20*, the AMAC representatives argued that they could not restrict the working hours of their female employees (presumably so that women would not have to travel to and from work in the late hours of the night) without jeopardizing global competition—the reason their companies are there in the first place.

It is our belief that what contributes to the feminicides is the lack of accountability by the nation-states or TNCs. Consequently, this has placed all border women in danger since the impunity exhibited by these institutions created a climate of injustice. Indeed, according to Cynthia Morales, the program director at the Center Against Family Violence in El Paso, Texas, it is not uncommon for men to transport their female partners to Juárez with the intention of murdering them since they figure that no one is going to be accountable for their death.

Another indication of the sexual conquest is one of the "popular" theories about the reasons women are being murdered: the theory suggests that the victims are leading double lives as prostitutes. Gaspar de Alba (2003) used the term "maqui-locas" to portray the perceptions of crazy and sexually provocative women working in maquiladoras. Indeed, when a young woman is reported missing, the mothers of the disappeared are frequently driven around the red-light district in search for the daughters, further perpetuating the perception or stereotype of this "double life."[2] A similar pattern of feminicides and discourses that victims were prostitutes is found in Chihuahua City, Mexico, where you can also find hundreds of maquiladoras. Many of these young women were students and/or employed in other types of business. The portrayal of the young women as whores in both cities is a public ridicule for the already distraught families of the victims (see Washington Valdez 2005; Wright 2001). Yet the validity of this theory is suspect given the fact that most of the women have disappeared in the middle of the day in downtown Juárez, one of the busiest parts of the city just fifteen minutes away from the international bridge dividing Juárez and El Paso (Washington Valdez 2005). Similarly, in Chihuahua, the young women are also disappearing in broad daylight, murdered, and never heard from again.

The ambiguous status of women in Juárez is well articulated by Esther Chavez Cano, an activist who passionately claims that the roots of feminicide lie in this contradictory view of women—when she goes to work, she is supporting her family; when she is killed, people claim that she is a prostitute not worth anything (Wright 2001). The image of the promiscuous woman is even expressed by the former president of the Maquiladora Association AMAC who critically asked if the women victims were last seen at their plants or at a bar (Wright 2001). Perhaps more damaging are perceptions that women who are perceived to be overstepping the boundaries of sexual morality are not entitled to justice.

This sexual conquest functions as a form of social reproduction in which gender, class, and racial oppression influence terror tactics by attempting to restore traditional gender relations by keeping women in the private sphere, outside of public spaces. This is even more serious when considering that most of the kidnappings have happened during the day, so it is not enough not to go out at night. Merely working, attaining an education, or just socializing with friends and relatives means taking the high risk of being raped and murdered.

Erasure of Memory: Activist Women Called *Malinches*

Juárez has been described as the "murder capital of the world for women and girls." With this reputation comes a backlash against women's rights groups and activist mothers by entrepreneurs in the city who claim that these groups have stigmatized the city with this emblematic frame of reference. Mexican activist women have also been portrayed in more recent years as liars or exaggerators who have embellished the exact number of murdered women in Juárez. Detractors have used arguments akin to the *malinche* critique claiming that activist women continue to proclaim the murders of women so as to draw attention to a city that is struggling to reclaim its dignity. Ironically, the same women working to end violence against "Other" women are embroiled in a struggle for self-preservation and dignity for all women at the northern Mexican border. Their acts of defiance and their struggle to preserve the memory of the murdered women are considered treacherous.

In a conceptual sense, like the women workers and murdered women of Juárez, activist women and mothers are depicted as *malinches* who betray the city's newfound image as a haven for tourism and modernity. Regardless of their activism, the "for sale" sign that globalization has latched itself onto shines as a beacon for border vices, TNCs, and industry to abuse, exploit, rape, and murder the women left in charge of lifting the city from poverty and its universally recognized mark as the "murder capital of the world." Even the local magazine *Industry*, published in El Paso, stated in an article titled "The Oasis Principle" that "this region [El Paso/Juárez] is far more complex than carelessly developed stories about drug trafficking or the excessive exposés about the murders in Juárez" (Sandoval 2006, 57). Although there are several unsolved cases of feminicide victims from Juárez, "local officials and business leaders have increasingly grumbled about the so-called 'myth' or 'black legend' of femicide that is allegedly giving Ciudad Juárez a bad name on the world stage" (Frontera NorteSur 2007). In effect, critics of these women, including local business leaders and local authorities, define women's activism as a form of female treachery to the city of Juárez.

These arguments have come full circle: not only are women exploited and killed, but they are now also blamed for their own violent victimization. The colonizer has again successfully colonized the "Other." The process of erasure in order to transform and resurrect the city, its image and reputation, and economy now lies on expunging the discourse of feminicides and the memories of these horrific deaths. Intimidation tactics and death threats have not swayed these women from their activism. In fact, the next strategy to be employed by the critics of these activists seems to be silencing the very icons that represent the murders.

Silencing of Bodies and Monuments

"Workers have started clearing a portion of the old cotton field where the tortured, raped and mutilated remains of 8 young women were discovered in November 2001. Located near the site of the new US Consulate in the border city, the cotton field is suddenly in the middle of a hot commercial zone" (Frontera NorteSur 2007). The historical memory of this crime scene turned public memorial with eight pink crosses representing the deaths of the eight women is now being prepared to make room for new hotels and other establishments. Since 2001, this space has represented social gatherings to mourn the murders of all women in Juárez. It has been transformed as an international and national space to mourn, plead, and protest. For years, families of the murdered women have requested that this field near a busy intersection—ironically, across from the Maquiladora Association—be transformed into a public memorial park to remember the murdered women. Apparently, the response they received was silence. As families discussed transforming this space into a memorial park, more concrete debris seemed to be placed around this homemade memorial.

According to Michel-Rolph Trouillot (1995), "Silences enter the process of historical production at four crucial moments: the moment of fact creation (the making of *sources*); the moment of fact assembly (the making of *archives*); the moment of fact retrieval (the making of *narratives*); and the moment of retrospective significance (the making of *history* in the final instance)" (26). Trouillot's basic model is a four-point process of creating memories and creating silences. His analysis offers a framework to understand what is being remembered and what is consciously erased. Memories are created by contemporary political contexts or situations, but in the case of Juárez, history is about what is happening in the present and what is intentionally being erased and replaced with images of modernity.

The erasure of memory of the feminicides is consciously done. "'One does not forget,' said Javier Camancho, the new owner of the cotton field property under development. 'It's sad what happened [the murders], but nothing is gained by the crosses, and one way of stopping this is by developing the border'" (Frontera NorteSur 2007). This new proprietor of a cotton field that is haunted with the deaths of eight women found in a ditch canal in 2001 points to economic development and its attendant neoliberal policies as a way to again lift the city from its preceding reputation. This is primarily the "historical production and refiguring of history and memory [which] is always a question of redefining for the middle class and the wealthy" (Leyva 2007). History is not just what is remembered but also what is consciously erased from memory, and those who seemingly engage in erasure are those with the most power and wealth who desecrate the created sacred space of historical and public memory.

Women activists of the families of murdered women have lacked financial clout to purchase this land and establish a memorial to their daughters. By acquiring the space through their protests and constant vigils, they empowered the memory of their daughters and kept their memory and this human rights movement alive. What is registered as public memory involved an act of conscious choice by the families and activists to retain the memory of murder victims and to never forget the atrocities of the past done to the citizens of the state of Chihuahua. Regrettably, though, the histories of people deemed important are remembered, but those histories of people deemed as unimportant are erased. Attempts to obliterate their images are monumental. "The bigger the material mass, the more easily it entraps us: mass graves and pyramids bring history closer while they make us feel small. . . . We suspect that their concreteness hides secrets so deep that no revelation may fully dissipate their silences. We imagine the lives under the mortar, but how do we recognize the end of a bottomless silence?" (Trouillot 1995, 30). Public spaces have been rearticulated and defined to remember, recognize, and commemorate poor, "brown," and "otherized" women, yet these spaces are intentionally removed disrespectfully in a poorly constructed strategy to create the imagery of a safe, modern, metropolitan city.

The memory of the hundreds of murdered women remains alive and well. What the city of Juárez and its entrepreneurs do not understand is that retaining the memory of the feminicide victims would demonstrate to the world that Juárez commemorates its dead and reserves a space to mourn the most precious of their city. On February 23, 2007, the seminude body of a woman was found on an empty lot near the Juárez airport south of the city (Frontera NorteSur 2007). Local media sources on both sides of the Mexico–U.S. border now fail to mention in any seriousness the feminicides still plaguing the city. The violent legacy and varied manifestations of border sexual conquests through exploitation of work or through the brutality of torture and violent killings cannot be erased from the international collective memory or those loved ones who remain to protest and tell the story.

CONCLUSIONS

Cuidad Juárez is located at the Mexico–U.S. border in a region historically marginalized at multiple levels—local, national, and even global. This region has undergone two waves of globalization due to political economic arrangements between Mexico and the United States. The women of Juárez have been the model export workers responsible for the development of the nation. They have experienced wage and sexual exploitation in maquiladoras and have been subjected to threats of sexual violence and sexual violence itself. Ultimately, they have also been silenced. Similar to Pateman's (1988) *Sexual Contract,* nation-states presented the treaties as a story of social and economic freedom, yet the contract is a sexual contract with a story of subjection in that it establishes access to women's bodies (i.e., sexual violence) and men's political right over women (i.e., as preferred laborers and victims of sexual violence).

Women have been treated in an inferior manner in civil society, and now it is compounded by neoliberal policies and globalized trade. Ultimately, women's rights are trampled on and consequently threatened, violated, and often killed. Previous UN treaties must maintain their enforcement on violence against women, and new treaties must reinforce women's rights as human rights with significant ramifications for nation-states that do not enforce those treaties or conventions.

Expanding the literature on structural violence, sexual violence, and the political economy, we propose that the violence in Juárez is an illustration of border sexual conquest. The manner in which TNCs search for an exploitable labor force in the "brown" developing world is an illustration of contemporary forms of Western imperialism. The estimated 440 women murdered and the possible thousands who have disappeared are contemporary forms of sexual conquest that surfaced within the context of globalization. Subsequently, border sexual conquest has become the new version of Pateman's *Sexual Contract* with what Vila (2003) argues as "women's open bodies" serving as the path for exploitation, subjugation, and, finally, murder and the silencing of women and memory.

NOTES

1. This work is from a proposed book project by Fregoso and Bejarano tentatively titled *Gender Terrorism in the Americas*.
2. Several of the victims' mothers in Juárez and Chihuahua have mentioned this to Cynthia Bejarano and Cynthia Morales.

REFERENCES

Alarcón, Norma. 1983. "Chicana's Feminist Literature: A Re-Vision through Malintzín/ or Malintzín: Putting Flesh Back on the Object." In *This Bridge Called My Back: Writings by Radical Women of Color*, edited by Cherríe Moraga and Gloria Anzaldúa. New York: Kitchen Table: Women of Color Press.

Almaguer, Tomas. 1994. *Racial Fault Lines: The Historical Origins of White Supremacy in California*. Berkeley: University of California Press.

Bales, Kevin. 1999. *Disposable People: New Slavery in the Global Economy*. Berkeley: University of California Press.

Baron, Larry, and Murray A. Straus. 1989. *Four Theories of Rape in American Society: A State-Level Analysis*. New Haven, Conn.: Yale University Press.

Beechey, Veronica. 1978. "Women and Production: A Critical Analysis of Some Sociological Theories of Women's Work." In *Feminism and Materialism*, edited by Annette Kuhn and AnnMarie Wolpe. Boston: Routledge & Kegan Paul.

Bhattacharyya, Gargi, John Gabriel, and Stephen Small. 2002. *Race and Power: Global Racism in the Twenty-First Century*. London: Routledge.

Bonilla-Silva, E., T. A. Forman, A. E. Lewis, and D. G. Embrick. 2003. "'It Wasn't Me!': How Will Race and Racism Work in 21st Century America?" *Political Sociology* 12: 111–34.

Bonilla-Silva, Eduardo, and Karen Glover. 2004. "'We Are All Americans': The Latin Americanization of Race Relations in the USA." In *The Changing Terrain of Race and Ethnicity: Theory, Methods and Public Policy*, edited by Amanda E. Lewis and Maria Krysan. New York: Russell Sage Foundation.

Bowden, Charles. 1996. "While You Were Sleeping." *Harper's Magazine*, December. dieoff.org/page77.htm (accessed February 18, 2007).

Bowman, Kirk S. 1994. "The Border as Locator and Innovator of Vice." *Journal of Borderlands Studies* 9, no. 1: 51–67.

Brah, Avtar. 1992. "Difference, Diversity, and Differentiation." In *Race, Culture, and Difference*, edited by James Donald and Ali Rattansi. London: Sage.

Brock, Rita Nakashima, and Susan B. Thistlewaite. 1987. *Casting Stones: Prostitution and Liberation in Asia and the United States*. Minneapolis: Augsburg Fortress.

Chasin, Barbara H. 1997. *Inequality and Violence in the United States: Casualties of Capitalism*. Atlantic Heights, N.J.: Humanities Press International.

Comisión Para Prevenir y Eradicar la Violencia Contra Las Mujeres en Cuidad Juárez. 2006. *Tercer Informe de Gestión*. Secretaría Gobernación.

Cravey, Altha. 1998. *Women and Work in Mexico's Maquiladoras*. Lanham, Md.: Rowman & Littlefield.

Federación Internacional de los Derechos Humanos. 2006. "Mexico: The North American Free Trade Agreement (NAFTA) Violations of Labour Rights." *Report: International Fact-Finding Mission* 448: 2.

Fernández-Kelly, Maria Patricia. 1983. *For We Are Sold, I and My People: Women and Industry in Mexico's Frontier*. Albany: State University of New York Press.

Franco, Jean. 1989. *Plotting Women: Gender and Representation in Mexico*. New York: Columbia University Press.

Fregoso, Rosalinda. 2006. "The Complexities of 'Feminicide' on the Border." In *Color of Violence: The INCITE! Anthology*. Cambridge, Mass.: South End Press.

Frontera NorteSur. 2007. "Bulldozing the Memories of Murdered Women." *Industry*, February 25. www.nmsu.edu/~frontera (accessed January 10, 2007).

Fuentes, Annette, and Barbara Ehrenreich. 1983. *Women in the Global Factory* (INC pamphlet). Boston: South End Press.

García y Griego, Manuel. 1996. "The Importation of Mexican Contract Laborers to the United States, 1942–1964." In *Between Two Worlds: Mexican Immigrants in the United States*, edited by David Gutiérrez. Wilmington, Del.: Jaguar Books on Latin America.

Gaspar de Alba, Alicia. 2003. "The Maquiladora Murders, Or, Who Is Killing the Women of Juarez, Mexico?" Latino Policy and Issues Brief No. 7. Los Angeles: UCLA Chicano Studies Research Center.

Gill, Anton. 1995. *Ruling Passions: Sex, Race, and Empire*. London: BBC Books.

Hunter, Margret L. 2002. "If You're Light You're Alright": Light Skin Color as Social Capital for Women of Color. *Gender and Society* 16: 175–93.

Jackson, Stevi. 1995. "The Social Context of Rape: Sexual Scripts and Motivation." In *Rape and Society*, edited by Patricia Searles and Ronald J. Berger. Boulder, Colo.: Westview Press.

Kline, Chris, and Reuters. 1998. "Murder Stalks the Women of Ciudad Juarez." CNN, May 8.

Leyva, Yolanda. 2007. "Monuments of Conformity: Commemorating and Protesting Onate on the Border." Public Lecture, Memory and Monuments: Commemorating and Confronting History on the U.S.-Mexico Border, University of Texas at El Paso, February 24.

Martinez Canizales, Georgina, and Cheryl Howard. 2006. "Mortalidad por Homicidio, una Revisión Comparativa en los Municipios de Tijuana y Ciudad Juárez, 1985–1997." In *Entre las Duras Aristas de las Armas: Violencia y Victimización en Ciudad Juárez*, edited by Patricia Ravelo Blancas y Héctor Domínguez Ruvalcaba. Mexico City: CIESAS.

McClintock, Anne. 1995. *Imperial Leather: Race, Gender and Sexuality in the Colonial Encounter*. London: Routledge.

Miller, Tom. 1985. *On the Border: Portraits of America's Southwestern Frontier*. Tucson: University of Arizona Press.

Mohanty, Chandra, Anna Russo, and Lourdes Torres. 1991. *Third World Women and the Politics of Feminism*. Bloomington: Indiana University Press.

Monárrez, Julia Fragoso. 2003. "Serial Sexual Femicide in Ciudad Juárez, 1993–2001." *Aztlan* 28, no. 2 (fall) 1–26.

Moraga, Cherríe. 1986. "From a Long Line of Vendidas: Chicanas and Feminism." In *Feminist Studies/Critical Studies*, edited by Teresa de Laureties. Bloomington: Indiana University Press.

Murguia, Edward, and Rogelio Saenz. 2005. "An Analysis of the Latin Americanization of Race in the United States: A Reconnaissance of Color Stratification among Mexicans." *Race and Society* 5: 85–101.

Murguia, Edward, and Edward E. Telles. 1996. "Phenotype and Schooling among Mexican Americans." *Sociology of Education* 69: 276–89.

Pateman, Carole. 1988. *The Sexual Contract*. Stanford, Calif.: Stanford University Press.

Rassekh Milani, Leila, Sarah C. Albert, and Karina Purushotma. 2004. *CEDAW, the Treaty for the Rights of Women: Rights That Benefit the Entire Community*. Washington, D.C.: Working Group on Ratification of the U.N. Convention on the Elimination of All Forms of Discrimination Against Women.

Rodríguez, Néstor P. 1995. "The Real 'New World Order': The Globalization of Racial and Ethnic Relations in the Late Twentieth Century." In *The Bubbling Cauldron: Race, Ethnicity, and the Urban Crisis*, edited by Michael Peter Smith and Joseph R. Feagin. Minneapolis: University of Minnesota Press.

Salzinger, Leslie. 1997. "From High Heels to Swathed Bodies: Gendered Meanings under Production in Mexico's Export-Processing Industry." *Feminist Studies* 23: 549–74.

———. 2003. "Re-Forming the 'Traditional Mexican Woman': Making Subjects in a Border Factory." In *Ethnography at the Border*, edited by Pablo Vila. Minneapolis: University of Minnesota Press.

Sandoval, Valentin. 2006. "The Oasis Principle: What Is It about El Paso's Social, Political, and Physical Landscape That Inspires Filmmakers to Make Movies?" *Industry*, August–September, 57.

Sassen, Saskia. 1998. *Globalization and its Discontents: Essays on the New Mobility of People and Money*. New York: New Press.

Scully, Diana, and Joseph Marolla. 1995. "'Riding the Bull at Gilley's': Convicted Rapists Describe the Rewards of Rape." In *Rape and Society*, edited by Patricia Searles and Ronald J. Berger. Boulder, Colo.: Westview Press.

Tiano, Susan. 1994. *Patriarchy on the Line: Labor, Gender, and Ideology in the Mexican Maquila Industry*. Philadelphia: Temple University Press.

Trouillot, Michel-Rolph. 1995. *Silencing the Past: Power and the Production of History*. Boston: Beacon Press.

Vila, Pablo. 2000. *Crossing Borders, Reinforcing Borders: Social Categories, Metaphors, and Narrative Identities on the U.S.-Mexico Frontier*. Austin: University of Texas Press.

———. 2003. "Gender and the Overlapping of Region, Nation, and Ethnicity on the U.S.-Mexico Border." In *Ethnography at the Border*, edited by Pablo Vila. Minneapolis: University of Minnesota Press.

Washington Valdez, Diana. 2005. *Cosecha de Mujeres: Safari en el Desierto Mexicano.* Mexico City: Océano.

Wright, Melissa. 1999. "The Dialectics of Still Life: Murder, Women, and the Maquiladoras." *Public Culture* 29: 453–73.

———. 2001. "A Manifesto against Femicide." *Antipode* 33: 550–66.

———. 2003. "The Politics of Relocation: Gender, Nationality, and Value in a Mexican Maquiladora." In *Ethnography at the Border*, edited by Pablo Vila. Minneapolis: University of Minnesota Press.

12

Israeli Fashion and Palestinian Labor during the Intifada

Mary Hovsepian

One of the first industries to meet the criteria of the circulation of capital is the apparel or garment industry. The concept, simply put, is to move the basic item, the commodity that is a good produced for exchange, through a process that ends up making money, or what Marx describes as the metamorphosis of the commodity into money (Marx 1981).

The garment industry was also one of the earliest industries to develop during the Industrial Revolution. The early industrialization of the garment industry was "natural" because for centuries prior to industrialization, sewing and garment work had been done on a piecemeal basis, mostly by farm women. Thus, the practice of producing garments by using women with little financial capital has been around for centuries (Williams 1944).

A brief history of the garment industry reveals two major players: the United States and Great Britain. From the 1700s to the present, these two countries have led the world in the production of cloth and completed garments. Both have employed similar strategies in order to be successful in this industry, namely, relying on former colonial relationships and the exploitation of vulnerable, mostly immigrant, women. The British needed to import cloth and did so from one of its colonies—India—and a former colony: the United States. The U.S. supply of cotton came primarily from the southern cotton-producing states such as Mississippi (a former slave state). In both Britain and the United States, the major garment production occurred in those countries' major cities, London and New York, respectively. In both of these cities, the labor power to produce the garments was drawn mainly from a population of poor, immigrant women (Chin 2005;

Louie 2001). For example, in New York City, the garment industry relies heavily on the exploitation of the newest wave of female immigrants; currently, the "sweatshops" are filled with Asian women and Latinas (Louie 2001).

With global expansion, the garment industry in the United States began to outsource parts of the production process to take advantage of cheaper labor markets in so-called Third World countries, namely, Mexico, China, and Singapore. What made this move so attractive to multinational corporations was the ability to exploit vulnerable women living in the Third World without having to bring them to live in the United States. Furthermore, because labor standards are significantly less rigorous in several of these Third World countries, multinational corporations are able to engage in labor practices that are even more exploitative and in more severe violation of human rights ranging from below-market wages to "sweatshop" conditions that demand too much output per hour, inhospitable working conditions, and no breaks to use the bathroom (Louie 2001). The case of the United States and Mexico not only is particularly interesting but, under different circumstances, would also provide for a full-blown comparison. Geographer Matt Rosenberg (2007) provides this description:

> Maquiladoras originated in Mexico in the 1960s along the U.S. border. In the early to mid-1990s, there were approximately 2,000 maquiladoras with 500,000 workers. In just a few years, the number of plants has almost doubled and the number of workers has more than doubled. Maquiladoras primarily produce electronic equipment, clothing, plastics, furniture, appliances, and auto parts and today eighty percent of the goods produced in Mexico are shipped to the United States. Maquiladoras are owned by U.S., Japanese, and European countries and some could be considered "sweatshops" composed of young women working for as little as 50 cents an hour, for up to ten hours a day, six days a week. However, in recent years, NAFTA [the North American Free Trade Agreement] has started to pay off somewhat—some maquiladoras are improving conditions for their workers, along with wages. Some skilled workers in garment maquiladoras are paid as much as $1–$2 an hour and work in modern, air-conditioned facilities. Unfortunately, the cost of living in border towns is often 30% higher than in southern Mexico and many of the maquiladora women (many of whom are single) are forced to live in shantytowns, surrounding the factory cities, that lack electricity and water. Maquiladoras are quite prevalent in Mexican cities such as Tijuana, Ciudad Juarez, and Matamoros that lie directly across the border from the interstate highway–connected U.S. cities of San Diego (California), El Paso (Texas), and Brownsville (Texas), respectively.

This chapter explores the labor practices and human rights violations in another former British colony: Palestine. Specifically, I examine the exploitative labor practices of Israel, a westernized, developed country that, like the United States and Britain before it, exploits another vulnerable population of "Third World women," those living in the occupied territories in Palestine. I demonstrate that just as is the case in the maquiladoras that the United States maintains in Mexico, the very circumstances of the Israeli garment industry in Palestine stand as a clear violation of human rights (Rosenberg 2007).

ISRAEL AND PALESTINE

As the border opened when Israel occupied the Palestinian territories of Gaza, the West Bank, and East Jerusalem, a subcontracting network of apparel assembly and homework expanded in the occupied territories influencing the opportunities available to Palestinian men and women. These new opportunities for work also imposed constraints. When a Palestinian mass-based uprising against the Israeli occupation began in 1987[1] calling for delinking from Israel and facing Israeli political repression, including Israeli control over Palestinian mobility to cross the border, instead of halting subcontracted assembly work, these practices proliferated and transformed ever more Palestinian homes in the occupied territories into assembly shop floors of the Israeli clothing industry (Hovsepian 2004).

Global subcontracting operations connecting the developed and the developing countries have been on the increase since the 1970s as part of the process of the restructuring of global capitalism (Bonacich and Applebaum 2000). The apparel industry has been at the forefront of the reorganization of global production, including the relocation of its labor-intensive production operations and deskilled tasks to the lower-wage regions of the world, tapping their female labor force (Bonacich et al. 1994; Fuentes and Ehrenreich 1983). Rarely, however, does the topic of global apparel production conjure the image of Palestinian laborers in the occupied territories let alone during periods of heightened and coordinated Palestinian resistance against the Israeli occupation, such as happened during the first uprising of December 1987.

Contributing factors to this oversight include the prevalent framing of the discussion on globalization in economic terms to the exclusion of the political or human rights framing and of the relationship between Israel and Palestine in political terms to the exclusion of the economic context. In addition, economic accounts of globalization give us the impression that capital flows across borderless states in search of cheap labor, ignoring how power and politics play a major part in reproducing the cheap labor so sought after by capitalists. In the occupied territories, Palestinian labor mobility and access to jobs are controlled by the context of occupation and resistance to it, albeit in a gendered fashion, and is not determined solely by an inherent economic logic (Hovsepian 2004). The companies' choice to outsource, offshore, or to keep production in the core is influenced by the availability of a labor force close at hand that can be forced to accept cheaper wages because of its vulnerable political status.

Using life and work history accounts of Palestinian workers and subcontractors,[2] I discuss how the increased uncertainty and limited mobility of labor during the uprising of 1987[3] resulted in the proliferation of apparel assembly work increasingly employing Palestinian male labor along with their female counterparts.

ON SUBCONTRACTING

Israeli fashion wear—usually women's fashion basics that have a longer shelf life than the high-end fashion wear—as well as jeans or denim pants are manufactured in the occupied territories' clothing workshops, while the Israeli firms, clustered in the garment district of Tel Aviv, retain control over the design, branding, and marketing of the commodities (Gereffi and Korzeniewicz 1994). The subcontracting arrangements between Israeli companies and Palestinian workshop owners in Gaza and the West Bank involve the provision of raw materials and pattern or precut pieces of fabric for assembly into a complete garment by Palestinian labor to be returned to Israel for sale in the domestic market or in the territories markets or to be exported to markets outside Israel.

The Israeli apparel firm represents what Collins (2003) refers to as a modified type of an apparel concern, one that orders clothing to be manufactured by others. Since the profits are realized in marketing, design, and retailing—typically activities that remain in core countries or core regions within countries, such as industrial districts in the core (and are thus core activities), and not in the manufacturing operation, which gets transferred into peripheral countries or peripheral regions within countries (and are thus peripheral activities) (Gereffi, Korzeniewicz, and Korzeniewicz 1994)—the cross-border production of garments ends up reflecting and reproducing the unequal power structure between Israelis and Palestinians.

Although some argue that fashion wear, unlike mass standardized production of basics such as T-shirts and jeans, requires flexible specialization in order for producers to respond just in time to changes in style and consumer demand and to be in proximity to markets (and thus logically they remain in the major cities of the core),[4] the fact remains that as long as the fashion garments are labor intensive, they will require cheap labor. For this reason, Gereffi (1994) argues, "it is the fashion oriented segment of the apparel commodity chain that is most actively involved in global sourcing"

(102). The choice to outsource, offshore, or to keep production in the core, as the subcontracted production across the Palestinian–Israeli border demonstrates, remains contingent on the availability of a labor force close at hand that can be forced to accept cheaper wages because of its vulnerable political status under occupation and is not determined solely by an inherent economic logic of short production runs that characterize fashion-sensitive clothing.

Gender, Work, and the Border

A devastated Palestinian economy in the wake of the 1967 war meant that Palestinians had to search for work inside Israel. Palestinians preferred to work in Israel rather than in the West Bank/Gaza Strip because the wages are relatively high in the former even if they are substantially below the average wage levels for Jewish workers. Although the gross earnings of Israeli workers are on average 17 percent higher than those of workers in the occupied territories (Samara 1992), the latter could expect to make up to 45 percent more in Israel than in the occupied territories (Semyonov and Lewin-Epstein 1987). The Israeli Central Bureau of Statistics estimated the number of the territories' workers in Israel at 108,000 in 1990, accounting for approximately 7 percent of the Israeli labor force (Heiberg and Ovensen 1993, 206, 218). When no permits are issued by Israel, the undocumented workers tend to constitute the majority, roughly two-thirds, of the territories' workers in Israel (Palestine Human Rights Information Center 1990).

Despite the Palestinian preference for work in Israel, gendered restrictions on mobility caused women to exercise restraint when it came to seeking work in Israel and pushed them to accept lower-paying jobs in the occupied territories. A sexual double standard applied to cross-border mobility and work in Israel. Men's work in Israel, while discouraged on nationalist grounds during periods of heightened nationalist mobilization, such as during the uprising of 1987, is generally tolerated and understood by society as a necessary evil in the absence of decent (well-paying) jobs in the West Bank/Gaza Strip. Women who worked in Israel since the 1970s, on the other hand, were not the recipients of such sympathy and continued to be labeled as "less respectable" and "immoral" (Moors 1989, 184; Warnock 1990, 126) and were actively prohibited and harassed on their way to work, especially during the uprising and its organized strike days (Hammami 1994).

Women, particularly from the villages, are sometimes prevented by the males in charge from working outside the home (Warnock 1990) since patriarchal norms deem it unacceptable for women, mostly poor women, to mingle with men to whom they are not related by blood. Women are under the direct control of their fathers, and once they are married, they are sub-jected to the control and authority of the husband; consequently, any other form of male dominance over women cannot exist at the same time for fear of diminishing or threatening male control within the family (Warnock 1990). It is a more serious taboo when the nonrelated men are from the group of occupiers who enjoy more power over both Palestinian men and women. In the context of political oppression (Warnock 1990), the repro-duction of the family as a symbol entails not only keeping women from the public sphere but also, more important, keeping them isolated and pro-tected from Israeli society (Rockwell 1985).

The Israeli firms managed to tap the segment of the territories' labor force that is limited in mobility and in job options and developed specific gen-dered constructions connected to being unmarried, young, poor, working class, and female from the rural areas and the refugee camps.

Although some women crossed the border to work in Israeli factories and agriculture, their presence is the hardest to estimate, especially since Israel discontinued categorizing the registered Palestinian workers by sex in 1974 (Hammami 1994; Samara 1992). The result was that a gendered organiza-tion of work was gradually shaped across the Palestinian–Israeli border with Palestinian male labor crossing the border to work in Israeli construc-tion and other blue-collar jobs in the service sector, such as in restaurants and hotels, and Palestinian women increasingly joining the clothing as-sembly workforce in the territories.

The clothing industry—based on subcontracting from Israeli firms—flourished under Israeli occupation. This sector has had a tremendous im-pact on Palestinian life, as it represented the largest sector, in terms of em-ployment, in the Gaza Strip and the second-largest sector in the West Bank.[5] Nonetheless, the available figures on official employment underestimate the actual number of workers in these workshops, overlooking the larger number of unlicensed workshops, ignoring the proliferation of informal workshops inside the territories' homes, and, most important, ignoring in-dustrial homework altogether.

In addition, the process of attaining a permit to establish any production firm in the territories always required the Israeli military governor's ap-proval (Samara 1992). Israel has allowed its commodities free access to the Palestinian territories but not the other way around and restricted most of what it imported from the territories to reexported Israeli goods, such as as-sembled apparel, and given preference in import–export licenses to Israelis. For example, Palestinian exports to Israel required a permit from the Israeli military governorate in the area in which the exporter resided, while the Is-raeli merchants market their commodities in the territories without the need for permission (Samara 1992).

The Palestinian Uprising and Work

Discussions of global restructuring have emphasized the role of female labor as new areas of paid work, albeit under difficult conditions, have opened up employment for women (Rai 2002). Women have been central to the new international division of labor and have always been the labor force of choice in the apparel industry. Since the uprising of 1987, Palestinian men have been taking over sewing assembly, and the territories' clothing assembly workers, especially in Gaza, stopped conforming to the stereotypical nimble-fingered image of the female global assembly workforce. The general exit permit that allowed Palestinians to cross the border to work in Israel ended, while the uprising demonstrations, other forms of resistance, and Israeli policies to crush the uprising, including curfews, prevented Palestinian labor from crossing the border to seek work in Israel and further limited job opportunities in the territories. Prior to the beginning of the uprising, 35 percent of the West Bank's labor force and 46 percent of the Gaza Strip's labor force were employed in Israel.[6]

Many of the Palestinian workshop owners in the West Bank argue that they were approached by men asking for work in assembly during the uprising. Some subcontractors obliged, while others refused because their workshops were located in close proximity to the home, and thus they deemed it unacceptable to admit male strangers to the house. Gaza subcontractors witnessed an increase in the number of men passing by their workshops to ask for work and a sudden disappearance of women from the assembly shop floor during the first year of the uprising. Nawal,[7] a Gaza City fashion wear subcontractor, recalls,

> In the past I used to take [women], the ones who go out to seek work, whose families started preventing them [from going to work]. From the beginning of the intifada, the number of girls working for me ceased completely, and now all I have is young men. I do not have girls.[8]

The imposition of the Islamic attire on women in Gaza is insufficient to explain why women left the workshops during the uprising and never came back. It is true that during the intifada years, the imposition of the *hijab*, or head cover, was enforced strictly on the women of Gaza by the Muslim brothers who came to call themselves "the Islamic Resistance Movements," or Hamas, in the spring of 1988, so that by December 1988 "it was almost impossible for the women to walk around in Gaza without wearing some form of head cover." (Hammami 1990, 27). Imposition of the *hijab* was also spreading in 1989 to the West Bank, and incidents of egg and stone throwing occurred even in East Jerusalem against women who did not comply (Hammami 1990).

Nonetheless, the uprising years witnessed an increase in single women quitting workshop work in large numbers because of family constraints on their mobility, concern for their safety in the streets, an increase in marrying off women at an early age because of school closures that demotivated parents to extend their daughters' adolescence until they had finished school (FAFO 1994; Hammami 1993), and extended workshop closures. In addition, young women usually quit workshop work in the event of marriage. Nawal, like other subcontractors in Gaza, remembers the period of the intifada and thereafter in workshops and recalls,

> I used to employ mostly women. I, as a woman running the workshop, I prefer women. . . . Their families used to say [before the uprising] "as long as it is with a woman let her go . . . if the factory does not have men let her go" . . . after the girls left [because of the closure of the workshop under extended curfews], I would go and ask her and they would tell me "No." He [the father] is afraid to have a girl go out. We in turn, were forced to allow men in.[9]

However, an ideology developed during the uprising years in the Gaza Strip that equated women's work in the subcontracting workshops with being collaborators for Israel and thus discouraged them from seeking work in workshops. According to the women's program officer of the Gaza City UNRWA Department of Social Services,

> During the intifada and the position of women in it . . . fearfulness came about because there was an association between the workshops having subcontracts with Israel and that the girls . . . rumors surfaced that they were collaborators, so out of fear for the girl's reputation they stopped working in these workshops, and the men worked in their place, especially the men who used to work inside Israel but stopped working there during the Intifada.[10]

The female labor force was thus replaced by a male labor force, mostly from the ranks of the youth. Labor mobility was further curtailed since the imposition of a permit policy strictly abided by since March 1993.[11] The subcontracting sector remained one of the few job options available in the Gaza Strip. I note that the labor market is also shaped by a system of age stratification whereby the territories have a young age structure: one of every two persons is under the age of fifteen years in the West Bank, and in Gaza the proportion is slightly higher (Palestinian Central Bureau of Statistics 1995).[12]

The boycott of Israeli work sites during the uprising was also more strictly imposed on women, causing many to quit their jobs in Israel and increasingly to quit working outside the home altogether (AbdelHadi 1992). This process caused a proliferation of industrial homework, and more women took on homework. For example, Um Samer from the Dheisheh camp in the West Bank[13] quit her work in an undergarment factory in Israel during the uprising. Yet, lacking financial resources, Um Samer (her husband has been unemployed since before the uprising) acted in a manner that has become increasingly common in the territories since 1967: she brought two sewing machines to the home and looked for Palestinian clothing workshops to give her work to assemble at home. According to her,

> We started to work with them [sewing workshops]. We said we couldn't continue to sit [without an income], for it seemed like it [the uprising] will not end. And this is a household with expenses and so on; this is not easy! So we contemplated: "what can we do?" We thought of buying two machines. We could not buy two machines with what we had, because we had already spent our money [during the early months of the uprising]. I used to spend [*sic*] there is no income at all. We made partnership with some people, I mean we entered, you can say, in a partnership . . . they brought the machines. People related to us—relatives.[14]

The uprising witnessed men working at home in assembly for Israeli firms as well. This was due primarily to the surrounding social conditions at the time, namely, curfews and strikes that limited male mobility. Israeli policies during the uprising included tax collection raids that were accompanied by the army, severe restrictions on marketing, control of labor entry into Israel, restrictions of movement in the territories, and curfews that ranged from a couple of hours to a number of days, in certain instances even a month (Palestine Human Rights Information Center 1993). The political situation often meant that workers could not reach the site of work, and workshop owners were afraid to open their workshops either because of strikes or because of curfews imposed by Israel. In response, workshop owners closed down the workshops and relocated the sewing machines into the workers' homes so that they could continue to work and overall production could persist. This was especially the case of workshops located in commercial nonresidential areas or those located in risky areas, such as in the vicinity of soldier outposts. In Nablus City in the West Bank, for example, one workshop was located in such a transparent location, and the owner had employed male labor in his workshop in addition to women. The subcontractor decided to shut down the workshop during the uprising. He laid off the women workers and gave the work out to the male workers to sew at home during the intifada because he was unable to open his shop as a result of the curfews and strikes:

> The first workshop was by the municipality playground. At one point the soldiers took over the playground and made it into a checkpoint. We had young men working for us, and every time they [demonstrators] burnt a tire in the street we had to clean it [soldiers ordered them to clean it]. And any time

anything happens [a political event, such as demonstrations, strikes, and so on] they [soldiers] would come and take it out on us. So we were forced to close down the workshop. And we gave each of the workers a sewing machine to work at home. I mean, a distribution operation. I mean, work went on but it was hard. I mean, instead of having everyone here with me, I started going around to their houses every day: I deliver to this one or take from that one, I mean the operation was hard but work was continued. . . . We used to bring the work home [bring the precut pieces from Israel to the subcontractor's home]. I would divide it into bundles of 50 pants, or 40 pants and then we deliver it to their homes. Of course, unless there was a curfew that is. Once they open (lift the curfew) we deliver and pick up from them.[15]

During the intifada, subcontracting for assembly not only was maintained but often increased. A Gaza clothing workshop owner new to assembly work for Israel explains why he transformed his workshop into an assembly workshop in 1987:

During the intifada, the situation got worse—the problems that occurred—so the work shrunk. There is no possibility for me to go out [of Gaza] and return—strikes, the "Ikhwan" [Muslim Brotherhood), and shooting, and what else—so I transferred my work into a producer for Israel, meaning working . . . and the situation is the same till now . . . and till now I work for Israel.[16]

Although Palestinian subcontractors could not cross the border to deliver the assembled apparel—unless they held an East Jerusalem identity card—many still managed to maintain their subcontracting arrangements with Israel. Saleem, a West Bank subcontractor for an Israeli export clothing firm holding a West Bank identity card, could not cross the border to deliver the assembled products into Israel because of the difficulty in getting an entry permit. Since Israeli managers started being afraid to enter the territories, Saleem, who had a long-standing relationship with the company, managed to pick up orders, deliver, and get paid at the border checkpoint. He recalls,

The intifada was a very difficult period because we could not get permits [to go to Israel and Jerusalem]. The Jews, who were dependent on our work, used to deliver it to the checkpoint [on the Jerusalem-to-Bethlehem road]. They come with their car bringing work, and receive the finished work. This was how we managed! We calculate the fees here, hand it to them there [at the checkpoint], and they bring us the money, also at the checkpoint. We did that for a long period![17]

The mobility of labor, commodities, and capital across the border is not free flowing but, rather, selective and has always been controlled by the party in power, in this case Israel. Because of the quotas that Israel imposes on imported goods from the territories, most of what Israel imports from the West Bank/Gaza Strip are "re-exported Israeli goods usually labor intensive textile, clothing, or leather goods that were originally imported on a subcontracted basis, and returned to Israel in finished form for sale, with most of the benefits accrued by Israel" (Benvenisti 1988, 11). To be sure, this process is similar to that which takes place in Mexico. (An explanation of the maquiladora process was given earlier in this chapter.)

Since 1993, under what has come to be referred to as the closure policy, Israel imposed stricter regulations on the mobility of labor and commodities, yet the restrictions on mobility under the closure policy exclude Israeli commodities, which have unimpeded access to the territories (Roy 1994). Ironically, the result was an expanded West Bank trade with Israel and Gaza trade with Israel but a decreased interregional trade between Gaza and the West Bank.[18]

CONCLUSION

> Two things are certain: the Jews of Israel will remain; the Palestinians will also remain. To say much more than that with assurance is a foolish trick. (Said 1980, 235)

This reality, so eloquently expressed by the late Edward Said, speaks to the contemporary reality of labor relations between Israel and Palestine.

For example, during one of the military incursions on August 2002 into the Palestinian territory, an Israeli soldier told the Israeli newspaper *Maariv* that the soldiers were shocked as they stumbled on large quantities of "illegal" clothing merchandise and designer clothes in the Palestinian cities. He said, "In all the houses on the street we saw boxes. We opened some of the boxes and found 'levis' and 'Crocker' jeans and lots of shirts from 'Castro' . . . we didn't do anything with them; it wasn't our job" (Berman 2002, 1). The newspaper report commented that the "illegal merchandise" is being distributed in Israel through a "sophisticated network of underworld connections" (Berman 2002, 1). These underground economies exist and will persist regardless of the type of crackdown or how often these crackdowns are released on Palestine labor. The intensity only strengthens the Palestine will to work. Why? Israeli capital is dependent on Palestinian labor, particularly the labor increasingly confined to the homes of the territories under the existing political conditions and ready to be tapped through subcontracting arrangements by Israeli merchants.

Since 1994, the Palestinian Authority became the largest employer of the male labor force in the Gaza Strip, reflecting the lack of other job opportunities in the private sector rather than the attractiveness of the Palestinian public sector positions since the salaries were inconsistent and low.[19] The subcontracting sector remains a better option under the prevailing conditions of

Israeli occupation. As the mobility of Palestinian labor into Israel is restrained by Palestinian patriarchal norms or the Israeli military occupation's directly imposed restrictions on the movement of individual Palestinians into Israel through curfews and border closures, labor market integration with Israel persists through the medium of subcontracting arrangements across the Israeli–Palestinian divide, tapping not only female labor but male labor as well.

As the data in this chapter clearly indicate, the structure of the Palestinian labor market allows Israel and Israeli firms to take advantage of a vulnerable population. This type of exploitation is similar to that which is prevalent in certain other regions, such as the U.S.–Mexico border, where U.S. companies, through the use of maquiladoras and NAFTA, engage in exploitation and violate the human rights of vulnerable, poor Mexican women. It is important to note that though the Palestinian–Israeli conflict shapes the situation there in ways that it does not along the U.S.–Mexico border, *both* situations persist because of power and stratification, based on class, race/ethnicity, nationality, and gender.

Finally, both situations are bolstered by the institutionalized power that resides in the governments of "First World" nation-states and that further facilitates the exploitation of labor and persistence of human rights violations in contiguous "Third World" countries. In order for economic reform to take place in either location, a critical analysis of individual power, institutional power, and national power, such as I have supplied here, will have to be conducted.

NOTES

1. On December 9, 1987, demonstrations and protests erupted in Gaza and spread throughout the occupied territories after an Israeli truck hit a Palestinian van in Gaza, killing four Palestinian workers. The date came to mark the beginning of an uprising against the Israeli occupation (McDowall 1994).

2. The data are from research fieldwork by the author conducted in the occupied territories between September 1995 and August 1996.

3. The right to move freely, apart from being as a basic human right an end in itself, facilitates access to jobs and influences work conditions. Controlling Palestinian mobility, including access to East Jerusalem and Israel, shaped work opportunities and influenced work conditions of the Palestinians in the territories and the organization of work in the West Bank/Gaza Strip.

4. In Britain, fashion wear is subcontracted to ethnic men in the inner city and employs ethnic women whose immigration status as "family" women who entered Britain to join their husbands restricts their work opportunities and predisposes them to accept work in subcontracting. See Phizaklea (1990, 2). For Los Angeles, see Bonacich and Applebaum (2000).

5. The Israel Central Bureau of Statistics (1993) did not provide any figures in terms of production by this sector.

6. Palestinian Central Bureau of Statistics (1995). See also Israel Central Bureau of Statistics (1993).

7. All the names are assigned by the author and thus are not the real names of those interviewed.

8. Interview, August 9, 1995.

9. Interview, Gaza City, August 8, 1995.

10. Phone interview (Gaza City, August 7, 1995) with Lillian Tarazi, UNRWA women's program officer during the uprising.

11. A permit policy was introduced in 1991 and has been more strictly applied since March 1993. See Diwan and Shaban (1999, 5). Israel closed off the territories and established permanent checkpoints on the border between the territories and Israel. To enforce the closure policy, the Israeli government established a permit system that required the Palestinians of the West Bank/Gaza Strip to obtain a permit (*tasrih*) to be allowed in Israel between 5:00 A.M. and 7:00 P.M. See Bornstein (2002, 2).

12. The 1993 labor force participation rate was 40 percent for the West Bank: 73 percent for men and 9 percent for women.

13. Interview, Dheisheh camp, April 13, 1995.

14. Interview, Dheisheh camp, April 13, 1995.

15. Interview, Nablus, January 8, 1995.

16. Interview, Gaza, August 9, 1995.

17. Interview, May 11, 1995.

18. Office of the Special Coordinator in the Occupied Territories (1997).

19. Interview with the family of a security officer in the Palestinian Authority who works in Jericho. Interview in Dheisheh camp, West Bank, April 13, 1995.

REFERENCES

AbdelHadi, Mahdi. 1992. *The Uprising and the Issue of National Development: A Socio-Economic Analysis of the Voluntary Organizations and other Popular Economic Forms.* Ramallah, West Bank: Beisan Center for Research and Development. (in Arabic)

Benvenisti, Meron, and Shlomo Khayat. 1988. *The West Bank and Gaza Atlas.* Jerusalem: West Bank Data Base Project.

Berman, Debbie. 2002. "Palestinian Counterfeit Industry Said to Be Funding Terrorism." *Israel Insider,* August 14, 1.

Bonacich, Edna, and Richard Applebaum. 2000. *Behind the Label: Inequality in the Los Angeles Apparel Industry.* Berkeley: University of California Press.

Bonacich, Edna, Lunie Cheng, Norma Chinchilla, Nora Hamilton, and Paul Ong, eds. 1994. *Global Production: The Apparel Industry in the Pacific Rim.* Philadelphia: Temple University Press.

Bornstein, Avram. 2002. *Crossing the Green Line between the West Bank and Israel.* Philadelphia: University of Pennsylvania Press.

Chin, Margaret. 2005. *Sewing Women: Immigrants and the New York City Garment Industry*. New York: Columbia University Press.

Collins, Jane. 2003. *Threads: Gender, Labor, and Power in the Global Apparel Industry*. Chicago: University of Chicago Press.

Diwan, Ishac, and Radwan Shaban, eds. 1999. *Development under Adversity: The Palestinian Economy in Transition*. Washington, D.C.: International Bank for Reconstruction and Development/World Bank.

FAFO. 1994. *Palestinian Society in Gaza, West Bank, and Arab Jerusalem: Summary of a Survey of Living Conditions*. Oslo: Institute for Applied Social Science.

Fuentes, Annette, and Barbara Ehrenreich. 1983. *Women in the Global Factory*. Boston: South End Press.

Gereffi, Gary. 1994. "The Organization of Buyer Driven Global Commodity Chains: How U.S. Retailers Shape Overseas Production Networks." In *Commodity Chains and Global Capitalism*, edited by Gary Gereffi and Miguel Korzeniewicz. Westport, Conn.: Praeger.

Gereffi, Gary, and Miguel Korzeniewicz, eds. 1994. *Commodity Chains and Global Capitalism*. Westport, Conn.: Praeger.

Gereffi, Gary, Miguel Korzeniewicz, and Roberto Korzeniewicz. 1994. "Introduction." In *Commodity Chains and Global Capitalism*, edited by Gary Gereffi and Miguel Korzeniewicz. Westport, Conn.: Praeger.

Hammami, Rema. 1990. "Women, the Hijab, and the Intifada." *MERIP*, May–August, 24–28.

———. 1993. "Women in Palestinian Society." In *Palestinian Society in Gaza, West Bank, and Arab Jerusalem: A Survey of Living Conditions*, edited by Marianne Heiberg and Geir Ovensen. Oslo: FAFO.

———. 1994. "Between Heaven and Earth: Transformations in Religiosity and Labor among Southern Palestinian Peasant and Refugee Women, 1920–1993." Ph.D. diss., Temple University.

Heiberg, Marianne, and Geir Ovensen, eds. 1993. *Palestinian Society in Gaza, West Bank, and Arab Jerusalem: A Survey of Living Conditions*. Oslo: FAFO.

Hovsepian, Mary. 2004. "Sewing Other People's Clothes: Gender, Nation, and Subcontracting across the Border between the Palestinian Territories and Israel." Ph.D. diss., University of Wisconsin, Madison.

Israel Central Bureau of Statistics. 1993. *Statistical Abstract of Israel*, no. 44. Jerusalem: CBS.

Louie, Miriam Ching Yoon. 2001. *Sweatshop Warriors: Immigrant Women Workers Take On the Global Factory*. Boston: South End Press.

Marx, Karl. 1981. *Capital*. Vol. 2. New York: Vintage.

McDowall, David. 1994. *The Palestinians: The Road to Nationhood*. London: Minority Rights Publications.

Moors, Annelies. 1989. *Restructuring and Gender: Garment Production in Nablus*. Occasional Paper Series 1, no. 3. Amsterdam: Middle East Research Associates.

Palestine Human Rights Information Center. 1990. "From the Field: A Monthly Report on Selected Human Rights Issues." *PHRIC* 1, no. 3 (November). Online publication (accessed January 15, 2008) www.pchrgaza.org.

Palestine Human Rights Information Center. 1993. "Israel's Closure of Occupied Territories Creates Military Enclave; Strangles East Jerusalem; Spells Loss of Income to Families; Denies Access to Medical Care, Schools, Jobs, Place of Worship." Press release. April 15.

Palestinian Central Bureau of Statistics. 1995. "Labor Force Statistics in the West Bank and the Gaza Strip." *Current Status Report Series*, no. 3, May.

Phizaklea, Annie. 1990. *Unpacking the Fashion Industry: Gender, Racism, and Class in Production.* London: Routledge.

Rai, Shirin. 2002. *Gender and the Political Economy of Development.* Malden, Mass.: Blackwell.

Rockwell, Susan. 1985. "Palestinian Women Workers in the Israeli Occupied Gaza Strip." *Journal of Palestine Studies* 14, no. 2 (winter):114–36.

Rosenberg, Matt. 2007. "Maquiladoras in Mexico: Export Assembly Plants for the United States." geography.about.com/od/urbaneconomicgeography/a/maquiladoras.htm (accessed June 22, 2007).

Roy, Sara. 1994. *The Gaza Strip: The Political Economy of De-Development.* Washington, D.C.: Institute for Palestine Studies.

Said, Edward. 1980. *The Question of Palestine.* New York: New York Times Books.

Samara, Adel. 1992. *Industrialization in the West Bank.* Jerusalem: AlMashreq Publications.

Semyonov, Moshe, and Noah Lewin-Epstein. 1987. *Hewers of Wood and Drawers of Water: Non-Citizen Arabs in the Israeli Labor Market.* Ithaca, N.Y.: Cornell University Press and ILR Press.

Warnock, Kitty. 1990. *Land before Honour: Palestinian Women in the Occupied Territories.* New York: Monthly Review Press.

Williams, Eric. 1944. *Capitalism and Slavery.* Chapel Hill: University of North Carolina Press.

Part 4

INTRODUCTION TO THE INTERSECTION BETWEEN GLOBAL AND LOCAL HUMAN RIGHTS

Earl Smith

Globalization, as a process, has many starting points. For Marx (1967), this new world economy begins as soon as large sea vessels travel the world looking for commodities that trade on the newly developing world market. In the work of Eric Williams (1944), globalization has its starting point with the movement of Africans to the New World in the seventeenth and eighteenth centuries. With scholars like Braudel (1982) and Wallerstein (1980), globalization begins with the development of the European world economy, roughly around the end of the seventeenth century. This is a period of intense exploration and colonization.

Yet when listening to colleagues and administrators on campus talk about "globalization" since about 2004, you would think that globalization, as a process, began in the late twentieth century.

Granted, my point of reference here is the growing movement of having university students study abroad as a clandestine way to increase campus enrollments without announcing that more and more students come to campus each year even if there are faculty/administration "agreements" on the size of each incoming freshmen class.

When students and their professors and the administrators who run the overseas study programs talk about globalization, it is as if they just discovered that there is a thriving world beyond our east and west coasts. More problematic, though, is that they never discuss the issues raised in this book and especially the types of issues raised in this part of the book.

For example, while safety is every parent's concern when sending their daughter or son overseas to study, of equal concern would seem to be the type of country to which they are traveling, the type of institution they will study or volunteer in, or to put the matter differently, how the people, ordinary citizens in these receiving countries, are treated.

Seldom are students challenged (void of the "sociological imagination" we teach in introductory sociology courses) to think about anything other than their own self-interest.

These chapters offer strategies for students to engage the nature of the relationships that the United States has with countries around the world. These chapters will help anyone see the ongoing struggle for human rights, even those that may seem unimportant and/or disparate, such as polluted drinking water, lack of political participation, and lack of due process.

Gouldner (1957), while not directly addressing issues of globalization, does get at the micro and macro issues as these relate to how citizens interact with each other at home and abroad, thus defining their social roles. I include Gouldner here because his framework provides a lens for understanding the local and global human rights struggles described in the chapters in this part of the book.

For example, Katz-Fishman and Scott describe the grassroots movements for human rights in the United States and abroad. This chapter fits nicely in this part with Blau and Moncada's chapter detailing the struggle for human rights by addressing the presence or absence of human rights in the constitutions of nation-states. These are then compared with the U.S. Constitution.

Smith and Hattery also use the Gouldner framework to explore the way in which local human rights are exported globally via the prison-industrial complex. The argument is grounded in the notion that the diabolical policies and practices that have been carefully recorded in prisons in Afghanistan, Iraq, and Guantanamo Bay, Cuba, all come from the annals of U.S. prison policy, which has a long history of prisoner abuse.

Finally, Embrick takes a long look at the book and closes his chapter with pointers on where we go from here. That is, depending on how the world turns, he looks at global relationships—old and new—and especially at the new economic relationships taking place between not only nation-states but also nation-states and corporate entities. This type of relationship was unheard of even twenty years ago.

REFERENCES

Braudel, Fernand. 1982. *The Structures of Everyday Life: Civilization and Capitalism, 15th–18th Century.* Vol. 1. New York: Harper & Row.

Gouldner, Alvin W. 1957. "Cosmopolitans and Locals: Toward an Analysis of Latent Social Roles." *Administrative Science Quarterly* 2 (December): 281–306.

Marx, Karl. 1967. *Capital.* Vol. 1. New York: International Publishers.

Wallerstein, Immanuel. 1980. *The Modern World-System I: Capitalist Agriculture and the Origins of the European World-Economy in the Sixteenth Century.* New York: Academic Press.

Williams, Eric. 1944. *Capitalism and Slavery.* New York: Capricorn Books.

13

Constitutions and Human Rights

Judith R. Blau and Alberto Moncada

The pace of constitutional innovation has been remarkable over the past two decades, which should be of special interest to sociologists. The most significant new development in constitutions is the elaboration of human rights provisions that are intended to enhance the economic and social security of citizens and to put societies on new trajectories that will maximally enhance equity and citizen equality and encourage social and cultural pluralism. Such developments clarify the pathways to harmonious communities and societies, and were all countries to follow the trajectories anticipated by their constitutions, we would have a far more peaceful world order. In this chapter, we set out to clarify the centrality of human rights in new and recently revised state constitutions, describe how anomalous the U.S. Constitution is, and clarify the importance of the international human rights framework as a model for state constitutions and regional charters. We also propose that these very recent developments in constitutions and charters are a response to globalization.

It is important to note initially that the United States has the oldest constitution in the world, and its human rights provisions are extremely skimpy by prevailing standards, limited to the civil and political rights spelled out in the first ten amendments and in a few subsequent amendments granting slaves their freedom, clarifying equality of citizenship, and giving women voting rights. The U.S. Constitution was written for an earlier epoch, before the expansion of capitalism, and for a nation whose citizens were largely agrarian. Playing a major role in the drafting of the Constitution was the framers' intention to accommodate slaveholders, promote the interests of landed and propertied elites, and protect the central government from popular challenges. While no other constitution is as old as the U.S Constitution, virtually all others encompass a full range of human rights. These new developments in state constitutions and legal frameworks have gone unnoticed in sociology, but they are highly relevant for sociologists because as states implement constitutions to become policies and programs, societies will be transformed. We draw in this chapter from our book *Justice in the United States*[1] but go further here and propose that these developments help us understand (using the language of the World Social Forum) that "A Better World Is Possible."

CONSTITUTIONS BY YEAR OF ADOPTION

We start with a very descriptive snapshot. Figure 13.1 is a scatter plot of countries, showing how many countries adopted a new constitution or substantially revised their constitution each year, from 1787, the year of the earliest constitution (that of the United States), through 2004, the last year in the series.[2] We exclude those few countries, such as Israel, that do not have constitutions.

As is evident, most activity by far occurs approximately in the past two decades. During this period, new states that were formed when the Soviet

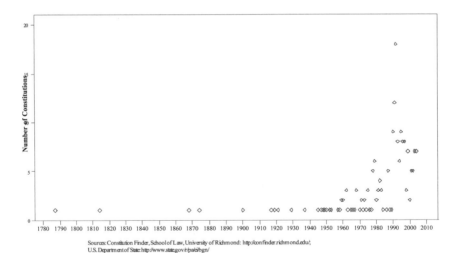

Sources: Constitution Finder, School of Law, University of Richmond: http://confinder.richmond.edu/;
U.S. Department of State: http://www.state.gov/r/pa/ei/bgn/

Figure 13.1. Number of New and Revised Constitutions by year of Promulgation (N = 191)
Sources: Constitution Finder, School of Law, University of Richmond: confinder.richmond.edu/; U.S. Department of State: www.state.gov/r/pa/ei/bgn/

Union broke up drafted their first constitutions. However, in the majority of cases, the high frequencies between 1980 and 2004 are the result not of state formation but of countries revising or rewriting their constitutions. As states such as Burkina Faso, Ghana, and Malawi advanced as democracies, they rewrote or substantially revised their constitutions. Yet there are also instances of old democracies revising their constitutions during this period, including the Netherlands (1983), Belgium (1994), Germany (1990), Australia (1999), Switzerland (2000), Greece (2001), and Monaco (2002). Earlier, before 1980, other old democracies revised theirs: Denmark (1953), France (1958), and Sweden (1975). Most striking, as we will discuss, is that these new and newly revised constitutions include expansive human rights provisions. To state this more precisely, a main reason why countries have recently revised their constitutions is to elaborate human rights provisions.

HISTORICAL DEVELOPMENTS IN HUMAN RIGHTS

When the framers of the Universal Declaration of Human Rights (UDHR) drafted the provisions dealing with civil and political rights (Articles 3 through 12 of the Declaration), they drew on the principles encompassed in the Bill of Rights of the U.S. Constitution, France's 1789 *Déclaration des droits de l'Homme et du citoyen*, English common law (including the 1215 Magna Charta and the 1679 Habeas Corpus Act), and provisions laid down by King Magnus of Norway in 1275. These foundational documents—and this tradition generally—are often referred to as "liberal rights," or "Western rights," which is to say they protect the individual against the state and draw from struggles waged by ordinary people against monarchical powers and a medieval order. They deal, in other words, with protections from the state and, for that reason, are sometimes called "negative rights." By now, every constitution in the world has these provisions, along with judicial systems that, at least in principle, protect these liberal rights.

The 1948 UDHR clarifies many other rights as well, and virtually all state constitutions use the UDHR as a model. In states with earlier constitutions, such as Finland, which has a 1919 constitution, and Norway with its 1814 constitution, there are provisions that link to the international human rights framework. For example, in Finland, the UDHR and UN human rights treaties are incorporated in their entirety into Finnish constitutional law. The more common practice is to elaborate human rights provisions within the constitution itself. All constitutions encompass liberal rights (civil and political rights) and, as we illustrate later, virtually encompass socioeconomic and other rights and identify particular groups that need special protections, such as children, women, and minorities that face discrimination, but also indigenous groups, linguistic minorities, and migrants.

Thus, human rights have expanded considerably at the level of the nation-state since the UDHR was approved, and the very conception of human rights has evolved and become more expansive. For example, the rights of gays and lesbians to marry or enter into civil unions is a topic that has made its way into deliberations about providing constitutional protections. The South African constitution is the first to extend equal rights to gays and lesbians.[3] Thus, while human rights law has rapidly expanded within most countries and leaders and the public try to respond to sources of insecurities and threats to human well-being and inequalities, these extraordinary developments have bypassed the United States, which remains stuck in the eighteenth century.

The U.S. Constitution does not contain most of the rights spelled out in the UDHR, including the right to a decent job and labor protections and rights to health care, education, housing, social security, and leisure and the rights of minorities, children, women, and the elderly. These are often referred to as socioeconomic rights. Why did the United States, particularly after being a pioneer on liberal rights, fall so far behind other countries on the elaboration of socioeconomic rights?

Because the UDHR is an international agreement and not a legal instrument, member states of the United Nations agreed to establish a treaty that would encompass all the provisions of the UDHR and would accompany monitoring and enforcement mechanisms. The United States rejected the idea of including labor, health care, social, and economic rights in a binding treaty, and, mostly at the insistence of the United States, UN member states divided the UDHR into two treaties, one that covered civil and political rights and the other that covered socioeconomic and cultural rights. Both went into force in 1976, with the United States ratifying only the first while most other countries ratified both.

Whose rights does the U.S. Constitution protect? In an 1886 case, *Santa Clara v. Southern Pacific Railroad*, Chief Justice Waite asserted in an oral argument, that "the court does not wish to hear argument on the question whether the provision in the Fourteenth Amendment to the Constitution, which forbids a State to deny any person within its jurisdiction the equal protection of the laws, applies to those of corporations. We are all of the opinion that it does."[4] And what is the precedent for this? In an earlier case that same year, *Southern Pacific Railroad* (118 U.S. 294), a court stenographer had made an error in transcription, giving Southern Pacific the rights of a person: immunity from state authority. When the error was discovered by a newspaper reporter, it was flashed to many newspapers via telegraph. Whatever their reasons, the justices did not revoke the error and embraced it as their own.[5]

Corporate personhood rights in the United States are extensive: 1) corporations and shareholders are immune from prosecution; 2) corporations are offered some First Amendment rights;[6] 3) under the Fourteenth Amendment, corporations may establish a business anywhere they want and have considerable power using eminent-domain provisions to seize land and threaten natural habitats; 4) under the Fifth Amendment, they may hire real persons who will protect their rights against self-incrimination;[7] (5) under the Fourth Amendment's search and seizure provisions, they are protected against surprise visits by government officials, such as Occupational Safety and Health Administration inspectors;[8] and 6) under due process provisions, corporations are protected in courts.[9] Moreover, they have the rights to airtime to lobby against legislation that they perceive as harmful to them,[10] and under the Sixth Amendment, they have the right to trial in criminal cases.[11] Because U.S. courts rejected in the famous 1886 case the idea that corporations and businesses were a matter of "special privilege" and instead a matter of "general utility with certain person-age rights," corporations and businesses have been shielded from considerable regulation and control by state authorities ever since.

Corporate rights, according to Carl Mayer, dramatically expanded in the 1990s, as the Supreme Court further elaborated its personhood rights while shrinking its responsibilities to workers, communities, consumers, and the environment.[12] Besides, Anthony Ogus explains, the U.S. Constitution is moot on contract rights, and that is why there are virtually no constitutional cases dealing with contracts that protect the contractual rights of people, such as their housing and employment rights.[13]

THE UDHR AND CONTEMPORARY CONSTITUTIONS

Human rights are rights held comprehensively and equally by all persons by virtue of being human.[14] A core principle of human rights is that humans have empathic regard for others. This ethical principle is ancient, emerging with the first human settlements, and can be found in all faith traditions. The first formal comprehensive international codification of human rights was the 1948 UDHR. One way to describe the provisions of the UDHR is that they correspond to historical epochs in the evolution of human rights. Drawing from Micheline Ishay's summary, we might think of the UDHR in terms of four pillars.[15] The first, covered in the first two articles of the Declaration, stands for human dignity that is shared by all humans. The second, specified in Articles 3 through 21, invokes the first generation of civil, political, and liberal rights that evolved during the Enlightenment and over which peoples in England, on the European continent, and in America struggled. The third, in Articles 22 through 26, addresses social and economic rights, and the fourth, encompassed in Articles 27 and 28, although somewhat rudimentary, highlights cultural rights and principles of solidarity.

Since 1948, this fourth pillar has been elaborated in other declarations and treaties in ways that affirm human rights in a globally connected world, including through the promotion of social and cultural pluralism and environmental rights and in recognition of the vulnerabilities of particular groups, such as women, racial and ethnic minorities, children, indigenous peoples, and the disabled. As the member states of the United Nations have responded to globalization in these ways, so have individual nation-states by revising their constitutions to encompass human rights provisions.

How do state constitutions reflect these developments in international human rights discourse and law? The easiest way to show this is to give examples from constitutions that illustrate the principles of each of these four pillars. As for the first pillar, constitutions typically state in their preamble or in an early article the inherent moral worth and equal dignity of all humans:

> Cameroon (Preamble): We the people declare that the human person, without distinction as to race, religion, sex or belief, possesses inalienable and sacred rights.

> Chile (Article 1): Men are born free and equal, in dignity and rights.

> Bulgaria (Preamble): By pledging our loyalty to the universal human values of freedom, peace, humanism, equality, justice and tolerance; by holding as the highest principle the rights, dignity and security of the individual; aware of our irrevocable duty to protect the national and state integrity of Bulgaria, hereby promulgate our resolve to create a democratic, law-governed and welfare state, by establishing this Constitution.

> Portugal (Article 1): Portugal shall be a sovereign Republic, based on the dignity of the human person and the will of the people and committed to building a free, just and solidarity society.

Pillar 3 encompasses economic and social rights, or the rights of security. None of these are included in the U.S. Constitution, but they are included in all new and recently revised constitutions, in other words, the majority of constitutions.[16] Such provisions include labor rights and the right to a job, provisions for maternal health, universal health care, housing rights, rights of the elderly and disabled, and rights of children:

> Bangladesh (Article 15): It shall be a fundamental responsibility of the State to attain, through planned economic growth, a constant increase of productive forces and a steady improvement in the material and cultural standard of living of the people, with a view to securing to its citizens—
>
> 1. the provision of the basic necessities of life, including food, clothing, shelter, education and medical care;

2. the right to work, that is the right to guaranteed employment at a reasonable wage having regard to the quantity and quality of work;
3. the right to reasonable rest, recreation and leisure; and
4. the right to social security, that is to say to public assistance in cases of undeserved want arising from unemployment, illness or disablement, or suffered by widows or orphans or in old age, or in other such cases.

Italy (Article 32: 1): The republic protects individual health as a basic right and in the public interest; it provides free medical care to the poor.

Paraguay (Article 54.1): Families, society, and the State have the obligation of guaranteeing a child the right to a harmonious, comprehensive development, as well as the right to fully exercise his rights by protecting him against abandonment, undernourishment, violence, abuse, trafficking, or exploitation. Anyone can demand that a competent authority comply with these guarantees and punish those who fail to comply with them.

Human rights that are defined by pillar 4 are the most recent and have quickly evolved as the world's peoples confront a more complex and interconnected world. What motivate the codification of rights here are concerns about groups whose members face discrimination, intergroup and intercultural relations, how best to advance cultural pluralism, and how to secure environmental protections. To illustrate these principles of protection of minorities, pluralism, and the way that environmental protections are linked with environmental sustainability, we cite a few examples of constitutions:

Algeria (Article 29): All citizens are equal before the law. No discrimination shall prevail because of birth, race, sex, opinion or any other personal or social condition or circumstance.

New Zealand (Section 20): A person who belongs to an ethnic, religious or linguistic minority in New Zealand shall not be denied the right, in community with other members of that minority, to enjoy the culture, to profess and practice the religion, or to use the language, of that minority.

Ethiopia (Article 39): Every nation, nationality or people in Ethiopia shall have the unrestricted right to self determination up to secession.

South Africa (Article 6.1): The official languages of the Republic are Sepedi, Sesotho, Setswana, siSwati, Tashivenda, Xitsonga, Afrikaans, English, isiNdebele, isiXhosa, and isiZulu.

South Korea (Article 35): All citizens have the right to a healthy and pleasant environment. The State and all citizens shall endeavor to protect the environment.

Spain (Section 3): The richness of the different linguistic modalities of Spain is a cultural heritage which shall be specially respected and protected.

It should be noted that all constitutions, without exception, include the provisions of pillar 2, namely, civil, political, and legal rights of citizens. Whether these rights or any other constitutional rights are fully protected or not is, of course, another matter, but the purpose of a constitution is to chart the way forward, not to describe the present circumstances. To illustrate, Eritrea, which does not have a functioning democracy, has a 1996 constitution that includes the principles of pillar 1 and all the rights of pillar 2, including guaranteeing citizen participation in all spheres, equality under the law, right to due process, protection from search and seizure, freedom of speech, and right to a fair trial. Its constitution also elaborates the provisions covered in the third and fourth pillars. The constitution is not currently in force but will be when the country becomes a functional democracy. (But it might be added that Americans no longer have secure rights to privacy, with electronic surveillance; torture is authorized by U.S. agencies, and many prisoners do not have rights to a fair trial.)

By highlighting these provisions, we would also like to convey that states are remaking themselves, relaxing their roles as top-down political entities as they depart from the Machiavellian conception that the state constitutes the body politic and in the direction of becoming a facilitator for complex societies. States also need to protect their citizens against the onslaught of globalization. Looking inward, they can do this through constitutional reforms. But another way that states respond to globalization is through the creation of regional alliances.

REGIONAL CHARTERS

As a response to greater global interdependencies and especially to the destructive effects of global, unregulated markets, countries have formed regional bodies for the purpose of trade and multistate environmental agreements but also to cooperate in ways that better protect their economies, natural resources, and peoples. The oldest of these is the European Union, established in 1982. Accompanying the political and economic activities of these alliances, these regional bodies have promulgated human rights charters that bolster state constitutions and address transborder human rights concerns, such as migration and trafficking. It is useful to briefly describe these charters and to suggest that they further bolster country constitutions and UN human rights agreements and treaties.

A particularly interesting one is the 1986 African (Banjul) Charter on Human and People's Rights because it encompasses not only political, civil, and socioeconomic rights but cultural rights as well, thereby further strengthening countries' authority to elaborate ethnic, tribal, and language rights in their own constitutions.[17] The African Charter has been elaborated further with the 1999 Optional Protocol on the Rights and Welfare of the Child and two new human rights instruments, the Optional Protocol on the Rights of Women and the African Youth Charter, the latter of which deals with the rights of adolescents. Both of these are now being circulated among member states for signatures and ratifications.

Asian countries adopted a charter in 1998 called the Asian Human Rights Charter—A Peoples' Charter,[18] which underscores the importance of basic rights as well as those of workers and women, and vulnerable groups, such as children. The Arab League's 1997 Charter on Human Rights[19] closely parallels the other charters while highlighting the connection between Islam and humanitarian values and those involving community, human rights, and freedom from domination. The most recent regional charter is the Charter of Fundamental Rights for the European Union (2000). Like all regional charters, it has provisions for rights that parallel the UDHR, including civil and political rights, rights of workers, and economic and social rights, and while it is somewhat more restrained than the African Charter on cultural rights, it includes environmental and consumer protections.[20] Finally, all thirty-five countries of the Organization of American States (OAS) are party to the American Declaration of the Rights and Duties of Man, a statement of principles. Accompanying this declaration are seven human rights treaties, including ones devoted to civil, political, economic, social, and cultural rights, among others. Out of the total of seven human rights treaties, the United States, an OAS member state, is a party to none.[21]

DISCUSSION

Although not pursued here systematically, it can be suggested that in spite of similarities across charters and constitutions in defining fundamental rights, there are remarkable differences that reflect differences in history, traditions, and cultures. Each has its own "personality" that shines through even though these documents are legal instruments that reflect a great deal of borrowing back and forth across countries and regions and especially borrowing from UN human rights instruments.[22]

Constitutions, to repeat, are not descriptive. Rather, they are the aspirations of peoples and reflect insistence that the state protect citizens and provide them with the support and resources they need to flourish and to build a better society. Although we did not provide examples, most state constitutions outline the duties and responsibilities of citizens to contribute, in turn, to society. The clear theme especially of constitutions is that societies are collectives, not aggregates, and that there are public goods, including equality and democracy.

One way of understanding the remarkable increase in the number of revised constitutions during the past two decades is that countries are responding to the threats posed by globalization and attempt to chart a course that will provide their citizens with greater security. Official documents that accompany new charters and constitutions support this conclusion.[23] There is abundant evidence that the effects of globalization on Third World countries have been detrimental, leading to greater poverty, fueling migration, and creating economic inequalities, and except for the wealthy, the citizens of affluent countries have not especially benefited by globalization

While the United Nations proper, along with its various specialized agencies (notably the Commission on Human Rights but also the UN Development Program, the Office for the Coordination of Humanitarian Affairs, UNESCO, the World Health Organization, and the High Commission for Refugees), advocates and promotes human rights, the economic agencies are, we believe, better allies of profiteers than of human beings. The structural adjustment policies of the International Monetary Fund have forced governments to cut social services and education budgets, the policies of the World Trade Organization have decimated the capacities of poor countries to develop their economies, and the infrastructural projects of the World Bank have led to the destruction of vast agricultural lands and benefit rich local elites in its urban projects. Globalization has been driven by multinationals but also by these international organizations.

There is no question that globalization has spurred legions of human rights activists into action, working in and on behalf of nongovernmental organizations and community-based organizations, and triggered the founding of the World Social Forum, which not only challenges neoliberalism but advances alternatives that are based on human rights principles. There are now vast and far-flung networks of people, communities, and organizations that pursue the advance of human rights, and, as we have shown, individual countries are developing the constitutional frameworks to help achieve this. This is what has become known as "the human rights revolution."[24] There is little evidence that Americans have joined this revolution, at least formally, and it is unlikely we can while we boast the "oldest constitution in the world." Were the United States, as an alliance of government and the people, to join the rest of the world in this revolution, amazing transformations would take place. Americans themselves would be the initial beneficiaries, but with a recovered reputation and improved world image, the United States could use its considerable power, influence, and resources to participate in the project of advancing that "Better World."

NOTES

1. Blau and Moncada (2006).
2. University of Richmond (www.confinder.richmond.edu).
3. South Africa Constitutional Court.
4. See Hammerstrom (2002).
5. The 1886 case of *Santa Clara v. Southern Pacific Railway* became the key precedent for subsequent decisions. With that, corporations became legal persons in the United States and gained the ability to challenge regulatory actions. In 1893, corporations won a major victory in the case of *Nohle v. Union River Logging*, which gave them Fifth Amendment due process rights against the federal government as well as state governments. The Fourth Amendment right against search and seizure has been used by corporations from having to open up their books. Fourth Amendment protections require inspectors from the Occupational Safety and Health Administration and the Environmental Protection Agency to produce a warrant in advance of an inspection, giving companies an opportunity to whisk irregularities out of sight. Many First Amendment free speech protections apply to corporations. See Reclaim Democracy (**www.Reclaimdemocracy.org**).
6. *National Bank of Boston v. Ebellotti* (1978); *Pacific Gas & Electric Co v. Public Utilities Communication* (1980).
7. *Hale v. Henkel* (1906).
8. *Hale v. Henkel* (1906).
9. *Noble v. Union River Logging R. Co.* (1903).
10. Myers (2000).
11. *Armour Packing Co v. United States* (1908).
12. Mayer (1990). See also Edwards (2002).
13. Ogus (1990).
14. For a written summary, see Blau and Moncada (2005).
15. Ishay (2004). We slightly modify her classification to distinguish more clearly political rights from social and economic rights.
16. Blau and Moncada (2006, 226–31).
17. African Union (1986).
18. The countries included in this Asian alliance (the Asian Human Rights Commission) are Bangladesh, Burma, Cambodia, India, Indonesia, Maldives, Nepal, Pakistan, the Philippines, Sri Lanka, and Thailand. See Asian Human Rights Commission (1998).
19. Arab League (1994).
20. European Union (2000).
21. Organization of American States (1969), Table of Ratifications, www.cidh.oas.org/basic.eng.htm.
22. See Heyns, Padilla, and Zwaak (2006).
23. See the pages of the European Commission, www.ec.europa.eu/justice_home/fsj/external/fsj_external_intro_en.htm; see also Howard-Hassmann (2005).
24. Blau and Moncada (2005).

REFERENCES

African Union, African (Banjul) Charter on Human and Peoples' Rights. 1986. www.africa-union.org/root/au/Documents/Treaties/Text/Banjul%20Charter.pdf (accessed April 8. 2007).

Arab League, Charter on Human Rights. 1994. www.law.wits.ac.za/humanrts/instree/arabhrcharter.html (accessed April 8, 2007).

Asian Human Rights Commission, Asian Human Rights Charter. 1998. material .ahrchk.net/charter/mainfile.php/eng_charter (accessed April 8, 2007).

Blau, Judith, and Alberto Moncada. 2005. *Human Rights: Beyond the Liberal Vision.* Lanham, Md.: Rowman & Littlefield.

——. 2006. *Justice in the United States: Human Rights and the US Constitution.* Lanham, Md.: Rowman & Littlefield.

Edwards, Jan. 2002. "Challenging Corporate Personhood." *Multinational Monitor* 23, nos. 10–11. Available at multinationalmonitor.org/mm2002/02oct-nov/oct-nov02 interviewedwards.html.

European Union, Charter of Fundamental Rights of the European Union. 2000. www.europarl.europa.eu/charter/pdf/text_en.pdf (accessed April 8, 2007).

Hammerstrom, Doug. 2002. "The Hijacking of the Fourteenth Amendment." reclaim democracy.org/personhood/fourteenth_amendment_hammerstrom.pdf (accessed April 8, 2007).

Howard-Hassmann, Rhoda E. 2005. "The Second Great Transformation: Human Rights Leapfrogging in the Era of Globalization." *Human Rights Quarterly* 27: 1–40.

Heyns, Christof, David Padilla, and Leo Zwaak. 2006. "A Systematic Comparison of Regional Human Rights Systems: An Update." *SUR: International Journal on Human Rights* 4: 163–71.

Ishay, Micheline. 2004. *The History of Human Rights: From Ancient Times to the Globalization Era.* Berkeley: University of California Press.

Mayer, Carl J. 1990. "Personalizing the Impersonal: Corporations and the Bill of Rights." reclaimdemocracy.org/personhood/mayer_personalizing.html (accessed January 18, 2008).

Myers, William. 2000. "The Santa Clara Blues." Corporate Personhood versus Democracy. www.iiipublishing.com/alliance.htm (accessed January 18, 2008).

Ogus, Anthony. 1990. "Property Rights and the Freedom of Economic Activity." In *Constitutionalism and Rights: The Influence of the United States Constitution Abroad,* edited by Louis Henkin and Albert J. Rosenthal. New York: Columbia University Press.

Organization of American States, Inter-American Commission on Human Rights, American Convention on Human Rights. 1969. www.cidh.oas.org/Basicos/basic3 .htm (accessed April 8, 2007).

South Africa Constitutional Court. www.concourt.gov.za/text/rights/know/homo sexual.html (accessed April 8, 2007).

University of Richmond, School of Law, Constitution Finder. www.confinder .richmond.edu (accessed January 18, 2008).

14

Twenty-First Century Globalization and the Social Forum Process: Building Today's Global Justice and Equality Movement

Walda Katz-Fishman and Jerome Scott

Today's globalization and neoliberal policies mean the rich get richer, the poor get poorer, and political repression and war intensify throughout the world as well as here in the United States. The struggle for basic human needs and collective human rights—economic, political, social, cultural, and ecological—takes place within the context of capitalist globalization and the emerging bottom-up movement for global justice and equality in the twenty-first century. We examine critical lessons from social history and social struggles and from political practice—organizing and educating. We understand the movement building process in terms of the overlapping stages of raising consciousness about the systemic root causes of our problems, creating a vision of the world we are fighting for, and developing strategy and tactics for transformation and liberation. We reflect on the seventh World Social Forum in Nairobi, Kenya, and lift up the first-ever United States Social Forum held in the summer of 2007 as part of the global social forum process and the movement for another world. We share our vision of a world where human needs and rights, community, and the planet are valued and put before market economics, profits, and the exploitation of people and nature. Another world is possible, another United States is necessary; and it is already happening.

TODAY'S MOVEMENT BUILDING MOMENT

In the opening years of the twenty-first century, the day-to-day realities in working-class and low-income communities across race, nationality, gender,

and generational lines are harsh. Life is harsh in some of the richest countries in the world. Crises are deepening and intensifying. The legacy of capitalism—as colonialism, imperialism, neocolonialism, and today's globalization—means ongoing exploitation and growing polarization between the
world's rich and the world's poor. The long reach of genocide and slavery
lives through white supremacy and racism. Patriarchy, gender, and sexual oppression are embedded in every aspect of daily life. War, militarism, repression, and occupation of our communities at home and abroad are ongoing.
Ecological and social destruction are now global.

Any semblance of a human needs–based society that embodies the collective rights of peoples, working classes, oppressed genders, and communities
has been destroyed by centuries of exploitation, domination, and multiple
oppressions. Yet the resilience and the power of peoples' struggles are strong
and, once again, are rising up. The question and the challenge is, What kind
of global justice and equality movement are we building to address these historical forces, to win and hold on to the victories and visions we have for our
communities and our planet, to transform society and the world we live in?

The bottom-up movement we are building is rooted in the convergence
of many fronts of struggle. It embraces struggles around work and wages,
housing, health care, education, women, youth, communities of color and
immigrant communities, disability, the environment, and peace. It is multi-
issue and multisector and crosses divides of race, nationality, class, gender,
sexuality, age, and ability. It is, therefore, multiracial, multigender, and
multigenerational. This movement is locally grounded, nationally net-
worked, and globally connected. While this movement draws from all
classes and sectors of society, it is a bottom-up movement because its demands and program put forward solutions to the problems of the very
poor, the working class, and the most oppressed in society, and it has the
voice and leadership of those most adversely affected at its center.

The emerging bottom-up movement in the United States represents a
similar constellation of forces that the larger discussion and practice of
"globalization from below" represents on the world stage. It is a people's
globalization in response to capitalist, neoliberal, and corporate globalization from above and is embodied in the World Social Forum and the social
forum process and the organizations, forces, struggles, and visions that this
process brings together (de Sousa Santos 2006; Prashad & Ballve 2006).

THE SOCIAL FORUM PROCESS: A MOVEMENT
BUILDING SPACE

The World Social Forum (WSF), inspired by the First Intercontinental *En-
cuentro* ("encounter") for Humanity and Against Neoliberalism organized

by the Zapatistas in Chiapas, Mexico, provides an important space and context for building today's bottom-up movement. The WSF, happening every January since 2001, is a popular civil society gathering of the world's worker, peasant, youth, women, and oppressed peoples' struggles. It takes place at the same time and is in response to the World Economic Forum in Davos, Switzerland—a gathering of global corporate and political elites who plan expansion of markets and profits at the expense of working people and the environment the world over. The WSF is an expression of the ongoing movement-building process that fights against global capitalism, its neoliberal policies, and U.S. empire and war. Its mantra, "another world is possible," challenges us to envision that "other" world we are struggling to create (Katz-Fishman and Scott 2004; Mertes 2004; Scott, Katz-Fishman, and Brewer 2005).

Perhaps one of the most important accomplishments of the WSF is that it has reclaimed a social and political space for anticapitalist and anti-imperialist dialogue and struggle for the peoples of the earth. The WSF process has generated powerful relationships and networks across national boundaries dealing with questions of land, poverty, and housing; labor and work; natural resources and water; women and gender; debt reduction to international financial institutions (the International Monetary Funds [IMF] and the World Bank); and others. More concretely, the WSF process has brought together forces within the United States and globally that have slowed the rapid pace of global neoliberal policies, such as the Free Trade Area of the Americas, that would extend the North American Free Trade Agreement to the entire hemisphere of the Americas. These "free trade" policies, in fact, benefit global corporations' drive for markets and maximum profits while ignoring workers' rights and environmental protections and fueling the "race to the bottom" (de Sousa Santos 2006; Prashad and Ballve 2006; Project South 2005).

The WSF process brought forth the call for a United States Social Forum (USSF). Grassroots Global Justice (GGJ), an alliance of sixty U.S.-based grassroots groups organizing to build an agenda for power for working and poor people rooted in the local-global justice movement, answered the call. GGJ came out of two recent trends: the growth of grassroots base-building organizations in the United States over the past thirty years in response to the crises of today's globalization and neoliberalism and the emergence of the global justice movement, represented in the WSF process. GGJ stepped forward to organize a consultation process and the formation of the National Planning Committee (NPC)—the coordinating body for the USSF—in 2004–2005.

The legacy of centuries of movement building in the United States, and especially its deep roots in southern resistance to indigenous genocide and African slavery with the powerful voices of women, led many activists to struggle for having the USSF in the American South. The NPC, also recognizing the strategic importance of the American South, selected Atlanta, Georgia, as the site for the USSF to be held June 27 to July 1, 2007. Within today's context of building a transformative and liberatory movement, organizing the USSF—as part of a world social forum process linking social movements locally, nationally, and globally—was the critical next step in gathering together the various fronts of struggle and creating a shared vision of the United States and the world we want and need for ourselves, our families and communities, our sisters and brothers in the global South, and the planet itself (www.ussf2007.org).

Building the USSF and the bottom-up movement within the United States was and is important for two critical reasons. The first is the reality of the global South inside the United States. Poverty, racism, sexism, homophobia, and the destruction of the social safety net and the public sector are pervasive throughout the United States, and these struggles are very much part of the social forum and movement-building process. The second is our international responsibility to be in unity with the struggles and movements of the global South for justice and equality. To stop U.S. imperialism, militarism, exploitation, and oppression throughout the world, we must stay the hand of U.S. empire and global corporations here at home. The USSF and ongoing social forum processes offer the opportunity to build an antisystemic and counterhegemonic movement in the United States in relationship to the global justice and equality movement growing around the world.

LESSONS LEARNED FROM HISTORY AND STRUGGLE FOR BUILDING TODAY'S MOVEMENT

We have to know our history so that we can understand the present moment and plan for our future. Here we share six key lessons from social history and social struggle that inform our movement-building processes in the early twenty-first century.

The Centrality of Oppression and Exploitation in the U.S. Context

The United States was forged in the genocide of indigenous peoples, the enslavement of African peoples, and the oppression and exploitation of peoples of color, immigrant and working-class communities, and women and youth. These oppressions and exploitations were reproduced in new ways in every century since the late 1400s, and those most adversely affected have consistently resisted and struggled for their freedom and liberation. Poverty, class inequality, white supremacy, patriarchy, and gender oppression have been part of the day-to-day lived experience of too many of the American people throughout history. Today's movement must recognize the historical roots and current expressions of these exploitations and oppressions and challenge them in all their forms. These realities and the people's struggles for justice and equality are central to our social history and movement-building practice.

We Get Only What We Are Organized to Take

Whenever gains were made, it was because of popular struggles of those most adversely affected. The reforms addressed the demands of that section of society leading the movement. For example, the New Deal addressed the demands of the powerful trade union movement, mostly white male workers in industry, but excluded agricultural and service workers, where most blacks, other people of color, and women were. The inclusion of poor people, African Americans, and other people of color and especially poor women of color did not happen until the war on poverty and the civil rights movement struggles for the expansion of the social contract and the social safety net. However, these gains are now under attack in the current period of global capitalism and neoliberal policies. So the demands we put forward in today's movement-building moment have to answer the problems of all those at the very bottom of society—the poorest and most oppressed among us.

We Need a Long-Term Outlook

The ruling class takes a long-term view. For instance, in 1944, they put in place the major international financial institutions (e.g., the IMF, the World Bank, and the General Agreement on Tariffs and Trade) that today, sixty years later, dominate the economic and political landscape of capitalist globalization and its neoliberal policies (Project South 2005). Our communities and organizations often focus on campaigns, mobilizations, and protests that defend existing policies under attack or that seek immediate or short-term policy changes to lessen our poverty and our oppression (e.g., defending affirmative action, raising the minimum wage, and saving public housing, education, and health care) without a long-term analysis. While these are important short-term struggles, they do not address and will not solve the structural root causes of our problems. Our bottom-up movement also needs a long-term strategic outlook that informs the tactics of our day-to-day struggle.

Unity of Theory and Practice

Whenever our struggles converged into a powerful movement, it was because people united theory and practice. That is, they acted and reflected and were intentional about the intellectual and subjective side of the movement as well as the action side. Some form of continuous education is key to ensuring that people entering the movement from all sectors of society, from all fronts of struggle, have a clear understanding of how the system works, of how sectors and issues converge, of what is going on, and of the direction the movement is heading.

This is particularly important if we are to bring scholars, students, and workers together as part of today's movement for social transformation. Political education is essential for having each section of society—both scholars and students and workers—appreciate and value the different knowledge and lived experience that each sector brings to the table and the larger struggle. Our movement needs to have study circles and popular education to ensure the broadest and deepest popular participation in the movement and to develop collective leadership from all sectors of society.

There Are No "Good Old Days"—What Is Our Vision and Strategy for the Future?

The major victories and reforms of the twentieth century (e.g., labor, civil rights, gender, sexuality, ability, the environment, and peace) were won through great struggles on the part of the people and made a difference in people's lives. But poverty is still with us, as are white supremacy, patriarchy, ecocide, and war. And today we find our hard-won gains under attack and rolled back. This is because we reformed the system but did not change it fundamentally. Today's movement needs a vision looking forward—there are no "good old days" to go back to. We also need to reflect on what it will take to hold on to our victories over the long haul. What is our consciousness and analysis of the system? What is our vision? What is our strategy, and how will we implement it in our daily work?

Electronic Technology Creates Abundance—Our Movement Can End Poverty and Misery

Today's capitalist globalization is happening in a new objective moment in social history. The global electronic age is based on electronics, which is labor-replacing technology. The industrial age was based on machines, which was labor-enhancing technology. This means several critical and new realities. Working people are needed less and less in the production, distribution, and communication processes of the market economy. With fewer good jobs and lower wages, working people the world over often cannot afford to buy the necessities of life. Because of this, it has become much harder for global corporations to sell all the goods and services produced by this highly productive technology. Within the context of the capitalist market, workers are in a spiraling crisis of poverty and all its social effects, and even global capital is facing a crisis of glutted markets. On the other hand, today's electronic technology (e.g., computers, robots, and all forms of automation) makes it possible to create an abundance of all the things we need (e.g., food, housing, clothing, health care, education, and transportation), while protecting the earth. Our movement needs to embrace the potential of this new technology that can truly liberate humanity if we transform society organized around private property and maximum profits into a cooperative and collective society organized to meet human needs and the collective rights of the peoples of the earth (Katz-Fishman and Scott 2005; Peery 2002; Project South 2005; Robinson 2005).

LESSONS LEARNED FROM POLITICAL PRACTICE— ORGANIZING AND EDUCATING

We have also learned critical lessons from our experience and day-to-day practice of movement building. It is important to sum these up to guide our work in bringing together our various fronts of struggle and our many organizations as we go forward.

This Is Very Hard Work over the Long Haul

Across race, nationality, class, gender, sexuality, age, region, and religion, we are building a transformative movement that has human liberation and protection of the planet at its center. This movement is anticapitalist, anti–white supremacist, and antipatriarchal and opposes all forms of oppression, inequality, and degradation of the environment. We are trying to do this from inside the "belly of the beast" within the context of centuries of "divide and conquer" by the ruling class, twentieth-century anticommunism of the McCarthy period, today's resurging economic and political crises, and practices and ideologies of racism, sexism, nationalism, and homophobia (Fried 1997). Needless to say, history and context makes theorizing, visioning, strategizing, and funding antisystemic struggles very hard work. It also means that we have to be in this work for the long haul.

We Have to Challenge Historic Divides inside the Movement

The powerful ruling class strategy of "divide and conquer" is so much a part of society across the globe that it too easily enters our political work and our movement. Divides and privileges based on race, class, nationality, language, culture, gender, sexuality, age, religion, and more are embedded in and reproduced by the economy, political and legal structures and processes, educational institutions, ideology, culture, media, the arts, and all aspects of social relations. Often those with power, privilege, and resources in the larger society (e.g., whites, people with more money, people with more formal education, men, heterosexuals, adults, citizens, and so on) bring their privilege and power into their organizations and the larger movement. In addition, working and low-income people bring ideologies and practices into their organizations and the movement that reproduce divisions from the larger society—such as white supremacy and racism, anti-immigrant stereotypes and actions, male supremacy, heterosexism, and ageism. Inside our movement—within and among organizations—we have to intentionally challenge these divides through dialogue, popular and theoretical education, and action and have internal processes for accountability and dealing with issues as they arise (Kelley 2002; Mohanty 2004).

We Have to Walk the Talk—Model the World We Are Trying to Create

People often ask how we can ever hope to build a movement to fundamentally change society when things are so unjust and unequal. It is essential that we strive inside our organizations and movement to "walk the talk"—to model the world we are trying to create. Concretely, this means that the power and leadership of people and communities at the grassroots are central in the process of creating liberation and that leadership needs to be collectively held and continually developed through education and practice. This leadership needs to be diverse in terms of race, gender, class, nationality, sexuality, and age, and we have to be very intentional about developing and lifting up the voices and leadership of those most adversely affected who are pushed forward in struggle. We also have to be intentional about creating inside our organizations structures and processes that are collective and cooperative. This requires, within our organizations, building relationships and building trust through dialogue and practice across divides. All of this takes time and patience.

Politics Leads and Requires Financial Independence

Much has been said about the relationship between money and politics, especially that those who have financial resources set the political agenda. This is truly problematic for today's organizations that claim that they are committed to social justice and social change but are part of the vast array of 501(c)(3) organizations with government tax-exempt status and funded in large measure by foundations and in a few cases by university affiliation. Organizations can apply to the Internal Revenue Service—the government taxing authority—for nonprofit or tax-exempt status. Many types of organizations are eligible (e.g., charitable, educational, service, advocacy, and research). To qualify for nonprofit status, organizations cannot run candidates for political office or support political parties that do and cannot spend over 15 percent of their budget on political lobbying. But organizations can run educational campaigns around political issues, and many do. The advantage of 501(c)(3) designation (named for the tax code law provisions) is that organizations are tax exempt; they pay no business taxes (except payroll taxes), and donations made to them are tax deductible for the donor. Most charitable foundations that fund grassroots organizations require that they have 501(c)(3) status or have a fiscal agent that does. Many nongovernmental organizations (NGOs) in the United States are part of the growing nonprofit sector. From within these organizations, we are having conversations and even conferences about the "501(c)(3)ing" of our justice and equality movement and often repeat the slogan "the revolution will not be funded."

Two of the most obvious challenges and contradictions are that funders set agendas and that funders foster turf issues and competition among organizations rather than cooperation and collaboration. Even progressive foundations and universities most often have a reform agenda and even more specific funding guidelines that constrain the political worldview and practice of their grantees. As a result, community-based organizations have lost the culture of grassroots fund-raising and resource gathering and find their very survival financially in the hands of external funding sources, most of which do not really want social transformation and human liberation. In addition, as a result of these dynamics, building collective and egalitarian structures and processes within our organizations and movement is very difficult.

It is important that movement-building organizations that take university and/or foundation resources not alter our vision and our work because of these grants. It is critical that we continue to develop our grassroots fund-raising as the only way to maintain our political independence and believe that we can and must "sell" our political analysis and our movement-building work to our members and supporters as a long-term strategy for our survival and for the larger project of human liberation.

Unite Organizing and Educating

Another challenge to long-haul and liberatory movement building is that inside many of our organizations, theory and analysis are less valued and given less time than direct action, campaigns, protests, providing services, and advocacy to address immediate needs or fight for short-term policy changes. Clearly, both short-term fixes and long-term transformative movement building need to be part of our agenda. Theory has to guide practice both strategically and tactically, and practice needs to inform theory development and application.

For us, theory is "living theory"—not theory as doctrine or dogma but theory as the intellectual side of political struggle and movement building for liberation. We took up popular education within the movement-building process to address this need of the movement and our organizations for reflection, analysis, and, as the movement developed, visioning and political strategy. It remains a challenge to get organizations to take time for reflection, education, and theory. But as crises have intensified and the movement has grown, organizations are a bit more willing to take the time to do this intellectual work of movement building.

Another challenge is the historic campus–community divide, particularly given the separation between radical and revolutionary activists and scholars as a result of the McCarthy era anticommunism and "witch hunts." For us, the challenge is connecting university-based intellectuals and movement-based intellectuals in a meaningful way within the movement-building process so that theorizing is rooted in political practice, practice is grounded in living theory, and both sections of society are part of the emerging social movement. As an organization that, from our beginning, intentionally sought to create a space to bring scholar and grassroots activists together on the basis of equality, we struggle to be a bridge between these communities and to the larger movement. We do this through relationship building and popular education in both movement spaces and campus and scholar spaces. Twenty years ago, this was very difficult work, and it remains difficult today. However, as activism and the movement have become more visible, more folks in both communities are willing to take time for the intellectual work of uniting theory and practice.

Think Outside the Box and Have a Bold Vision and Long-Term Strategy

The ideological hegemony of the corporate and political elite permeates peoples' formal education and mass culture and thus their consciousness. We often view capitalism, racism, patriarchy, homophobia, and so on as "permanent" structures and social relations rather than as ever-changing structures and ideological constructions. So it is vital that we do the critical work of political education, through poplar education and living theory, to guide the movement through the consciousness, vision, and strategy stages. Understanding social history and the crisis of global capitalism in the electronic age moves those most adversely affected to begin to envision a world and a United States that is not capitalist, not white supremacist, not patriarchal, and not homophobic. We have seen this need and desire for visioning and a growing need for concrete next steps. Through the theoretically grounded popular education tools we developed to explore consciousness, vision, and strategy, we are able to be part of pushing the movement-building process forward in this historic moment.

FROM NAIROBI TO ATLANTA:
ANOTHER WORLD IS HAPPENING

Central to this historic moment is the WSF and global social movement process in response to deepening crises of global capitalism and neoliberal policies over the past two decades. While global capital and global corporations increasingly dominate the world in pursuit of markets, maximum profits, and the accumulation of great wealth, growing poverty is the reality of billions of people the world over, including here in the United States. Poor and working people are in a "race to the bottom." This means loss of land, jobs, wages, the right to organize, and collective bargaining rights. It gives rise to new forms of forced labor and human trafficking that disproportionately affect poor women and children (Project South 2005; Robinson 2005).

Oppression and repression based on race, nationality, citizenship status, religion, gender, sexuality, and class intensify. In the post-9/11 era, the "war on terror" is the excuse to suspend civil rights and civil liberties and to pour more and more money into prisons, border walls, and wars at home and abroad. Militarism is on the rise in our local communities and in communities across the globe; violence and rape against women and children is on the increase (Project South 2004; Robinson, 2005).

Deregulation and privatization of public goods and services is widespread. Basic social needs, such as water, food, housing, health care, education, and energy, are available only through the market, and many people cannot afford these necessities with their meager earnings. Environmental destruction and global climate crises affect our daily lives but also the very survival of the planet (Project South 2005; Robinson 2005).

The urgency of these problems is awakening communities everywhere, and social struggles around all these issues are emerging. Many communities and struggles are gathering in social forum spaces (de Sousa Santos 2006; Prashad and Ballve 2006). Following are some reflections on the seventh WSF in Kenya and the first-ever USSF.

Africa and the WSF 2007

In January 2007, the world came to Africa to talk about the problems of the world (not just the problems of Africa), such as extreme poverty, ongoing war, genocide, millions dying from illness and hunger, millions living in slum communities, and the privatization of all social needs (e.g., water, housing, health care, and education). We also came to discuss ways to collectively build the global social movement necessary to resolve these problems and create the world we envision. This is a world organized around the values of justice, equality, diversity, and peace. Cooperative and globally interconnected communities will protect, produce, distribute, and sustain the resources of the earth on the basis of human need, and all humanity will be free to develop to the fullest potential.

The seventh WSF took place in Nairobi, Kenya, from January 20 to 25, 2007, within the context of the African continent. That continent's rich history and culture and human and natural resources have been dominated and exploited by centuries of colonialism, neocolonialism, and today's global capitalism. The legacy of this violence, repression, and theft of Africa's peoples, their labor, their land, and their resources continues to hang heavy in the air. The widespread and grinding poverty is challenged daily by the tactics of survival: economically, socially, and culturally. The people's resistance is vibrant, and their social struggles are growing.

The WSF 2007 in Nairobi, which brought together 60,000 participants, was a powerful and instructive experience. The massive contradictions of the larger society were also found inside the social forum. The most obvious include corporate sponsorship and commercialism, special contracts for government officials, a large police presence to keep the "order," highly visible church participation, NGOism (i.e., large and well-funded NGOs attempting to silence grassroots and low-income organizations and voices), and slum dwellers fighting to get into the space because of the cost. The entry fee of 500 Kenyan shillings, the equivalent of one week's pay for the average Kenyan, was waived after protests. Another demonstration closed down the prime-spot restaurant and bar run by a top government official, but only after the demonstrators drank and ate everything they wanted.

But the overwhelming reality of WSF 2007 remains the resilience and rising power of the many fronts of struggle in a way not seen before in social forum spaces. African and Kenyan social struggles were highly visible and brought a clear voice. Feminists, led by African women, were well organized and brought forth demands for ending all forms of violence against women and girls (whether violence in war, domestic violence, or physical and cultural violence against their bodies), demands for economic and political equality, and demands for full access to treatment and drugs for HIV/AIDS. The LGBT (lesbian, gay, bisexual, transgender) community was more present and militant than in earlier social forums, calling for equality and an end to all forms of oppression. The youth from the slum dwellings of Korogocho and Kibera—two of the largest slums with roughly 200,000 and an estimated 1 million residents, respectively—fought their way into the WSF and offered workshops and tours to share their day-to-day realities and struggles. The organizing efforts within these slum dwellings are connected to the International Association of Slum Dwellers, linking hundreds of thousands of slum dwellers across the globe and participating in the social forum and movement-building process.

The historic tension within the social forum between using the forum as a space for debate and as a social movement-building space has been answered for the moment—the Social Movements Assembly has asserted itself and now shares the space. We united behind the slogan of the social movements: "The social forum is not for sale."

The fourth day, organized by the Social Movements Assembly, was a compelling movement-building process. It began with an open-mike session in the morning, followed by thematic assemblies to plan coordination and action throughout the year in the various fronts of struggle (e.g., workers, women, antidebt, antiwar, antiprivatization, the People's Assembly, and so on). The day ended with a gathering of 2,000 participants where socialism was put on the table as part of our vision for the future, coordination of days of action for January 2008 (in the place of a 2008 WSF) was discussed, and the convergence of our fronts of struggle into a unified movement became the overarching challenge.

This intentional process led by the Social Movements Assembly was, for us, the highlight of WSF 2007. What we take away is how to make this a reality.

The social forum process has its own set of contradictions. The leadership of the WSF, the International Council, is composed of many members who represent both reformist political tendencies as well as revolutionary tendencies, who are largely European and Brazilian, and who are majority scholars rather than social movement activists. At the same time, within the Social Movements Assembly are revolutionary organizations and activists who are gathering their forces and gaining strength. This sets the basis for intense political struggle. The question is, Will they continue to be able to share the social forum space?

Another key political question is, How do we build into the social forum process ongoing political education, analysis, vision, and strategizing? As we plan for coordinated days of action and global campaigns in January 2008 and throughout the year, we also need to pay attention to and create the intentional space for collective study and dialogue to deepen our consciousness and our intellectual grasp of the systemic nature of our problems and crises and the transformative quality of our struggles.

The Road to Atlanta and the USSF

What does this mean for the USSF and building a transformative movement in the belly of the beast? It means, most strategically, that we in the United States—activists and organizations—have the responsibility to build a U.S. movement worthy of uniting with our brothers and sisters in the global South.

As we were gathering our forces in the United States and planning for the USSF over the past three years, this was our strategic goal. It set the basis of our struggle to get the USSF to the American South, the historic location of the most intense repression and exploitation and equally intense resistance and struggle, and to ensure leadership from organizations led by people of color and of low income.

To make this happen, GGJ, an alliance of sixty grassroots organizations representing people of color and low-income communities in the United States, took the lead in forming the NPC, as mentioned previously the co-ordinating body of the USSF. The NPC, which consists of over forty organizations, led by mostly working-class folks and people of color, had the overall responsibility of organizing the USSF. The site we selected was Atlanta, Georgia, home to centuries of struggle for racial, economic, and gender justice and equality.

As USSF organizers, we identified four additional goals to move us toward realizing our overall strategic goal of a powerful and transformative U.S. movement:

- Convergence of our diverse fronts of struggle
- Linking local and global organizing
- Creating organizational infrastructure and coordination, and re-sources—building trust, relationships, and networks across historic divides and collective and grassroots resource mobilization
- Envisioning another United States as part of another world

Another United States Is Happening

After three years of organizing and planning, the USSF held in Atlanta from June 27 to July 1, 2007, generated a buzz across the United States. The question is, Why? This is what we think. First, the social forum process was initiated by social movements of oppressed and exploited peoples in the global South; no one group in the United States "owned" it. Second, the social forum was brought home to the United States by grassroots organizations—organizations led by people of color and of low income. Third, the social forum was and is a convergence process of all our fronts of struggle; it is multi-issue and multisector and inclusive of all who are struggling for justice, equality, and peace. Fourth, the social forum was and is a space where a broad range of political analysis is welcomed, from progressive to revolutionary.

The mantra of the social forum process, "another world is possible," takes on new meaning for the United States in the historical context of having hosted the first USSF in 2007. Another United States is necessary. It remains the ongoing task of the U.S.-based bottom-up movement to envision it and develop the political strategy required. This is why the USSF was the place to be in the summer of 2007 for activists, for movement builders, and for visionaries. There will be future social forums in the United States and around the world. So even if you missed the USSF in 2007, be there next time to help make it happen! (Visit www.ussf2007.org.)

REFERENCES

de Sousa Santos, Bonaventura. 2006. *The Rise of the Global Left: The World Social Forum and Beyond*. London: Zed Books.

Fried, A., ed. 1997. *McCarthyism: The Great American Red Scare—A Documentary History*. New York: Oxford University Press.

Katz-Fishman, W., and J. Scott. 2004. "A Movement Rising." In *An Invitation to Public Sociology*. Washington, D.C.: American Sociological Association.

———. 2005. "Global Capitalism, Class Struggle, and Social Transformation." In *Globalization and Change: The Transformation of Global Capitalism*, edited by B. Berberoglu. Lanham, Md.: Lexington Books.

Kelley, R. 2002. *Freedom Dreams: The Black Radical Imagination*. Boston: Beacon Press.

Mertes, T., ed. 2004. *A Movement of Movements: Is Another World Really Possible?* New York: Verso.

Mohanty, C. T. 2004. *Feminism without Borders: Decolonizing Theory, Practicing Solidarity*. Durham, N.C.: Duke University Press.

Peery, N. 2002. *The Future Is Up to Us: A Revolutionary Talking Politics with the American People*. Chicago: Speakers for a New America.

Prashad, V., and T. Ballve, eds. 2006. *Dispatches from Latin America: On the Frontlines against Neoliberalism*. Cambridge, Mass.: South End Press.

Project South, ed. 2004. *The Roots of Terror: Yesterday's Struggles, Today's Lessons, Tomorrow's Victories*. 2nd ed. Atlanta: Project South. Available at www.projectsouth.org.

———. 2005. *Today's Globalization: A Toolkit for Popular Education in Your Community*. 2nd ed. Atlanta: Project South. Available at www.projectsouth.org.

Robinson, W. 2005. *A Theory of Global Capitalism: Production, Class, and State in a Transnational World*. Baltimore: Johns Hopkins University Press.

Scott, J., W. Katz-Fishman, and R. Brewer. 2005. "Global Movement on the Rise: World Social Forum 2005—Brazil." *As the South Goes . . .* 13: 10–11.

15

The Globalization of the U.S. Prison-Industrial Complex

Earl Smith and Angela Hattery

Human rights principles are contained in national and international law. Ensuring that business operations are consistent with these legal principles helps companies avoid legal challenges to their global activities. In recent years, U.S. and European courts have accepted or instigated lawsuits alleging that multinational companies have contributed to human rights violations in third world countries.

—Business for Social Responsibility (2003)

In the last 3 decades The Prison Industrial Complex has been developed in the US. It is a confluence of special interests that has given prison construction in the United States a seemingly unstoppable momentum. Since 1991 the rate of violent crime in the United States has fallen by about 20 percent, while the number of people in prison or jail has risen by 50 percent. Increases take place because of the imprisonment of people who have committed nonviolent offenses. Instead of community service, fines, or drug treatment, they get a prison term, by far the most expensive form of punishment. Politicians, both liberal and conservative, have used the fear of crime to gain votes; Impoverished rural areas where prisons have become a cornerstone of economic development are on the rise; Private companies tap into $35 billion a year spending on prisons. Spending on corrections since 1980s increased 5 times; there are more than 1000 vendors that sell corrections paraphernalia; the growth projected 5–10% annually; Private prisons keep 90,000 prisoners from 27 states. "Bed brokers," rent a cell facilities ($20 to $60 a day with $2.50–5.50 commission per man-day); trucking prisoners hundreds of miles through the country—threat to public order; escapes; Wackenhut

Corrections, second largest private-prison company has ravenous $1 billion a year profits; U.S. Corrections Corporation, the largest private-prison company wants to buy and run all state of Texas' prisons; Globalization of the private-prison business: British private-prison company, Securicor, operates two facilities in Florida; Wackenhut Corrections is now under contract to operate prison in England, three prisons in Australia, and a prison in Scotland. It is actively seeking prison contracts in South Africa. One pay phone in prison generates $15,000 a year and MCI installs phones for free.

—Schlosser (1998, 51–77)

Incarceration has become a multibillion-dollar industry[1] that relies on incarcerating more than 2 million citizens on any given day in the United States. We are, in fact, addicted to incarceration.[2] In order to fully understand this addiction, we compare incarceration rates in the United States to those in other countries, both those with good human rights records and those with poor records.[3] Why is the United States addicted? This chapter utilizes the concept of the prison-industrial complex, first coined by Eric Schlosser (1998) and Angela Davis (1998), in order to examine the complex configuration comprised of the U.S. prison system, multinational corporations, small private businesses, and the inmate population in the social and political economy of the twenty-first century United States.[4] Second, we focus on the ways in which inmates in the United States, primarily African American men, provide a pool of highly exploitable labor that allows all types of industries, from agriculture to multinational corporations like Microsoft, to turn record profits. Specifically, we argue that the current system of incarceration in the United States mimics the slave plantation economy of the South. And the products and profits of this modern-day slave economy are exported each day through the expansion of global markets: in a system where "societies have no borders." Finally, we examine the ways in which the United States also exports prison practices by using administrators in U.S. prisons to set up and run our prisons abroad (Abu Ghraib and Guantanamo Bay) and by exporting detainees to countries that do not adhere even nominally to UN conventions[5] regarding prison torture. We note that because the human rights violations associated with U.S. global prison practices occur on foreign soil, they are largely ignored.

STATISTICS ON PRISONS IN THE UNITED STATES

We begin with some background on the state of prisons in the contemporary United States.

The Growth of Prisons: Institutions and Population

The number of prisons has grown, as has the number of Americans incarcerated (see figure 15.1). In 2005, more than 2.6 million[6] Americans (or .7 percent of the U.S. population) were incarcerated in nearly 1,700 state, federal, and private prisons, with many more under other forms of custodial supervision, including probation and parole (Harrison and Beck 2005).

Furthermore, despite the fact that we think of certain other countries as being dominated by incarceration, the United States incarcerates a higher proportion of its population than all other developed countries and many in the developing world (Mauer 2003). Specifically, we note that in the United States, a significantly higher proportion of citizens are incarcerated than in nation-states such as China (see figure 15.2), the incarceration practices of which are frequently the target of investigations and reports by human rights watch groups such as Amnesty International (Amnesty International 2005).

This steep growth in incarceration can be traced to the implementation of the drug reform laws that began in the 1970s. Under these laws, many possession offenses were recategorized as felonies, mandatory minimum sentences were imposed, convicts were required to serve at least 80 percent

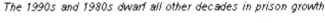

The 1990s and 1980s dwarf all other decades in prison growth

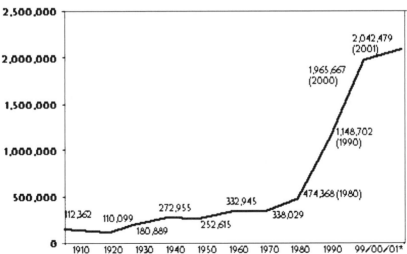

Figure 15.1.   The Punishing Decade: Number of Prison and Jail Inmates, 1910–2000
Source: Justice Policy Institutes analysis of U.S. Department of Justice Data.
*1999, 2000, and 2001 are Bureau of Justice Statistics Estimates of What Could Be the Year End Totals.

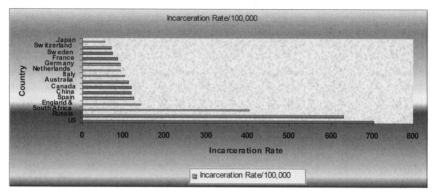

Figure 15.2.   Incarceration Rates by Country
(Mauer 2003:2)

of their sentences, and, more recently, the "three strikes and you're out" laws were implemented (Hattery and Smith 2007).

Race and Incarceration

Of the 2.6 million Americans who are incarcerated, 1 million, or 43 percent, are African American men (see table 15.1). In other words, more than 40 percent of *all American* prisoners—men and women—are African American *men*. African Americans make up nearly two-thirds (62 percent) of the male prison population, yet they make up just 13 percent of the U.S. male population (Roberts 2004). Furthermore, African American men are seven to eight times more likely to go to prison than their white counterparts. And *nearly one in three African American men will be incarcerated during their lifetimes.*[7]

Coupled with the prison boom has been an unprecedented collaboration with the capitalist economy in the United States such that, in 2006, nearly 100 national and multinational corporations, as well as small townships and even colleges and universities, do business in or with prison industries. And, by and large, the individuals working to create the products are African American men who earn below-market wages.

Table 15.1.   Probability of Incarceration for men by Race

90 out of every 1000 men will be incarcerated in their lifetimes

44 out of every 1000 white men
160 out of every 1000 Hispanic men
285 out of every 1000 African American men

THEORETICAL FRAMEWORK: THE PURPOSE OF PRISON— REHABILITATION OR A TOOL OF CAPITALISM?

In this chapter, we utilize data on the prison-industrial complex (PIC) and prison industries in particular to pose the question, What is the purpose of prisons? Is it the rehabilitation of the inmates or the exploitation of prison labor for profit-making corporations?

The deliberate implementation over the past two decades of sentencing policy can be characterized as using prisons as catchments for the undesirables in our society (Chasin 2004).[8] Furthermore, prisons provide a "captive" population, one that is highly vulnerable and one that has increasingly been exploited for its labor. University of Wisconsin sociologist Professor Erik Olin Wright (1997) put it thus:

> In the case of labor power, a person can cease to have economic value in capitalism if it cannot be deployed productively. This is the essential condition of people in the "underclass." They are oppressed because they are denied access to various kinds of productive resources, above all the necessary means to acquire the skills needed to make their labor power saleable. As a result they are not consistently exploited. Understood this way, the underclass consists of human beings who are largely expendable *from the point of view of the logic of capitalism*. . . . Capitalism does not need the labor power of unemployed inner city youth. . . . The alternative, then, is *to build prisons and cordon off the zones of cities in which the underclass lives*.[9] (153, emphasis added)

According to Wright, prisons can be seen as a form of modern-day genocide, a strategy for removing unwanted, unnecessary, unuseful members of a capitalist society. It is a system whereby the privileged can segregate or cordon off these unwanted members of society without the moral burden of genocide. It is easy to see how prisons accomplish this goal: they remove individuals from society and permanently (in many states) disenfranchise them from the political realm (Hattery and Smith 2007; Pager 2003). Prisoners and ex-convicts become virtual noncitizens, unable to challenge the economic, social, or political power structures.[10]

We argue that while Wright was astute in his observations that prisons provided a mechanism for removing the "unexploitable" labor from society, we argue that this formerly "unexploitable" class of Americans has now been redefined as highly exploitable by national and multinational corporations. Taking the lead from prison labor that has been around for a century or more, from agricultural labor at prison farms like Parchman and Angola to the license plate factories that were popular in the middle part of the twentieth century, dozens of Fortune 500 companies have moved at least part of their operations into prisons. As the data will demonstrate, this transition to prison labor allows corporations to significantly cut their labor

costs, thus maximizing and accumulating their profits, much like planta-
tions, shipbuilders, and other industries did during the 200-plus years of
slavery in the United States.[11]

Human Rights and Prison Labor

Human rights are basic standards of treatment to which all people are entitled,
regardless of nationality, gender, race, economic status or religion. Human
rights fall into five general categories: economic, social, cultural, political and
civil (Business for Social Responsibility 2003).

Yet, as Moncada and Blau (2006) so aptly point out, for a variety of reasons
the United States has not chosen to protect the human rights of its own citizens and, more troubling, has chosen to continue to engage in the practice
of human rights violations in the name of laissez-faire capitalism all around
the globe.

The relationship between incarceration and human rights has long been
contested. On the one side are those who argue that when someone com-
mits a crime, he or she chooses to give up his or her claim to rights. On the
other side are those who argue that though inmates should be deprived of
citizenship rights (the right to vote, the right to freedom of movement, and
so on), they should not be deprived of basic human rights (such as life, liberty, and security of person) that are guaranteed in the international declaration of human rights (www.un.org/Overview/rights.html).

Human rights advocates such as Amnesty International and the Juvenile
Justice Project of Louisiana (JJPL) have sued for human rights protections
for inmates and in the case of JJPL were successful in closing a children's
prison, Tallulah, notorious for human rights violations. However, most of
the attention of these groups has focused on basic human rights violations
(safe food and housing) and capital punishment.[12] We argue here that the
exploitation of vulnerable labor also constitutes a type of human rights violation not at all dissimilar to the use of child labor and sweatshop labor
abroad. Prisons are like sweatshops and, as such, operate on the principle
of low- to no-wage labor as the mechanism that drives the profit margins.
Furthermore, as explicated by the Business for Social Responsibility (2003):

While human rights principles were originally intended to limit state action towards individuals or groups, several human rights principles relate directly or
indirectly to private sector actions. These include the avoidance of child labor
in global manufacturing, non-participation in state action depriving citizens of
basic civil liberties, and the avoidance of forced prison labor.

Finally, we argue that this relationship between the capitalist economy and
the prison system that characterizes the PIC creates a feedback loop. The more

prisons that are built for profit rather than rehabilitation, the more people who must be incarcerated. Prisons make money only when the cells are occupied. Similarly, the more prisons provide labor for corporations, the higher the demand for prison labor and the more prisons will be built. Thus, we suggest that the PIC and its attendant industries contribute to the increased rates of incarceration in the United States and the continued exploitation of labor, primarily African American labor, resulting in major human rights violations of the most vulnerable and marginalized citizens of the United States.[13]

The Economics of the PIC: The Case of the Corrections Corporation of America

The Corrections Corporation of America (CCA) builds and staffs prisons. Currently, it has 67,000 beds (approximately 62,000 inmates) in sixty-three facilities—from California to Oklahoma to Montana to the District of Columbia—and has plans to build more. This private corporation, founded in 1983, trades on the New York Stock Exchange with posted annual earnings in 2005 of over $1.2 billion (CCA 2005).

Clearly, there is big money to be made in the incarceration industry. We begin by examining the ways that private prison corporations like CCA make money. We point out that though in some cases the government pays part of the cost of incarceration, the inmates themselves seldom contribute to the cost of their own incarceration.[14] And it is quite expensive to house a single prisoner in a jail or prison. Rough estimates indicate that it costs most states more to house a single prisoner per year ($23,183.69) than to educate a citizen in college for that same year.

Hence, there has to be another method to pay for, in both the public and the private facility, the built environment of the prison. Even the most basic economic analysis would note that the prison loses money when there are empty cells. Thus, just like college campuses must enroll enough students to fill the dorms, prisons rely on being at "full capacity," so, as some others have also suggested (see Mauer and Chesney-Lind 2002), part of the explanation for the rise in incarceration rates is the fact that building and expanding prisons means that we must continue to fill them. We must impose harsher and longer sentences, and we must continue to funnel inmates into prisons. We argue here that this funnel is being filled primarily by the vulnerable, unempowered populations, primarily the young, poor, African American men that Wright (1997) describes. Reiman (2007) underscores our main point about the overrepresentation of minorities and the poor within the U.S. prison population:

> My point is that people who are equally or more dangerous, equally or more criminal, are not there; that the criminal justice system works systematically

not to punish and confine the dangerous and the criminal, but to punish and confine the poor who are dangerous and criminal. (153)

Private commerce that utilized prisoners as labor has been under way for centuries in Anglo societies, dating back to the 1600s and before (Hallett 2004). This fits with the findings of Oshinsky (1997) showing that on the backs of prison labor, postbellum capitalism flourished.

During the twentieth century, penal capital moved from the raw convict leasing system characterized by Oshinsky to a service economy that mirrors the larger U.S. economy (Oshinsky 1997). From an economic perspective, this penal capital allows a middleman like Signature Packaging in Washington State, which moves products such as Starbucks coffee, to win contracts and outbid other packagers because they use prison labor. They do not have to pay market wages, they do not pay health insurance or vacation benefits, and they do not have to worry about severance pay or layoffs.

One aspect of the PIC that has perhaps received less attention is the role that the use of prison labor plays in the postindustrial political economy of the United States at the beginning of the twenty-first century. There are many types of industries that utilize prison labor, including construction, road maintenance, and agriculture. We focus here on one illustration that has an international scope: service sector labor (for a lengthy discussion of prison labor, see Hattery and Smith 2007; Smith and Hattery 2007).

Service Sector Work

Perhaps the most recent change in inmate labor and the one that seems to be the most controversial and disturbing is the use of inmate labor for a variety of service sector work that is subcontracted through "middlemen" for some of the nation's leading manufacturers. There are estimates that on any given day, the average American uses thirty products that were produced, packaged, or sold out of a prison. Through this type of service sector work, prison industries have truly infiltrated the global market:

> Another source of profit for private companies is prison labor. Companies that use prison labor include IBM, Motorola, Compaq, Texas Industries, Honeywell, Microsoft, Boeing, Starbucks, Victoria's Secret, Revlon, Pierre Cardin. (Evans 2005, 217–18)

One can easily come to the conclusion that this is a positive movement in the evolution of prisons because it provides work, it teaches job skills that are transportable, and it allows inmates to earn some money while they are on the inside. However, critics, including many inmates at the Twin Rivers Corrections Unit in Oregon, are skeptical of the underlying reasons for this evolution in prison industries. They do not necessarily believe it is indicative of a *rehabilitative movement* in prisons but rather is driven entirely by companies seeking another way to maximize their profits (Barnett 2002):

> Others suspect that DOC's motives are more pecuniary than pure-hearted, noting that by shaving nearly 50 percent off the top of an inmate's paycheck, the department slashes its own expenses while subsidizing the companies in the program, which aren't required to pay for inmates' health insurance or retirement. "They figure that if somebody's sitting around, doing their time and doing nothing, they don't make any money off them," Strauss says. . . . Richard Stephens, a Bellevue property-rights attorney, is suing DOC on the grounds that the program is unconstitutional, allows businesses that use prison labor to undercut their competitors' prices, and unfairly subsidizes some private businesses at the expense of others. . . . *Private businesses are "paying prison workers less than they're paying on the outside, but they aren't reducing the markup to the consumer"* they're pocketing the profits. Another key difference, Wright notes, is that prisoners can just be sent back to their cells whenever business goes through a lull; "on the outside, they have to lay off workers. It's much more difficult," Wright says. (A7)

The use of inmate labor allows middle-level companies like Signature Packaging to underbid their competitors by cutting their labor costs. And prisons benefit as well because by engaging their inmates in this sort of economic production and then charging inmates for their own incarceration, they are able to keep the costs of running the prison down. Wright, an inmate at Twin Rivers, sums it up:

> "They need to know that they are buying these products from a company that is basically getting rich off prisoners." Wright, sent to Twin Rivers for first-degree murder in 1987, *believes parents would be disturbed to know that their child's Game Cube was packaged by a murderer, rapist, or pedophile.* "These companies spend a lot of money on their public image," Wright says, "but then they're quick to make money any way they can." (Barnett 2002, A7)

International Human Rights and the Extension of the PIC

The international PIC is gaining in acceptance as an international tool of capitalism primarily through the exportation of products manufactured inside prisons, allowing U.S.-based corporations to compete with companies that have "outsourced" their manufacturing to places like China and Singapore. And this practice allows these companies to meet the requirements of "Made in the U.S.A." and access the associated privileges while still posting profits similar to those that engage in outsourcing.

China has been the focus of much attention from human rights watchdogs, including Amnesty International, which in a recent report documents human rights violations connected to prison labor (Amnesty International

2005). As a result, the official position of the U.S. government is to ban the import from China of products manufactured using forced prison labor (U.S.-China Economic Security Review Commission 2005). Yet "for reasons of sheer economic and political self-interest, and owing to its liberal traditions, which are antithetical to collective endeavors, the United States has remained aloof from this 'human rights revolution'" (Moncada and Blau 2006, 115).

The data presented here indicate that many of the same human rights violations we abhor in China occur in U.S. prisons, specifically the hyperexploitation of labor.[15] Yet even the most ardent American human rights advocates seldom focus their attention on what is happening in their own backyards, nor do they ask questions about the products they consume on a daily basis.

THE PIC, HUMAN RIGHTS, AND THE EXPLOITATION OF AFRICAN AMERICAN LABOR

Corporations that appear to be far removed from the business of punishment are intimately involved in the expansion of the prison industrial complex (Davis 1998, 16).

Specifically, we have argued that the PIC and its attendant "prison industries" mimics the slave mode of production—that, in the end, wealthy whites (primarily men) are profiting by not paying a living wage to African American inmates (also primarily men). Thus, corporations are engaging in an exploitive labor practice, termed by Marx the extraction of surplus value (Marx and Engels 1990). By not paying what the labor is worth when inmates are working on farms, building furniture, or assembling products for giant multinational corporations like Microsoft and McDonald's, corporations make additional profits. And when large corporations such as these engage in this practice, they also receive an unfair advantage over their competitors. Finally, we must note here that the whole scene is reminiscent of the "plantation economy" of seventeenth-, eighteenth-, and nineteenth-century America. The slaves were black chattel. They had no rights, and they were a captive labor force. *All of this* is the same for today's prisoner (Smith and Hattery 2007).

The consent decree between prisons and private companies and government has been shattered. No longer will the private prison companies honor the agreement that prison goods be for use within prisons and sold only to government agencies. Now, the prison industries will sell to the highest bidder. With profits from this industry now soaring to nearly $2 billion a year, it is a monster fully out of control. We turn now to a discussion of the exportation of torture through U.S. prison practices abroad.

Exportation of Torture

The PIC has gone international in other ways as well, from simply being depositories for "terrorist enemies of the US"[15] (Herbert 2006a) in U.S.-run prisons abroad (Abu Ghraib and Guantanamo) to detaining and exiling these enemies of the state in countries that blatantly refuse to abide by the UN treaties on prison torture. We begin by examining the exportation of torture practices abroad.

Global Workers: Guards and Prison Administrators

Although global markets have existed for centuries and Marx was one of the first to comment on this (Marx and Engels 1990), Friedman (2006), in his brief history of the technology of the world, notes that in the third millennium not only are "goods" markets global but increasingly so are labor markets. Not only does he document the ways in which U.S. multinational corporations are able to move workers back and forth across international borders with ease, but he also demonstrates the way in which this transfer of labor is designed to transfer labor practices as well. (For a discussion of U.S.–China relations, see Friedman 2006, especially chapters 9 and 10.)

As news of the horrors of prison torture of Iraqis by Americans in the notorious Abu Ghraib[17] hit the headlines, Americans were stunned to learn about the various types of torture that our own citizens, both civilian and military, were utilizing against Iraqi detainees. Despite the fact that the Bush administration labeled these detainees as well as those detained in Guantanamo Bay as "enemies of the state" and thus not entitled to the protection of the Geneva Convention (see *New York Times* 2006), Americans nevertheless reacted strongly to the images and tales of torture they read and heard about taking place in this faraway land.

Yet, for those who study prisons, these tales were no surprise. Why? Because observers of U.S. prisons have long documented similar types of abuse (Elsner 2004; Mauer 2003). Moreover, as the details from Abu Ghraib and Guantanamo spilled out, the names of those involved rang familiar. As we document here, many of the men charged with setting up Abu Ghraib and designing protocols for both Abu Ghraib and Guantanamo had honed their prison administration skills and torture techniques in the U.S. prison system (Caldwell 2004). We argue not only that prison administrators were exported to Iraq but also that they took their torture tactics with them and were allowed to "flourish" away from the watchful eyes of "watchdog" groups in countries where there was no adherence to UN conventions regarding torture.

As early as May 2003, Attorney General John Ashcroft recruited several former prison administrators in the United States and appointed them to the International Criminal Investigative Training Program (ICITAP) (Caldwell 2004).[18] Among the men who served as part of the ICITAP team that set up Abu Ghraib were Terry Stewart (Arizona Department of Corrections), Gary DeLand (Utah Department of Corrections), John Armstrong (Connecticut Department of Corrections), and Lane McCotter (Texas, New Mexico, and Utah departments of corrections). Together these men have decades of experience administering prisons in the United States, and all of them have faced multiple charges of human rights violations both as prison administrators and as individuals. For example, Terry Stewart was accused of human rights violations when he detained several hundred inmates he thought were responsible for a prison fire shackled, on their bellies, outside in the Arizona heat for *four days*. Under John Armstrong's watch,

> In 1999, Timothy Perry, a 21-year-old mentally ill prisoner, was beaten to death by guards at Hartford Correctional Center. Perry put up no resistance when guards entered his cell and beat him to death. To cover up the murder, the guards continued to act as if Perry was alive and put him in four-point restraints. A nurse even injected Perry's corpse with Thorazine, a psychotropic drug that he was allergic to. At no time did anyone bother to call a doctor or to check if Perry was breathing. All was caught on film. None of the staff involved in Perry's murder were disciplined. The state of Connecticut paid $2.9 million to Perry's estate for the murder. (Caldwell 2004)

Similarly, O. Lane McCotter, who has worked in several prison systems in the West, including in Texas and Utah, has also faced allegations of torture of inmates under his supervision:

> In Utah, McCotter served five years as director of Corrections. In July 1994, prisoner Lonnie Blackmon was stabbed 67 times by another prisoner in a Utah state prison while eight guards looked on and did nothing. The lawsuit filed by Blackmon's family said that Blackmon was placed in an area of the prison that housed a majority of white supremacist gang members. Guards cuffed Blackmon and left him in the area "defenseless." While Blackmon was being stabbed, cameras were recording everything. The guards had a high-pressure hose and weapons at their disposal, yet no one acted. . . . In March 1997, the death of another prisoner was also caught on tape. Michael Valent, a 29-year-old schizophrenic, died of a blood clot that had formed in his legs and traveled to his lungs after being strapped naked to a restraining chair for 16 hours. Prison officials claimed that Valent had been restrained in the chair because he was banging his head against the wall and posing a threat to his own safety. . . .

The videos show the 115-pound Valent in his cell with a pillowcase wrapped around his head, some claim to shut out the voices in his head, while the guards forcibly remove him from his cell and cut off his clothing. He was then strapped to the chair, the leg restraints strapped to the tightest level. After 16 hours, Valent was removed from the chair, and he died in the shower three hours later. Valent's death was ruled a homicide, and his mother received a $200,000 settlement. McCotter claimed that Valent could've developed those clots anywhere. (Caldwell 2004)

Thus, we suggest that the U.S. government knowingly employed prison administrators with known records of human rights violations to set up and administer U.S. prisons abroad—namely, Abu Ghraib and Guantanamo—under the auspices of ICITAP. The descriptions provided here are remarkably similar to the images that came onto our television screens and across the Internet illustrating the abuses in Abu Ghraib and Guantanamo. Here is a description from an FBI account after a visit to Guantanamo:

"On several occasions witnesses saw detainees in interrogation rooms chained hand and foot in fetal position to floor with no chair/food/water; most urinated or defecated on themselves and were left there 18, 24 hours or more," according to one FBI account made public. . . . One FBI witness saw a detainee "shaking with cold," while another noted a detainee in a sweltering unventilated room was "almost unconscious on a floor with a pile of hair next to him (he had apparently been pulling it out through the night). (CNN 2007)

Next we examine the practice of shipping detainees to countries that patently refuse to abide by the UN conventions on torture.

Shipping Detainees to Other Countries

Bob Herbert of the *New York Times* first broke the story of Canadian citizen Maher Arar, who was detained by the United States for more than a year in Syria:

Arar was detained at New York's John F. Kennedy Airport in 2002 during a stopover on his way home to Canada from a vacation with his family in Tunisia. . . . He said he was chained and shackled by U.S. authorities for 11 days during interrogation and then flown to Syria, where he was tortured and forced to make false confessions. . . . He was released 10 months later, with Syrian officials saying they had no reason to hold him further. (CNN 2007)

Arar's case, with the help of *New York Times* op-ed contributor Herbert (2006b), brought widespread attention to a longtime practice engaged in by the CIA. Although the CIA has been in the business of international detainment for decades, Amnesty International (2006) reports that these rendition practices have changed and increased since September 11:

> Since 11 September the focus of rendition practice has shifted emphatically; the aim now is to ensure that suspects are not brought to stand trial, but are handed over to foreign governments for interrogation—a process known in the USA as "extraordinary rendition"—or are kept in US custody on foreign sites.

Newsweek confirms the existence of a special CIA plane that is specifically used for the CIA's rendition program:

> NEWSWEEK has obtained previously unpublished flight plans indicating the agency has been operating a Boeing 737 as part of a top-secret global charter servicing clandestine interrogation facilities used in the war on terror. (Hirsh, Hosenball, and Barry 2005)

We argue that this practice, like those practices in Abu Ghraib and Guantanamo, is justified under the aegis of the "war on terror" yet amounts to nothing short of the globalization of American prison torture practices.[19]

CONCLUSIONS

> Human rights advocates and foreign leaders have repeatedly called for its [Guantanamo Bay] shutdown, and the prison is regarded by critics as proof of U.S. double standards on fundamental freedoms in the war on terrorism (*USA Today* 2007).

In this chapter, we sought to expose two main issues. First, we identified examples of human rights violations perpetrated in U.S. prisons. Second, we exposed three processes by which these human rights violations are exported to the world's America. With regard to human rights violations perpetrated in U.S. prisons, we focused on two illustrations: the PIC and U.S. international prison practices, namely, the construction of U.S. prisons on foreign soil and the rendition of "enemies of the state" to prisons in countries that do not abide by human rights standards. At the time of the writing of this chapter, in the summer of 2007, the U.S. government had released the news that it plans to build a new international prison to house "enemy combatants" in Afghanistan (*USA Today* 2007). We can only speculate that the same staff employed to set up Abu Ghraib and Guantanamo Bay will find "new work" in setting up this latest institution for torture.

With regard to the PIC, we argue that it is a system that exploits inmates by engaging them in labor market work without adhering to labor market standards. Inmates are paid wages that are far below market value (typically forty to fifty cents per hour), they are not supplied with any benefits, and often their working conditions do not meet Occupational Safety and Health Administration standards. For example, at Parchman prison, inmates work in textile factories sewing uniforms, and these factories have no air conditioning. By any standards, the working conditions to which they are subjected constitute a violation of their human rights.

Added to this is the fact that prisons in the United States are filled with African American men. Thus, to use the language of Wright (1997), the PIC is a tool used not to rehabilitate but to cordon off African Americans much as they were cordoned off during slavery and Jim Crow segregation and to exploit their labor for individual and "class" gain.[20] Effectively, prisoners have suddenly been identified and reconstituted as the latest, greatest captive group whose labor can be exploited. And while inmates may see small benefits associated with the opportunities for labor that are created, as the inmates at Twin Rivers Correctional Facility so eloquently articulate, the PIC is a complex system that is not about rehabilitating inmates but rather about making money for a host of national and multinational corporations. Private prison corporations, such as CCA, make money by housing prisons and "leasing" their labor to the multinational corporations that make money and see soaring profits by paying below-market wages to inmates who labor for them.

Second, we demonstrated that the exploitation and human rights violations occurring in U.S. prisons are exported: both in tactics (such as at the Abu Ghraib military prison[21]) and in consumer goods. We note that just as the United States became the richest nation on earth by its extensive 250-year reliance on exploiting slave labor, today U.S.-based corporations secure their place as the richest companies in the world by exploiting vulnerable, mostly African American prison labor. Furthermore, it is clear that the building of U.S. prisons on foreign soil is attractive to the U.S. government for the same reasons that U.S.-based multinational corporations outsource manufacturing to places like Singapore and China. Not only can factories take advantage of exploiting labor and reducing their labor costs, but they are typically set up in countries that have fewer and less rigorous standards for workers' rights; for example, U.S. corporations are allowed to employ children under the age of sixteen, they are not held to maximum daily or weekly hours worked per employee, and they can legally run what amount to sweatshops. The building of U.S. prisons in countries like Iraq and Afghanistan provides the same attraction: prisons can be built and run without adherence to basic standards and laws, at least nominally, on U.S. soil.

Finally, we argue that the United States, the world's self-appointed jailer, skirts the very human rights models it exports to lands as vast as Iraq and Israel (see Elsner 2004) by engaging in unsanctioned torture in prisons in the United States as well as in prison and renditions practices abroad.

Specifically, the exportation of these practices, under the guise of the "war on terror," stands as a flagrant act of hypocrisy and contributes significantly to human rights violations both at home and abroad.

NOTES

1. Corrections Corporations of America, a private prison company, reported revenues of $1.2 billion in 2005 (www.correctionscorp.com).

2. Although one reviewer for this chapter was not happy with the use of the term "addiction" to note the high levels of incarceration in the United States, we first heard the term "incarceration addiction" in the keynote address delivered by Marsha Weissman at the University of North Carolina Law School annual conference on Race, Class, Gender, and Ethnicity (CRCGE) in February 2006. Therefore, we will use the term herein and are indebted to Marsha for bringing this to our attention.

3. See, especially, Office of the United Nations High Commission on Human Rights, www.ohchr.org/english/law/treatmentprisoners.htm (accessed October 29, 2006).

4. Mills (1956) first utilized the term coined by President Dwight D. Eisenhower, the "military-industrial complex," to refer to the complex political economy of the United States. No one, not even the president, could have imagined that such a speech would be the basis for discussing a similar relationship in the new millennium, but this time the interlocking relationships are the prison system, business, and the African American male population.

5. The UN Conventions on torture can be accessed at www.hrweb.org/legal/cat.html.

6. Figures on incarceration vary depending on what types of institutions (jails, prisons, military prison, and so on) are included in the count.

7. And, although we did not speak directly to this piece of the racialization of the American prison, we note that it is the most racially charged environment on earth: the American prison. Recently, the U.S. Supreme Court ruled that segregation in the prison system violated the 1954 decision in *Brown v. the Board of Education* and required that the California prison system desegregate its prison population (Gumbel 2005).

8. Chasin (2004) makes this point over and over. See, especially, pp. 235–39.

9. Wright (1997).

10. And the very fact of cordoning off some individuals means that the goods and riches of society are accessible only to those citizens who are *not* cordoned off. As Zinn and Dill (2005) note, every system of oppression has as its reflection a system of privilege. That which cordons some off "cordons" others in.

11. Evidence has surfaced that prestigious Ivy League Brown University was built on the fortunes the Brown family amassed in the slave trade. "Slavery was an integral part of the developing economy of colonial and post-Revolutionary Rhode Island. In the early and middle 1700s, members of the Brown family participated in the slave trade while simultaneously developing other enterprises. Slaves were employed at the family's spermaceti candle works and iron foundry, among other busi-

nesses, and almost certainly were used for farm work and household labor. In addition, while managing the 1770 construction of the College Edifice (later renamed University Hall), Nicholas Brown & Company apparently utilized some slave labor. In addition, at one time or another ships owned by Brown engaged in the triangle trade that brought slaves to the Caribbean and to America" (Nickel 2001).

12. Oshinsky (1997) notes that in response to anti–capital punishment protesters, the warden put the electric chair in the bed of a pickup truck so that he could move the executions around the prison grounds, thus avoiding further protests.

13. We note that institutional review boards recognize that inmates are vulnerable populations and that special considerations must be taken when doing research inside prisons. Yet there are no guidelines we can identify that require that companies that utilize prison labor conform to similar considerations that recognize and protect the special vulnerabilities associated with incarceration.

14. Some state and private prisons have adopted a requirement that inmates work, typically contracts they fill for private corporations ranging from Microsoft to Victoria's Secret, and the inmates are required to pay a sizable portion of their paychecks back to the prison, effectively paying for their own incarceration. For example, Oregon enacted legislation that required that all able-bodied prisoners in the Oregon state prison system engage in productive work.

15. In addition, the United States exports the exploitation of human rights via prison labor through the exportation of prisons themselves. The CCA operates several prisons abroad, including in Puerto Rico, Great Britain, and Australia.

16. Skilled in the area of torture, the U.S.-run international PIC covers the globe tracking down innocent human beings and abusing both their civil and their human rights (Herbert 2006b). Dana Priest (2006) revealed that the CIA operates a large overseas prison system in at least eight countries, including Thailand, Afghanistan, and eastern European countries.

17. Abu Ghraib is a prison in Baghdad, Iraq, that was used as a detention and torture center under the Saddam Hussein regime. Shortly after the United States invaded Iraq in March 2003, the U.S. military took over this site and converted it into a detention and torture center for use by American civilian and military personnel.

18. According to Caldwell (2004), the ICITAP has been in place for at least four decades, and its primary mission is to set up prisons and train prison staff in countries that are "clients" of the United States.

19. Using torture (both physical and psychological) as a way to coerce prisoners to give up information came to light in America with the Internet publication of the demeaning pictures detailing army prison guards torturing Iraqi detainees. What was surprising for many was that some of the guards were women who used prohibited sex practices in front of and in some instances on the Iraqi prisoners. The most infamous, of course, was then-Private Lindy England.

20. So that it is clear, we make a disclaimer here. We are not advocating the abolishment of prisons as a form of punishment for those who commit crimes. Prisons should be for violent criminals like John Robinson, who abducted women and children over the Internet and lured them to his rural Iowa home and then raped and murdered them, stuffing several of the dead into fifty-five-gallon drums. People who are addicted to marijuana and crack should not spend fifteen to twenty-five years in prison but should receive treatment for their illness.

21. The exportation/internationalization of the PIC is clearly seen at Abu Ghraib. The building and running of the military prison was under the direction of Lane Mc-Cotter, former director of the Utah state prison system. It was in Utah, under McCotter's watch, that prisoners were inhumanely treated, shackled to boards for days. In addition, former Army Specialist Charles A. Graner Jr., the ringleader of the torture at Abu Ghraib, learned his craft at State Correctional Institution-Greene in southwestern Pennsylvania. There, Graner routinely beat prisoners, often laughing while doing so.

REFERENCES

Amnesty International. 2005. *Amnesty International Report 2005 the State of the World's Human Rights.* London: Amnesty International.

———. 2006. "UNITED STATES OF AMERICA Below the Radar: Secret Flights to Torture and 'Disappearance.'" web.amnesty.org/library/Index/ENGAMR510512006 (accessed July 15, 2007).

Barnett, Erica. 2002. "Prison Coffee: Starbucks Admits Its contractor Uses Prison Labor." *Michigan Citizen* 24: A7.

Business for Social Responsibility. 2003. *Overview of Business and Human Rights.* San Francisco: Business for Social Responsibility.

Caldwell, Leah. 2004. "The Masterminds of Torture, Humiliation and Abuse: From Supermax to Abu Ghraib." *Prison Legal News,* October 15. www.prisonlegalnews.org.

Chasin, Barbara. 2004. *Inequality and Violence in the United States: Casualties of Capitalism.* Amherst, N.Y.: Humanity Books.

CNN. 2007. "FBI: Workers Saw Prisoner Abuse at Guantanamo." January 7. Available at www.cnn.com/2007/WORLD/americas/01/02/guantanamo/index.html.

Corrections Corporation of America. 2005. *Annual Report.* New York: Corrections Corporation of America.

Davis, Angela Y. 1998. "Masked Racism: Reflections on the Prison Industrial Complex." *Colorlines Magazine,* September, 11–17.

Eisenhower, Dwight. 1961. "Eisenhower's Farewell Address to the Nation." January 17, 1961, the White House. The Avalon Project at Yale Law School. www.yale.edu/lawweb/avalon/presiden/speeches/eisenhower001.htm (accessed February 16, 2006).

Elsner, Alan. 2004. "If US Plays Global Prison Ratings Game, It Ought to Play by Its Own Rules." *Christian Science Monitor,* March 4. Available at www.csmonitor.com/2004/0304/p09s01-cogn.html.

Evans, Linda. 2005. "Playing Global Cop: U.S. Militarism and the Prison Industrial Complex." In *Global Lockdown: Race, Gender, and the Prison-Industrial Complex,* edited by Julia Sudbury. New York: Routledge.

Friedman, Thomas L. 2006. *The World Is Flat: A Brief History of the Twenty-First Century.* New York: Farrar, Straus & Giroux.

Gumbel, Andrew. 2005. "Californian Jails End Racial Segregation." *Independent News,* February 25. www.independent.co.uk.

Hallett, Michael. 2004. "Commerce with Criminals: The New Colonialism in Criminal Justice." *Review of Policy Research* 21: 49–62.

Harrison, Paige M., and Allen J. Beck. 2005. *Prisoners in 2004*. Washington, D.C.: Bureau of Justice Statistics.

Hattery, Angela, and Earl Smith. 2007. *African American Families*. Thousand Oaks, Calif.: Sage.

Herbert, Bob. 2006a. "Dangerous Territory." *New York Times*, December 19.

———. 2006b. "Our Dirty War." *New York Times*, April 20.

Hirsh, Michael, Mark Hosenball, and John Barry. 2005. "Aboard Air CIA." *Newsweek*, February 28.

Marx, Karl, and Friedrich Engels. 1990. "Economic Manuscript of 1861–63: A Contribution to the Critique of Political Economy." In *Marx/Engels: Collected Works*. Vol. 32. New York: International Publishers.

Mauer, Marc. 2003. "Comparative International Rates of Incarceration: An Examination of Causes and Trends." www.sentencingproject.org (accessed July 23, 2003).

Mauer, Marc, and Meda Chesney-Lind. 2002. *Invisible Punishment*. New York: New Press.

Moncada, Alberto, and Judith Blau. 2006. "Human Rights and the Roles of Social Scientists." *Societies Without Borders* 1: 113–22.

New York Times. 2006. "President Bush's Speech on Terrorism: Bush on CIA Prisons" September 6. Transcript.

Nickel, Mark. 2001. "A Special Report: Slavery, the Brown Family of Providence and Brown University." Available at www.brown.edu/Administration/News_Bureau/Info/Slavery.html.

Oshinsky, David M. 1997. *Worse Than Slavery: Parchman Farm and the Ordeal of Jim Crow Justice*. New York: Free Press.

Pager, D. 2003. "The Mark of a Criminal Record." *American Journal of Sociology* 108: 937–75.

Priest, Dana. 2006. "Officials Relieved Secret Is Shared." *Washington Post*, September 7, 2006. accessed: January 15, 2007.

Reiman, Jeffrey. 2007. *The Rich Get Richer and the Poor Get Prison*. Boston: Allyn & Bacon.

Roberts, Dorothy E. 2004. "The Social and Moral Cost of Mass Incarceration in African American Communities." *Stanford Law Review* 56: 1271–1306.

Schlosser, Eric. 1998. "The Prison-Industrial Complex." *Atlantic Monthly* 282: 51–77.

Smith, Earl, and Angela Hattery. 2007. "If We Build It They Will Come: The Relationship between Private Prisons, Incarceration Rates, and Prison Industries in the US." *Societies Without Borders* 2: 276–92.

USA Today. 2007. "U.S. Building Afghan Prison, Not Guantanamo Alternative." June 23.

U.S.-China Economic Security Review Commission. 2005. *U.S. China Security Review Commission Policy Paper on Prison Labor and Forced Labor in China*. Washington, D.C.: U.S.-China Economic Security Review Commission.

Wright, Erik. 1997. *Class Counts: Comparative Studies in Class Analysis*. New York: Cambridge University Press.

Wright Mills, C. 1956. The Power Elite. London: Oxford Press.

Zinn, Baca, and Bonnie T. Dill. 2005. "Theorizing Differences from Multicultural Feminism." In *Gender through the Prism of Difference*, edited by Maxine Zinn, Pierrette Hondagneu-Sotelo, and Michael Messner. New York: Oxford University Press.

16

America's World and the World's America: Conclusions and Recommendations for Addressing Inequalities and Human Rights Violations

David Embrick, Earl Smith, and Angela Hattery

> The negative side to globalization is that it wipes out entire economic systems and in doing so wipes out the accompanying culture.
>
> —Peter L. Berger[1]

We began this book by looking at globalization and the existence of a global economy as an old phenomenon rather than something recent. This may seem contradictory to recent discourse on globalization, but, as we pointed out earlier, capitalist expansion, often crude and in many instances used as a justification for prevailing notions of white supremacy, has been around for centuries (Cox 1964). Indeed, when considering events in our history such as the chattel slave trade, the exploitation of resources such as diamonds and rubber in Africa (Williams 1944), and the genocide of Native Americans in the United States in the name of Manifest Destiny, the only good (and recent) thing about globalization is the ease by which we are able to travel and communicate with one another across the globe. Of course, new technology allows Western industrialized countries like the United States and Great Britain to communicate with one another. It also allows developed nations to easily connect with so-called Second and Third World countries. Yet with new technology inevitably comes new forms of economic, labor, and resource exploitation. With emerging and groundbreaking technology come increased environmental concerns and new ways in which to pollute the planet. And with such great technology come more violations of human rights.

The chapters in this book are indicative of the cutting-edge research and theoretical insight on some of the most current and pressing issues facing the United States and the global world. We leave no stone unturned and recognize that part of the problem of inequalities lies not only with right-wing conservatives and moderates but also with the most liberal of individuals and organizations. Indeed, in chapter 2, research scholar Eduardo Bonilla-Silva presents a critical analysis of the tenets of the human rights movement and their initiatives. His fundamental argument is that the human rights tradition remains limited by its own white-centered analysis and solutions to the social and racial injustices of the world. Bonilla-Silva's argument is that data are collected, researched, and analyzed, and then models are developed in the shroud of whiteness. Bonilla-Silva's insight into the limitations of the human rights tradition provides a path from which we can create more meaningful and fruitful solutions that address, if not entirely solve, all the attendant global inequalities currently existing. The first step is to increase our knowledge and understanding of what *we must do* as scholars and activists if we are to move one step closer to global social and racial justice.

One of the major rules of being an effective scholar is the ability to critique one's own work or the shortcomings of one's perspective. In this book, we have taken every precaution to ensure that we do not fall into the trap of presenting globalization from a strictly Western mainstream perspective. With that in mind, we have taken what we believe is a holistic and critical human rights approach on current issues such as race, gender, reparations, imprisonment and immigration, and so on. Our aim with these chapters is twofold: first, we wish to shed light on exactly how the United States continues to allow inequalities to persist in its borders, and, second, it is our intent to illustrate the varied ways in which the United States is a major contributor of inequalities outside its borders.

We see this not as a concluding chapter but as a golden opportunity for further discussion on the issue of globalization and the role of the United States as both a technological and economic leader of the global world and a major purveyor of global inequalities. To that end, we ask the tough questions. What does it mean to live in a country that, on the one hand, is awed for its freedoms and sheer economic, societal, and military might yet, on the other, is seen as a rogue nation from which its self-congratulations are mostly products of exploitation and human suffering? Further, what does it mean to live in a nation that was fundamentally built as a safe haven to escape British tyranny yet engages in tyrannical behavior of its own? And what does it mean to live in a place that is so contradictory in its desire to create a diverse and inclusive society while maintaining multiple systems of domination that undermine this articulated goal? What does it mean to be in a society that claims to be color blind yet continues to be stratified by color? Finally, of course, what does globalization hold for our future?

In the remaining pages of this chapter, we revisit the arguments made throughout this book and attempt to weave their commonalities together to get a sense of the larger scope of existing global inequalities. Specifically, we draw your attention to four major focal points that, tied together, represent a large picture of the impact of the United States on the rest of the world: the U.S. impact on the global world; the United States as an importer/exporter of social, racial, and global injustices; the need for reparations; and immigration. We then proceed to discuss our thoughts for the future on these issues if the United States continues its ruthless trajectory of exploitation and other human rights violations. Finally, we conclude by offering talking points and critical thought questions for each of the sections designed to give the reader a chance to synthesize the various sides of overtly contentious debates, such as reparations or immigration policy or the more subtle forms of racial and gender inequalities that are less openly discussed and often ignored.

U.S. IMPACT ON THE GLOBAL WORLD

We are at a critical juncture in American history. That is, we are at a point in time where even the smallest neglect on our part can have dramatic implications for years to come. For instance, as we write this, the sheer neglect of our country in the past eight years (and even well before then) over the issue of global warming has finally reached a point where government officials are taking notice. But is it too late? Should we be worried that by January 2007, news reporters were touting that this was New York's first snowless winter since 1877? According CNN.com (2007), the Christian Aid Agency has predicted that by 2050, there will be 1 billion people displaced by global warming. This is in addition to the 10 million refugees and over 24 million people who are already displaced because of wars and oppression. Further, there are dire consequences associated with a rapidly melting polar ice cap and numerous melting glaciers around the world. With the sea level slowly rising, we face not only loss of precious freshwater reserves but also frequent and unpredictable natural disasters, the most recent tragedies being the tsunami off the Indian Ocean in 2004 that killed over 300,000 people and, closer to home, in 2005, Hurricane Katrina, which severely battered the coastlines of Mississippi and Alabama and completely devastated New Orleans and other parts of Louisiana. Although it is too simple to say that the United States should shoulder the brunt of the blame for global warming, according to the U.S. Energy Information Administration, it is very true that the United States is, by far, the largest single emitter of carbon dioxide (as a result of the burning of fossil fuels), a leading cause of global warming (see Dowell 2007). And while almost every industrialized country in the world has taken action to deal with global warming and with human rights (Blau and Moncada 2005), the United States has systematically sided with major corporations such as ExxonMobil, which would rank as the sixth-largest expender of carbon dioxide if it were a country, to block federal legislation to limit greenhouse gases and other forms of pollution.

Consider too the bombing of Afghanistan or the war against Iraq and its "still to be found" weapons of massive destruction. Was this about oil? Or was this simply another "war of choice" as argued by John Tirman (2006), where President Bush, like many of his predecessors, decided that war is the single best way to power? Either way, as the price of oil goes up, so too does the demand for new forms of energy. And, as demand for more energy-efficient fuels such as corn-based ethanol goes up, so too the price of milk and eggs goes up. And, in the meantime, we are still waging a war in the Middle East and tragically losing more soldiers every day.[2]

The history of the United States and its role as a force for spreading "democracy" and "freedom" is really a mis-history of epic proportions. In fact, the failure to recognize history is not only one of the greatest challenges that today's academics face but also one of the central issues of importance when trying to understand the contemporary role of the United States in our globalized world. The fact that many countries do not recognize the United States as a legitimate and sincere force of good is a cause for concern. Further, most Americans do not recognize or fail to understand that the United States has a bad habit of creating rather than repairing havoc around the globe. For instance, according to the 2007 Failed State Index[3] (issued by *Foreign Policy* magazine and the Fund for Peace), Iraq is now ranked number two (out of 177 countries) in terms of instability and this is in spite of billions of dollars of foreign aid and over 150,000 American troops stationed in the country. Put another way, Iraq is currently the second most unstable country in the world. Some could argue that Iraq was already on its way to being unstable, regardless of United States intervention, and would have wound up taking second place in the race to the bottom sooner or later. On the other hand, just three years ago, Iraq ranked two slots higher at number four, with much less foreign aid. Similarly, one could argue that the consistent refusal by the United States to lend aid (although the United States quickly found reasons to lend aid in Kuwait and other oil-rich countries) or ignore human rights conditions in countries such as Sudan has led to dire consequences for those countries. According to the 2007 Failed State Index, Sudan is ranked as the *most unstable country in the world*, with over 2 million people having died since its independence in 1956 and approximately 4 million people having been displaced since that time.

THE NEED FOR REPARATIONS

Making a decision to become a more egalitarian and democratic society does not begin by dismissing all the past atrocities that have occurred on one's soil. The healing process does not begin with our words and actions today. And, as the chapters in part 2 suggest, the question of reparations has no easy answers. There are both practical and philosophical considerations that must be weighed carefully.

Practically speaking, the United States has a long history of exploitation that began 400 years ago at Jamestown. The colonists and settlers brought with them knowledge and ideologies that were developed in an agricultural economy. Thus, it is not surprising that the early settlers saw the vast tracts of land in the "new world" and launched what would become one of the largest and most productive agricultural movements in the history of humankind.

In order to increase their success, these agriculturalists engaged in two practices that ultimately created one of the most well-embedded systems of racial domination on the planet: the genocide of the Native Americans and the importation of Africans as chattel slaves. Wright (1997) eloquently articulates these practices as embedded in set of exploitive class relations. He argues that the Native Americans were determined to be unexploitable by the colonists—they could not be forced to work on the land, they were not cooperative, and they had their own well-established societies—and therefore the strategy for dealing with them was two pronged: genocide and removal. In contrast, the Africans who were stolen from their homeland and defined as chattel—they could be bought and sold like animals, they were slaves for life, and they passed their status on to their children—were highly exploitable. Thus, every measure was taken to ensure they survived so that their labor could be used to build the vast fortunes that characterized the families of the founders of the United States.

The reparations movements, as addressed in chapters 4 to 6, are primarily about redressing the centuries of exploitation that both the Native Americans and the African slaves and African American slaves experienced at the hands of white colonists. In the practical sense, proponents of reparations provide evidence for the vast fortunes that were built off the free labor, such as the Brown family that founded Brown University, and argue that the descendants of those exploited should be in some way compensated for their contributions. (Similar arguments are made on behalf of the descendants of "displaced" Native Americans from places like Manhattan, the land of which is worth today billions of dollars.) Practically speaking, many wonder how the redistribution of wealth (or land) would be implemented. Proposals range from government payouts to the descendants of these injustices (similar to the payouts to the Japanese Americans who were interred during World War II) to government-sponsored educational trust funds for members of racial/ethnic minority groups that were exploited during the first 300 years of this country.

The philosophical arguments focus more on the need to recognize the injustices of the past, the need for white Americans to "own" these injustices, and some action to be taken to both symbolically and in a real way "right the wrong." Proponents of this perspective argue that in order to begin the process of dismantling the racialized system of stratification that was created by these systems of exploitation in place during most of U.S. history, some good-faith attempts must be made that formally recognize the injustice (some states, for example, have officially "apologized" for slavery) and provide access to opportunities such as education and work that have been denied racial and ethnic minorities, specifically Native Americans and African Americans. The chapters included in this text were designed to ask the questions and encourage the reader to grapple with these complex issues.

IMMIGRATION

Recent data on U.S. population suggest that the minority population will surpass the population of whites within the next twenty-five to fifty years (Bean and Stevens 2003). This dramatic demographic shift has profound implications for the way researchers examine and understand race, gender, and diversity in the United States. As the immigration debate heats up in America, so too is there a rise in the racial discrimination against Mexican American and other Latino American groups as well as against Mexican and Latino immigrants coming into the United States (for research on group threat, see Burr, Galle, and Fossett 1991; Fossett and Kiecolt 1989). The issue for current and future researchers is what these demographic changes mean for a society that prides itself on its diversity yet is deeply ambivalent about racial and ethnic integration on social, economic, and political levels.

As with the issue of reparations, immigration is at the center of political debate in the United States. Immigration presents both philosophical and practical quandaries that the chapters in part 3 of the book attempt to address. Philosophically, one of the major issues centers on the inscription on the Statue of Liberty, one of the most potent symbols of the United States. Her message implies that the United States is a place that welcomes those from other lands who bring their talents to U.S. soil where they "melt" into the existing population, barely distinguishable a generation after arriving here. Yet several of the chapters in this text focus on the severe discrimination that immigrants, particularly those from

Mexico and the Caribbean, face when they come to the United States presumably to seek a better life and better work than existed in the communities of origin. We apply the same question to immigration that we applied to race: at both the individual and the institutional level, how can we reconcile the cognitive dissonance that inevitably arises around the immigration debate. We extol the virtues inscribed on the Statue of Liberty, but do we really mean "Give us your poor, your tired, your huddled masses longing to be free?"

In addition, the immigration debate is confounded with debates about work, discrimination, access, and citizenship. Who should be allowed to enter the United States, under what conditions, and with what access to opportunities that exist here? Who benefits and who is hurt by immigration? Many big businesses that are traditionally very conservative side with liberals on immigration because for them the issue is about securing a highly vulnerable and thus highly exploitable labor force. Finally, in chapter 8, Goldsmith and Romero consider one of many types of discrimination faced by immigrants, especially those from the "global South": racial profiling. Specifically, they consider the use of "Mexicanness" as a category for legal racial profiling.

Does citizenship imply social inclusion, and, if not, what are the implications for granting citizenship to economically and socially established immigrants living in the United States? What are the consequences for not doing so? What is the relationship between immigration and citizenship? Chapter 7 addresses these questions by focusing on the human rights violations that are inherent in current immigration patterns.

THE UNITED STATES AS AN IMPORTER/EXPORTER OF SOCIAL, RACIAL, AND GLOBAL INJUSTICES

In part 4 of the text, the authors examine the role of the United States as an importer and exporter of social, racial, and global injustices. As we noted at the beginning of this chapter, globalization is not new. What is new is the magnitude. As Thomas Friedman (2006), noted op-ed contributor for the *New York Times* argued in his book *The World Is Flat*, technology now allows any person with a computer and an Internet connection to participate in globalization. As with most "advances," there are both good and bad, both intended and unanticipated consequences (Merton 1976). And such is the case with social and racial injustices. In its infancy, the United States firmly established itself as an "importer" of injustice. Not only did the colonists bring with them systems of domination including patriarchy and class-based stratification, but they almost immediately joined the European movement of importing Africans as chattel slaves. This, along with the near genocide of the Native American population, laid the groundwork for a system of racial domination that may be unparalleled elsewhere.

Once the United States gained international recognition and some power, it quickly moved into the business of exporting injustice. This has occurred by many pathways, including the outsourcing of low-skilled jobs to poor countries with highly vulnerable populations that can be exploited to the outsourcing of some of the worst torture practices that are now administered in U.S. prisons all over the globe. In chapter 15, Hattery and Smith document how these practices become intertwined with the rise of exploitative prison labor practices. These examples illustrate the ways in which the United States is able to engage in high-level human rights violations globally while still presenting herself as a beacon of democracy and meritocracy (see chapter 13). Fundamentally, this book has been put together to expose these practices both inside and outside the U.S. borders as well as to expose the high level of hypocrisy and disconnect between our "talk" and our "walk."

WHERE DO WE GO FROM HERE? FIGHTING THE "GOOD FIGHT"

For all that is said about the United States of America at the end of the day, it remains a great country. That is, politics and politicians aside, there remains great potential for the United States to become a progressive leader in an ever-growing global society. And while we, as editors of this book, may rant about America's many shortcomings, the truth of the matter is that we enjoy living and working here. We enjoy great American pastimes such as baseball and football. In particular, we enjoy our jobs as professors, the "last good job in America," according to Stanley Aronowitz (2001). Moreover, the United States has produced some great intellectuals, activists, poets, and writers. It is, after all, home to the first American sociologist, W. E. B. Du Bois, and countless other great leaders, such as Martin Luther King Jr., President John F. Kennedy, and Malcolm X. And finally, we enjoy the many freedoms that we often take for granted, such as free speech and the ability to shop where and when we want. And, as citizens, we are not forced to wake up every morning at 6:00 A.M. to blaring speakers informing us that it is time to get up and exercise.[4]

However, the United States is also a time bomb, ever ticking and waiting to be set off. Thus, it is up to us to make sure that this never happens. It is up to us to make sure that we are all educated about the world and, in particular, how the United States contributes to the social and racial injustices that occur throughout the world. But how exactly can we, as individuals, go about addressing inequalities that have haunted us since well before the

British vessels *Treasurer* and *White Lion*[5] sold their cargoes of slaves to the Virginia settlement of Jamestown in 1619? What kinds of policy suggestions can we recommend that can be easily implemented yet are strong enough to actually create change for the better? What policy recommendations can we suggest, given the scope and magnitude of some of the inequalities presented in this book, that have not been thought of or even implemented at some previous level? Those questions are never easily addressed in research journals and in scholarly texts. We attempt to do so in the next section.

Policy Recommendations

Like most books dealing with racial and social justice and global inequalities would suggest, there is no simple way to address these issues with policy recommendations that are often overlooked by government officials and policy advocates alike. In fact, since the days of the Kennedy/Johnson Great Society programs with the passage of equal housing laws, equal schooling laws, equal pay laws, the Voting Rights Act and so on, every conceivable statute and law on the books allows for statements, like we make in this chapter, that America is a great country. Here, however, we draw on the authors of our text to provide some insight on what went wrong and what is wrong.

Individual

Examine your own beliefs, ideologies, and practices. Own your own privilege. Work to reduce your own prejudices. Practice social justice in your personal and professional life. Learn what diversity is and how to work toward diverse communities at home, school, and work. For example, do not decry segregated schools in your community and then make justifications for sending your children to private academies. Hold lawmakers and law enforcers accountable. And, perhaps most important, join a social movement.

Institutional

Examine the articulated missions of the institution with special attention to the dissonance between that which is extolled and that which is practiced. Make human rights, not profit making, the central mission of the institution. Seek more and more innovative ways to diversify the institution. Institute practices such as living-wage policies and antidiscrimination practices in lending, hiring, and access to education and at all stages of the criminal justice system. Work for change.

National

Practice what you "talk about"; practice what you preach. Governments need to engage in the same type of self-reflection that we recommend to individuals. Examine beliefs, ideologies, and practices. Carefully examine inconsistencies between articulations of beliefs (constitutions) and practices. Make human rights a central part of the national agenda and then create legislation to ensure that human rights of all citizens will be protected above and beyond all other self-interests. This includes living-wage legislation, the *enforcement* of civil rights legislation, fair-lending legislation, reconstituting education as a basic human right, and reforming all aspects of the criminal justice system. Walk the walk, do not just talk the talk. Stop the importation and exportation of social and racial injustice. Finally, appoint and elect leaders with the courage to put aside the interests of those currently in power and work for a society of diversity and inclusion where the rights of all are held sacred.

Where Do We Go from Here?

> The twentieth century came to a close in an atmosphere astonishingly reminiscent of that which had presided over its birth—the "belle époque" (and it was beautiful, at least for capital).

—Samir Amin (2000)

We conclude this chapter and this book with words from Malcolm X (n.d.), the great American civil rights activist and leader. The first of his quotes reflects the totality of what we have tried to accomplish with this book:

> You're not to be so blind with patriotism that you can't face reality. Wrong is wrong, no matter who does it or says it.

America is no longer the isolated superpower that it was in the nineteenth century and the beginning of the twentieth. It has developed economic relationships on a global scale unheard of even in the past twenty years. And although the United States slowly lost its appetite for expansionism as it crept into the twenty-first century, the idea of Manifest Destiny takes on a whole new meaning for transnational corporations whose business is essentially the exploitation of labor and land of mostly so-called Third World people and nations.

These major American businesses operate best when backed by government. Thus, companies such as ExxonMobil (Dowell 2007) and Haliburton (see CorpWatch 2007) would not have experienced the phenomenally massive bottom-line growth that they did were it not for their relationship with the U.S. government and the mostly blind eye that is given to their practices. In turn, these massive corporations are able to engage in slave and child labor such as Nike in Pakistan and Coca-Cola in the sugarcane fields of El Salvador (see Lobe 2004). Today, these practices are unheard of in America. The end result is a reality that few Americans want to admit: that the United States continues to sanction and even encourage racial and social injustices in the name of democracy and the free market. However, as Malcolm X suggested once upon a time, "wrong is wrong," regardless of who does it.

So where do we go from here? The wonders provided to travelers by globalization are mostly ones afforded to the wealthier global citizens. Unfortunately, over half the world's population owns barely 1 percent of the global wealth (Davies et al. 2006). And regardless of how the world turns, unless there is significant change that alters what Immanuel Wallerstein and other scholars such as Samir Amin have labeled a world systems global marketplace,[6] there is little hope that we will see a more just and equal global future. That said, there are two things that have historically proven to be effective at creating social change: youth and coalition building. The need for youth as a social catalyst is crucial for creating change for a better world (see Bonilla-Silva 2006). Somewhere between Reaganomics in the 1980s and today, the power of youth to make real social change got lost in the era of electronic communication and perhaps the new and expanding multimedia. However, if we really want to look at the impact of youth in creating viable and concrete social movements that lead to social change, all we need to do is look at the role of youth during the civil rights era and especially the Selma-to-Montgomery march.[7]

The second crucial piece for creating effective social change lies in coalition building. However, the coalition building should be centered on the needs of the oppressed. As Bonilla-Silva pointed out in chapter 2 of this book, effective collectivities must work "toward group-level solutions for the 'problems' faced by the oppressed people of the world." The current issue at hand should not be equality for all, as it may be a realistically unachieveable goal. Even were it achieveable, how long should we expect oppressed people to stay oppressed while we "figure" things out? Indeed, the question should be, How do we lift oppressed people out of their poverty-stricken or war-torn conditions—immediately? Hope is not lost completely, however. As we put the final touches on this book, the first United States Social Forum is taking place in Atlanta, Georgia. Led in part by Project South, an institute designed to research and eliminate poverty and genocide, a local-global justice movement is being developed as a countermovement to the growing global inequalities that plague our world (see chapter 14).

There is still so much to be done. Inequalities do not solve themselves, and neither will progression occur when there is all talk and little activism.

This book was developed in part to stimulate discussion toward activism. It was developed not simply as a critique of the United States and its contributions to global inequalities in the twenty-first century but as a focal point from which we dissect some of the larger issues that plague us today. We conclued with a second quote from Malcolm X, one that directly reflects what we editors hope to achieve with this book and where we hope fruitful debate will lead to:

> Speaking like this doesn't mean that we're anti-white, but it does mean we're anti-exploitation, we're anti-degradation, we're anti-oppression.

TALKING POINTS

The purpose of talking points is to critically think about and synthesize the various debates raised in each part of this book. We offer these points in the hope that they will stimulate further discussions into each of the subject areas.

Part 1

1. What are some of the implications of Bonilla-Silva's argument in chapter 2 that the radical call to drop "identity politics" divests rather than invests efforts to create a larger, human rights-based movement?
2. The United States represents a hodgepodge society of various racial and ethnic groups, the majority group being white. However, the world's population is overwhelmingly comprised of nonwhites. What are the implications of these demographics in terms of creating a global community?
3. As the minority population slowly increases in number in the United States, what effect will this have on the mostly white male power structure that currently runs corporate America?
4. Consider the word *diversity*. Have you ever heard the word? In what context did you hear it? Was the word clearly defined when you heard it, and, if so, how was it defined?
5. With perhaps the exception of education, there is no other area in American society where the use of the term *diversity* has created such fervor of curiosity, debate, and criticism. Since the civil rights triumphs of the 1960s, laws have been created to outlaw formal employment discrimination against women and minorities. However, persistent racial, ethnic, and gender inequalities at all levels of the corporate world raise interesting questions about the sincerity of companies and

organizations that claim to be interested in maintaining a diverse and equal opportunity workforce. What would such questions look like?

Part 2

1. After reading chapters 4 through 6, what are your thoughts on the issue of reparations?
2. Even though it has been over 140 years since slavery was considered legal in the United States, there are many victims still alive who survived the brutal oppression that existed during apartheid in America. Do you believe that, at the very least, these remaining victims should be compensated for past wrongdoings that were committed against them or their loved ones? Why or why not?
3. As you have read in chapter 5, many other countries have issued reparations to groups that were previously mistreated within their borders, either in the form of monetary compensation or in the form of a national public apology. Do you think that the United States, as one of the wealthiest nations in the world, has a moral obligation to at least acknowledge its role as a major oppressor of various minority groups over the course of its history?
4. Can you think of alternative ways that we can solve the issue of reparations in the United States, particularly in regard to African Americans?
5. The issue has been brought up many times that before we give reparations to African Americans, we need to consider reparations for Native Americans. Arguably, Native Americans have been victims of nothing less than genocide as a result of European colonization and its policies that ranged from Manifest Destiny in the early to mid-1800s to the General Allotment Act of 1887 and termination in the latter half of the twentieth century.[8] What do you think about this argument?

Part 3

1. After reading chapters 7 through 12, what have you learned that you did not already know about immigration issues?
2. In chapter 7, Golash-Boza and Parker address the issue of immigration and specifically the guest worker program through the lens of human rights. If you were appearing on *Lou Dobbs* today to discuss immigration, how would you counter his arguments that a guest worker program is the ideal solution to the immigration "problem" facing the United States at the beginning of the twenty-first century?

3. There are many forms of racial/ethnic discrimination that are documented by the U.S. government every year. Given the claim in the U.S. Declaration of Independence and the civil rights legislation of the 1960s, how do you evaluate the legality of racial profiling as outlined in chapter 8? In addition, what factors play into the ability of Hispanics to access the American dream as argued in chapters 9 and 10?

4. The majority of chapters in part 3 (and throughout the book) have focused on racial injustice. In the final chapters in this part, the authors take on the intersection of race and gender oppression. How are race and gender oppression linked? How are they similar, and how are they different? What role do the United States and other developed countries (e.g., Israel) play in perpetuating gender inequality, gender discrimination, and even gendered violence through the class exploitation inherent in setting up factories across international borders?

Part 4

1. Trace the development of constitutions, especially the U.S. Constitution. Compare your notes after reading chapter 13 with what you learned in high school civics class. What role do constitutions play in movements for social justice?

2. Describe the development of the World Social Forum, a social movement, as described by Katz-Fishman and Scott in chapter 14. What lessons can be applied from such a large social movement to local grassroots movements in your own institutions (school, college, or workplace) and communities? Decide on an issue you would like to address and, using Katz-Fishman and Scott's work as a guide, outline the grassroots movement you would like to start.

3. The fundamental question raised in chapter 13 is the purpose of incarceration in the twenty-first-century United States. Summarize the ways in which prison labor is now used in the production of goods and services. Were you surprised by some of the corporations that use prison labor? Think about whether you believe inmates should work and under what conditions. Design a proposal for the use of prison labor (or not) by corporations based in or doing business in the United States.

Overall Questions

1. Reflect on your understanding of race, human rights, and inequalities before you read the chapters in this text. Has the text provided you with new information? What kind?

2. Has the text provided you with a more complex understanding of the relationships between race, human rights, and inequalities?
3. Make a list of the problems or issues you find most pressing today.
4. Taking one of the issues or problems you identified, develop a fact sheet about that issue or problem, articulate a solution, and then outline an action plan for tackling that issue or problem.

NOTES

1. This quote was taken from "An Interview with Peter L. Berger," *The Christian Century* 29 (1997): 972–78.

2. According to Antiwar.com, the official number of U.S. soldier deaths is 25,950 with an estimated number of deaths ranging from a low of 23,000 to a high of 100,000. For a comparison of what these casualties mean, there were 47,424 combat-related deaths during the Vietnam War and 33,741 deaths during the Korean War.

3. See link for Foreign Policy Magazine and the Failed State Index at www.foreign policy.com/story/cms.php?story_id=3865&page=7.

4. For those of you who are wondering what we are talking about here, this is a common practice in many communities in Vietnam. These communities are surrounded by loudspeakers that serve to give public announcements and news flashes to outlying villages and towns. However, as a preventive measure for obesity, the government has decided to use the speakers to wake up its citizens and request that they begin their morning exercise.

5. According to a new study by retired Berkeley historian Engel Sluiter, the slaves who were forced to relocate to Jamestown were originally forced to board a Portuguese slave ship in Angola. Two British pirate ships with Dutch flags seized the Portuguese slave ship along with all its cargo and proceeded to sell the slaves to various colonies along its route. According to Sluiter, the slaves were not of various ethnic backgrounds but rather represented one ethnic group with a common Bantu language (Rein 2006).

6. The world system analysis or "world system theory" is a concept developed primarily by Immanuel Wallerstein. It is a macrolevel Marxist perspective that seeks to explain the capitalist economy on a global scale. In this analysis, Wallerstein argues that the Western industrialized countries exploit other countries in a complex network of unequal economic exchanges. This endless level of exploitation serves to keep the industrialized Western nations (or core countries) wealthy and Second and Third World countries at an extremely poor level of dependence that ensures their continued participation and exploitation as a periphery country (Wallerstein 1974).

7. There are a number of good essays and books on the role of young people in this sector of the civil rights movement. See, especially, Hine, Jakoubek, and Dolan (1994).

8. For more information on this topic, see Cornell (1988).

REFERENCES

Amin, Samir. 2000. "The Political Economy of the Twentieth Century." *Monthly Review* 52, no. 2. www.monthlyreview.org/600amin.htm (accessed November 13, 2007).

Aronowitz, Stanley. 2001. *The Last Good Job in America: Work and Education in the New Global Technoculture*. Lanham, Md.: Rowman & Littlefield.

Bean, Frank D., and Gillian Stevens. 2003. *America's Newcomers and the Dynamics of Diversity*. New York: Russell Sage Foundation.

Blau, Judith, and Alberto Moncada. 2005. *Human Rights: Beyond the Liberal Vision*. Lanham, Md.: Rowman & Littlefield.

Bonilla-Silva, Eduardo. 2006. *Racism without Racists: Color-Blind Racism and the Persistence of Racial Inequality in the United States*. Lanham, Md.: Rowman & Littlefield.

Burr, Jeffrey A., Omer R. Galle, and Mark A. Fossett. 1991. "Racial Occupational Inequality in Southern Metropolitan Areas, 1940–1980: Revisiting the Visibility-Discrimination Hypothesis." *Social Forces* 69, no. 3: 831–50.

CNN.com. 2007. "Global Warming Heats Up Refugee Crisis." *Science and Space*, June 18. Available at www.cnn.com/2007/TECH/science/06/18/warming.refugees.reut.

Cornell, Stephen. 1988. *The Return of the Native: American Indian Political Resurgence*. New York: Oxford University Press.

CorpWatch: Holding Corporations Accountable. 2007. "Ongoing Investigations into Halliburton as of April 2005." www.corpwatch.org/article.php?id=12266 (accessed July 10, 2008).

Cox, Oliver. 1964. *Capitalism as a System*. New York: Monthly Review Press.

Davies, James, Susanna Sandstrom, Anthony Shorrocks, and Edward Wolff. 2006. *The World Distribution of Household Wealth*. New York: World Institute for Development Economics Research of the United Nations University.

Dowell, LeiLani. 2007. "U.S. Biggest Culprit of Global Warming." *Workers World*, January 15. www.workrs.org.

Fossett, Mark, and K. Jill Kiecolt. 1989. "Relative Size of Minority Populations and White Racial Attitudes." *Social Science Quarterly* 70: 820–35.

Friedman, Thomas. 2006. *The World Is Flat: A Brief History of the 21st Century*. New York: Farrar, Straus & Giroux.

Hine, Darlene, Robert Jakoubek, and Sean Dolan. 1994. *Pursuing the Dream: From the Selma-Montgomery March to the Formation of Push (1965–1971)*. Boston: Chelsea House.

Lobe, Jim. 2004. "Coke Benefiting from Child Labor in Sugar Cane Fields." *Organic Consumers Association*, OneWorld.net.

Merton, Robert K. 1976. *Sociological Ambivalence*. New York: Free Press.

Rein, Lisa. 2006. "Mystery of Va's First Slaves Is Unlocked 400 Years Later." *Washington Post*, September 3, A01.

Tirman, John. 2006. *100 Ways America Is Screwing Up the World*. New York: Harper-Perennial.

Wallerstein, Immanuel. 1974. *The Modern World System I: Capitalist Agriculture and the Origins of the European World-Economy in the Sixteenth Century.* New York: Academic Press.

Williams, Eric. 1944. *Capitalism and Slavery.* Chapel Hill: University of North Carolina Press.

Wright, E. O. 1997. *Class Counts: Comparative Studies in Class Analysis.* New York: Cambridge University Press.

X, Malcolm. 1965. *The Autobiography of Malcolm X.* New York: Ballantine Books.

———. n.d. www.cmgww.com/historic/malcolm/about/quotes.htm (accessed January 24, 2008).

Index

About the Contributors

EDITORS

Angela J. Hattery, Ph.D., is associate professor in sociology and women and gender studies at Wake Forest University. She completed her B.A. at Carleton College and her M.S. and Ph.D. at the University of Wisconsin, Madison before joining the faculty of Wake Forest in 1998. Her research focuses on social stratification, gender, family, and race. She is the author of numerous articles, book chapters, and books, including *African American Families* (2007) *Women, Work, and Family: Balancing and Weaving* (2001), and her forthcoming book *Intimate Partner Violence* (2008).

David G. Embrick is an assistant professor in the Department of Sociology at Loyola University, Chicago and a faculty fellow at the Center for Urban Research and Learning. He received his Ph.D. from Texas A&M University in 2006. He is a former American Sociological Association MFP Fellow and has published in a number of journals, including *Sociological Forum, Race and Society*, and the *Journal of Intergroup Relations*. He is currently working on a book project that examines the discrepancies between corporations' public views and statements on diversity and their implementation of diversity as a policy. He argues that corporate managers use diversity as a mantra while they maintain highly racially inequitable work environments. David is also working on a multiuniversity project with several other colleagues examining the differences between student racial attitudes in different academic environments (e.g., public vs. private and faith-based vs. secular universities).

Earl Smith, Ph.D., is professor of sociology and the Rubin Distinguished Professor of American Ethnic Studies at Wake Forest University. He is the director of the Wake Forest University American Ethnic Studies Program. He is the former chairperson of the Department of Sociology, Wake Forest University (1997–2005). Prior to his appointment at Wake Forest University, he was the dean of the Division of Social Science at Pacific Lutheran University (PLU) in Tacoma, Washington. He also served as chairperson of the Department of Sociology at PLU. He has numerous publications in the area of professions, social stratification, family, and urban sociology and has published extensively in the area of the sociology of sport. His most recent books include *Race, Sport and the American Dream* (2007) and *African American Families* (2007).

AUTHORS

Amy Ansell is associate professor of sociology at Bard College. Her current research interests revolve around the intersection of white racial attitudes and color-blind politics in debates surrounding rights, multiculturalism, and citizenship in the United States, Europe, and postapartheid South Africa. Publications include *Race and Ethnicity: The Key Concepts*, with John Solomos (forthcoming); *New Right, New Racism: Race and Reaction in the U.S. and Britain* (1997); *Unraveling the Right: The New Conservatism in American Thought and Politics* (1998); and other reviews and essays in *Ethnic and Racial Studies, American Journal of Sociology, Critical Sociology, Contemporary Sociology*, and *Politikon*.

Cynthia Bejarano is a native of southern New Mexico and the El Paso–Juárez border and an associate professor of criminal justice at New Mexico State University (NMSU). Her publications and research interests focus on border violence at the U.S.–Mexico border; race, class, and gender issues; and Latino youths' border identities in the Southwest. Bejarano is the author of *"Qué Onda?" Urban Youth Cultures and Border Identity* (2005). Bejarano is also the principal administrator for the NMSU College Assistance Migrant Program and cofounder of Amigos de las Mujeres de Juarez, a nonprofit organization working to end the violence against women in Chihuahua, Mexico, and the borderlands. She is currently working, with colleague Rosa-Linda Fregoso, on a new book: *Gender Terrorism Feminicide in the Américas*.

Judith Blau is professor of sociology at the University of North Carolina, Chapel Hill, and president of Sociologists Without Borders, US. Her recent collaborative books are: *Human Rights: Beyond the Liberal Vision* (2005), *Justice in the United States: Human Rights and the U.S. Constitution* (2006), *The Public Sociologies Reader* (2006), and *Freedoms and Solidarities: The Pursuit of Human Rights* (2007). She is the coeditor of *Societies without Borders* and is working on a volume on collective goods and human rights that will accompany a coedited volume, *The Leading Rogue State: The US and Human Rights*.

Eduardo Bonilla-Silva received his Ph.D. in sociology from the University of Wisconsin, Madison in 1993. He is a professor of sociology at Duke University. So far, he has published three books: *White Supremacy and Racism in the Post-Civil Rights Era* (2001), *Racism without Racists* (2006), and *White-Out* (2003, with Ashley Doane). He is the 2007 recipient of the Lewis A. Coser Award for Theoretical Agenda-Setting awarded by the theory section of the American Sociological Association.

David L. Brunsma received his Ph.D. from the University of Notre Dame (1998) and is currently associate professor of sociology and black studies at the University of Missouri, Columbia. His primary research is in racial identities, racial inequalities, racism, and human rights. He has published ten books, including *Mixed Messages: Multiracial Identities in the Color-Blind Era* (2006), *Beyond Black: Biracial Identity in America* (2002), *The Sociology of Katrina* (2007), and *The Leading Rogue State: The United States and Human Rights* (2008).

Karen Manges Douglas is assistant professor of sociology at Sam Houston State University. She received her Ph.D. from the University of Texas at Austin. Manges Douglas has published in the areas of race/ethnicity, welfare, and poverty.

Joe R. Feagin is Ella C. McFadden Professor at Texas A&M University. Among his fifty books, some coauthored, are *Systemic Racism* (2006), *Liberation Sociology* (2001), *Racist America* (2000), *The First R: How Children Learn Race and Racism* (2001), *Racial and Ethnic Relations* (2008), *The Many Costs of Racism* (2003), *White Men on Race* (2003), *Black in Blue: African-American Police Officers and Racism* (2004), and *Two-Faced Racism* (2007). He is the 2006 recipient of a Harvard Alumni Association achievement award and was the 1999–2000 president of the American Sociological Association.

Tanya Golash-Boza received her Ph.D. from the University of North Carolina, Chapel Hill (2005) and has a joint appointment in sociology and American studies at the University of Kansas, where she teaches classes on racism and globalization. She has published articles on Latino racial identity in *Social Forces, International Migration Review,* and *Ethnic and Racial Studies.* She is currently working on a book on constructions of blackness in Peru.

Pat Rubio Goldsmith is associate professor and chair of the Department of Sociology-Anthropology at the University of Wisconsin, Parkside. He earned a doctorate's degree from the Department of Sociology at the University of Arizona. He has published in journals including the *Sociology of Education* and *Social Problems.* In addition to research on immigration and human rights, he is conducting research on the causes and consequences of racial segregation.

Mary Hovsepian, Ph.D., is visiting assistant professor at Duke University. Her research specialties are in the areas of economic change and Third World development, globalization, political sociology, and the Middle East. Her book manuscript, *The Politics of Commodity Chains,* is under way.

Walda Katz-Fishman received her Ph.D. from Wayne State University and is a scholar activist and professor of sociology at Howard University. She is board chair of Project South: Institute for the Elimination of Poverty and Genocide and sits on the National Planning Committee of the United States Social Forum. She is a contributing editor to popular education tool kits and books, including *The Roots of Terror, Today's Globalization, The Critical Classroom,* and *Readings in Humanist Sociology.* She was corecipient of the American Sociological Association 2004 Award for the Public Understanding of Sociology.

Linda Lopez is the program director for cross-directorate activities in the Directorate for Social, Behavioral and Economic Sciences at the National Science Foundation. Prior to joining the National Science Foundation, she worked at the American Political Science Association and Chapman University in the Department of Political Sciences. She specializes in American politics with a particular focus on racial and ethnic politics and the representation of women of color in state legislatures. She is currently working on research that examines the role that skin color plays in perceptions on discrimination in the workplace and education settings among Latina/o populations. She received her Ph.D. from the University of Southern California.

Alberto Moncada has a Ph.D. in public law from Madrid University and in sociology and education from London University. He has taught at universities in Spain, the United States, and Peru; was the first rector of the University of Piura, Peru; and has directed research projects, including one on the links between American and Spanish culture. He is the author of thirty books and currently vice president of UNESCO's Valencia Center and president of Sociologists Without Borders, International. He frequently appears on Spanish television and radio.

M. Cristina Morales received her Ph.D. from Texas A&M University and is currently an assistant professor of sociology at the University of Texas at El Paso. Her research areas of interest include social inequality (race/ethnic, gender, and immigration/citizenship) and social demography (labor and immigration). She has published in the areas of immigration, race and ethnic demography, spatial inequality, and education.

Douglas A. Parker received his B.A. in English-language arts from San Francisco State University and his M.A. and Ph.D. in sociology from the University of California, Berkeley, and is a professor of sociology at California State University, Long Beach. Previously, he taught at Queen's University at Kingston, Ontario, and Colorado College and was employed in the epidemiology division of the National Institute on Alcohol Abuse and Alcoholism, where he was the principal investigator for a study of occupational conditions, drinking patterns, and psychological functioning among 1,367 full-time employed men and women in metropolitan Detroit. He has published papers in sociological, public health, and substance abuse journals and chapters in books and research monographs.

Mary Romero is professor of justice studies and social inquiry at Arizona State University. She is the author of *Maid in the U.S.A.* Recent publications include *Blackwell Companion to Social Inequalities* (2005) and *Latina and Latino Popular Culture* (2002). Her most recent articles are published in *Critical Sociology, Law and Society Review, British Journal of Industrial Relations, Cleveland State Law Review, Villanova Law Review, DePaul Law Review, Journal of Gender, Social Policy and the Law, Denver University Law Review,* and *Harvard Educational Review.*

Mercedes Rubio lives in Washington, D.C., and is assistant director for training in the Division of Adult Translational Research and Treatment Development at the National Institute of Mental Health (NIMH). Prior to joining NIMH, she was director of the Minority Affairs Program, program director and co–principal investigator on an NIMH/National Institute of Drug Abuse T-32 Diversity Training Grant, and staff sociologist at the American Sociological Association. She received her B.A. in sociology at California State University, Bakersfield, and her M.A. and Ph.D. in sociology from the University of Michigan.

Rogelio Saenz is professor of sociology at Texas A&M University. He received his Ph.D. from Iowa State University. He has published widely in the areas of demography, race/ethnicity, Latina/os, and inequality. He is a coauthor of *Latinas/os in the United States: Changing the Face of América* (2008). He received the American Sociological Association Latina/o Sociology Section's Distinguished Contributions to Research and Scholarship Award in 2005.

Jerome Scott, a labor and community organizer and educator, is director of Project South: Institute for the Elimination of Poverty and Genocide in Atlanta, Georgia. He is a contributing editor to four popular education tool kits, including *The Roots of Terror* (2004) and *Today's Globalization* (2005). He serves on the Coordinating Committee of Grassroots Global Justice and the National Planning Committee of the United States Social Forum. He was corecipient with Walda Katz-Fishman of the American Sociological Association's 2004 Award for the Public Understanding of Sociology.

James M. Thomas is a doctoral student of sociology at the University of Missouri at Columbia. His areas of interest are grounded in race and ethnic relations, culture and identity, and human rights and social justice. He has presented his own work on the subject of reparations and morality at the annual meetings of the Southern Sociological Society and the Association of Black Sociologists. His current body of work focuses on problematizing the notion of authentic selves within the literature on identity.

Ruth Thompson-Miller is a doctoral student at Texas A&M University. She received her B.A. in anthropology from the University of Florida, where she was a Ronald E. McNair Scholar and a University Scholar. She graduated summa cum laude. In 2006, she received the American Sociological Association/ National Institute of Mental Health Minority Fellowship. She has forthcoming articles in the journal *Counseling Psychologist*, *The Sociology of Racial and Ethnic Relations*, and the *International Encyclopedia of the Social Sciences*.